This book is from the
personal library of:

John M. Crager

If found please return.

BY THE NUMBERS

Using Facts and Figures
to Get Your Projects,
Plans, and Ideas
Approved

Joseph McLeary
Richard Haasnoot
Joyce McLeary
Susan Drake

AMACOM
American Management Association
New York • Atlanta • Boston • Chicago • Kansas City • San Francisco • Washington, D. C. •
Brussels • Mexico City • Tokyo • Toronto

This publication is designed to provide accurate and authoritative information in regard to the subject matter covered. It is sold with the understanding that the publisher is not engaged in rendering legal, accounting, or other professional service. If legal advice or other expert assistance is required, the services of a competent professional person should be sought.

Library of Congress Cataloging-in-Publication Data

By the numbers: using facts and figures to get your projects, plans, and ideas approved/Joseph McLeary . . . [et al.].
    p. cm.
    Includes index.
    ISBN 0-8144-0499-5
      1. Business presentation. 2. Communication in management. 3. Persuasion (Psychology) 4. Commercial statistics. 5. Information resources. I. McLeary, Joseph Webb.

HF5718.22.B9 2000
658.4'5—dc21

                                                99-059434

Printing number

10 9 8 7 6 5 4 3 2 1

From JCM and JWM: *To all our children who have taught us the most about turning innovative ideas into action!*

From SMD: *To Scott, Colleen, Gabriel and Faith, and to Susan Gross, for her cool head and loving heart.*

From RDH: *To the wise teachers who have crossed my path on this journey. I am blessed by your love and joy.*

In Loving Memory of James A. Thomas, III.

CONTENTS

Foreword

Having spent my career seeking sustenance for the innovative souls who populate our corporations, I know the challenges inherent in being an idea person and in trying to bring ideas to the market place. In the romantic ideal, fresh ideas and the creative people who birth them would be nurtured as precious newborns. In fact, some rare, amazing companies create "incubators" for just this purpose. I have been fortunate to work in a number of these situations, and participating in birth is an exhilarating experience.

Such utopian situations are seldom the case. Few Benjamin Franklins are valued in their own time. Innovation often comes about in spite of corporations; or, possibly more often, when the people inside a corporation finally abandon their hope of accomplishing things in traditional ways and instead leave the confines of corporate life for entrepreneurial pursuits. It's not that our corporate leaders don't need and appreciate innovation; it's simply that the normal methods of maintaining order in a business are counterproductive to engendering innovation. The term *creative organization* is an oxymoron, because creativity requires breaking the rules.

You can't break the rules and also maintain order.

If this sounds defeating, I don't want it to be. For all the people who must leave the organization in order to follow their hearts, there are millions of others inside corporations who approach their jobs in large and small creative ways every day. They are the heroes of corporate life, and they have and will succeed in bringing new ideas to the forefront working within the system. At 3M, where I helped create an executive innovation boot camp, stories abound of the innovative products that grew out of the corporate pool, not outside it.

Being successful as an innovator on the inside takes a unique blend of skills and character attributes that go far beyond the ability to think creatively. First, it takes unending energy and patience. Executives must be educated about what reality will be in the future and must be shown how a big new idea will help create that reality. That takes skill in persuasion and negotiation, the know-how to make a business case for your ability to gain allies and the willingness to share credit. Most important, it takes hardheadedness and, as my third-grade teacher used to say, stick-to-itiveness.

Expand your horizons. Don't limit yourself to what is in your world, but give yourself every opportunity to see the bigger picture. You must help management see things in a different way, and believe that the different way will be handsomely rewarded.

There are people who cannot function within a corporate setting, and they must leave, for their sake and for the sake of their organizations. Those people who are willing to work within the system will change the face of business. It takes both to create bold expression in our lives.

Dr. Robert S. Sullivan, Dean
Kenan-Flagler Business School
University of North Carolina

Acknowledgments

This book would not have been as enlightening without the incredible insights and experience of the wonderful people who shared their stories and suggestions. With much gratitude, we want to thank: Lisa Albanese, Carol Coletta, Jerry Daly, Judy Edge, Barbara Garner, Kenneth Glass, Lawrence Ladove, Ray Lewis, Debbi Fields Rose, Dr. G. Richard Shell, Dr. Robert S. Sullivan, Ronald Terry, Betsy Williams, and Brandt Wright.

In addition, we want to thank our wonderful and tireless agent, Sheree Bykofsky, who has been so kind and encouraging through this endeavor, and our editor, Ray O'Connell, the most patient person in the world.

Introduction

"What could be worse than having a million dollar idea
that you can't even give away?"

Jerry Daly

Your heart pounds. You smile. You have a sense of lightness. Excitement abounds. You are inspired. Life has new meaning. You can't wait to share with others.

What's the object of all this positive energy? An idea.

When you get a new idea, especially what feels like a big idea, it transforms you. It is one of the most positive experiences we have. It is often close to the feeling of falling in love.

The experience of getting a new idea is wonderful. What follows that experience can also be fun and exciting, when you have a plan and know what it takes to carry an idea from conception to reality.

This book provides you with the plan you need to develop, nurture, and sell your idea within an organizational environment. Your four authors have drawn upon their collective experiences in a wide range of organizations—large, small, public, private, friendly, and combative. We have sold many ideas and we have also been unsuccessful several times. The latter have been some of our better learning experiences.

Ideas, especially big ideas, are often the fun part of our jobs and careers. We have written this book in the spirit of enabling you to have fun from the first to the last step in the process. Enjoy!

What's the Big Idea?

Post-It Notes. Banking at automatic tellers. Disposable diapers. Frequent flyer programs. They're all products or services that have become standard in our lives. All ideas born of the creative people who make our corporations run.

Success Is a Numbers Game

What does it take to give bright ideas their start? It's true that inventiveness and creativity are among the qualities required to bring a new concept to fruition. But being able to dream is only the smallest piece of success. Underlying the genius of concepts like Velcro and cell phones are hard work and numbers.

Perhaps you're one of those people whose brainstorm will revolutionize our lives. But how will you get it off the ground? Can you maneuver through your company's bureaucracy to give your brainchild life?

Dreaming a dream is one thing, but bringing the dream to the market is another dimension entirely. Business is all about making money, which means the bottom line *is* the bottom line. Some ideas put money on the bottom line, some don't. If you're the proponent of an idea, the first question you'll ask yourself is: What is this idea's potential? Will this product, business line, or cost-saving program either make or save money?

If the answer is yes, can you prove it beyond a shadow of a doubt? And can you convince others of its value?

You see, enthusiasm is not enough. To make an idea succeed, you must be a practical idealist. As publisher C. D. Jackson said, "Great ideas need landing gear as well as wings" (Boone, 1992). That's not always an easy proposition.

This book is all about how to give your idea landing gear. It describes a methodical process you can use to prepare your idea for approval. With it as a guide, you can build your knowledge of the things that could contribute to your idea's success, and find out (before it's too late) what could determine its downfall.

At Pfizer Pharmaceuticals . . . the R&D gang proposes literally thousands of ideas for new drugs. Out of every hundred, only half are considered worthy of pursuing to the development stage. After a second cut, only ten make it to the processing stage. Out of those ten, only one makes it through the required tests, protocols, and approvals to arrive on the shelves of our local pharmacies.

At DuPont it can take as many as two hundred fifty raw ideas to yield one major marketable product. (Kanter et al., 1997)

The Need to Sell Your Idea

Every day CEOs and their executive committees turn down ideas, some good, some bad. That's because ultimately a company's time and money are limited. Projects compete for resources, which means even some good ideas won't get approved.

Sometimes the decision to go with a project, or not to go with it, is simply a subjective call, based on gut feel. Or perhaps the numbers don't look promising enough. But too often a project is shelved because the person presenting it doesn't know how to prove its value to the company or how to gain wide-scale approval. That may be because of insufficient information. Unsupported assumptions. Unprofessional presentation. Inability to answer tough questions. And all of those add up to one thing: poor selling.

Perhaps you've never thought of selling as a preliminary step, but as something you do after you've got the project up and running. Aren't ideas launched because of an innovative concept with healthy projected revenues? Yes . . . and no. It helps to have a great idea. But inside a corporation great ideas don't stand on their own. Making creative things happen is not a solitary journey. Intrepreneurs—entrepreneurs with salaries—must harness their desire to blast off on new adventures, taking the time to load other passengers on their starships.

Call it persuasion or call it selling. To give your project the best possible chance for success, you have to convince one or several key people that the product or service you're promoting will create sufficient benefit to make it worth your company's time. Your ability to do that will be what turns a concept into a number on your company's bottom line . . . and yours.

Selling is what it takes to get a new business off the ground, to implement a business extension, or to get the sign-off on an employee program or a financial strategy. So if you have an idea that you're sure can revolutionize your company's product line, save money, or help retain employees, how should you go about selling that idea to your senior management?

The Steps to Success

There are three phases in getting an idea off the ground:

1. Get an idea . . . and sell it.
2. Develop the idea . . . and sell it.
3. Move the idea to market . . . and really sell it!

This book describes the elements of the selling proposition. Each chapter covers one of the steps you should take to give your project the best chance of gaining support:

- Research your idea from all standpoints.
- Develop a comprehensive plan.
- Build a support network.
- Develop a presentation that meets your audience's needs.
- Prepare to present.
- Deliver your idea.
- Celebrate your success!

You'll find our approach to be strategic as well as tactical, because the process of creating and implementing a concept requires both the ability to think big and the ability to attend to the tiniest detail.

Most of the work takes place long before the formal presentation. Do your prep work well and you'll pave a smooth road to getting those budget dollars.

What determines your success?

It is the value you add to your idea, starting with the moment the idea first appears. When inspiration strikes, be open to expanding and building on the idea to make it even bigger. As you research your idea, do so with an open mind that adds value to it. As you prepare to present your idea to decision makers, you will have opportunities to strengthen elements of the plan. Take those opportunities.

Don't allow your idea to remain unchanged from the moment of conception. Nurture it at each stage and watch it grow and become even stronger than you might have first imagined and hoped for.

Do all of this with a sense of adventure and fun. If the process becomes drudgery, step back and take a deep breath. Reconnect with the spirit you had when you conceived the idea. Bring the fun and the positive energy back into the process. Let it guide you and you will be successful even if the decision maker says, "No."

Our hope for you in this book is that your journey is full of fun, excitement, and success. We hope the ideas and experiences we share with you contribute to that journey.

CHAPTER 1

Ideas and Idea People

"Ideas are refined and multiplied in the commerce of
minds. In their splendor, images effect a very simple
communion of souls."
Gaston Bachelard (1884–1962), French scientist,
philosopher, literary theorist

There's no telling where an idea may come from. 3M regularly
discovers multimillion-dollar ideas from the most ordinary everyday events. Take Scotchcast, a fast-drying, lightweight orthopedic
casting material that resulted from the CEO breaking his leg and
having to wear a heavy, bulky plaster cast. Among its internally generated uses are sandpaper, masking tape, transparent tape, reposi-
tionable notes, adhesive-backed surgical drapes, reflective sheeting
for traffic safety, diaper tape, electrical tape, and maintenance-free
respirators. (Kanter et al., 1997)

The idea may spring from your own brainstorming, or it might spring from an idea planted by an executive hoping an intrapreneur will pick it up and run with it. You may sometimes hear management ask an apparently casual question, such as, "What do you think about that new service program our competitor announced?" The manager may be tossing out ideas, sometimes in an attempt to evaluate people by seeing who jumps on it.

Debbi Fields, founder and chief cookie lover of Mrs. Fields Cookies, says that her company's best ideas come from her front line people who deal directly with the customers. One of her most successful products came from a very simple idea: making cookies in the shape of hearts and selling them on Valentine's Day. Prior to heart-shaped cookies, Valentine's Day for Mrs. Fields Cookies was a low-volume day, as people passed its stores to buy candy in heart-shaped boxes. Now Valentine's Day is among their highest volume days, demonstrating that ideas do not need to be revolutionary to make a big difference.

She also says that suppliers and distributors can contribute greatly to new ideas and improvements. Since companies are mutually dependent on these partners, it behooves everyone to work together to create a better overall process.

In today's world, innovation opportunities abound. Not only has technology provided unlimited possibilities for process improvements and new business opportunities, customers and employees are much more demanding in what they want from corporate relationships, requiring corporations to anticipate and respond to their changing needs. The old days of sticking with the status quo, or doing business because "that is the way we have always done it," are gone forever. In addition, corporations are competing with small entrepreneurial companies every step of the way. For corporations to survive, they must rely on talented, creative individuals who are not only visionaries, but are dedicated to the corporate community.

Do You Have What It Takes?

To be able to sell your idea you must master a variety of skills: organizing, networking, speaking, negotiating, along with a host of character traits such as patience, persistence, and political savvy. G. Richard Shell, Director of the Wharton Executive Negotiation Workshop and author of *Bargaining for Advantage: Negotiation Strategies for Reasonable People* (1999) says,

> You must be relentlessly persistent, patient, and lucky. The first two create the opportunity for luck to happen. Sometimes getting organizations to change only a few degrees requires massive amounts of effort, so patience and persistence are vital. And, be strategic. Timing is everything. In fact, timing is as critical as content.

According to Betsy Williams, VP of Human Resources at Nielsen Media Research, a person who wants to get a new idea sold "must be totally aware of their corporate culture and its strategic objectives. They also have to be politically astute and know who to involve and who not to involve. They must be excellent communicators, which is different from sales, to answer the questions they'll be asked." She goes on to say that most people who cannot get their ideas sold can blame their lack of success on one of two reasons: "1) a person may know their idea inside and out, but cannot sell it or understand the political plays within the company, and conversely, 2) he may be an excellent salesperson but cannot deliver or follow through."

Chances are you're an intrapreneur, a person who can turn vision into action, always looking for ways to take advantage of opportunities within the corporate setting. Intrapreneurs and entrepreneurs have much in common, but there are some distinct differences as well. Figure 1.1 highlights these traits.

The biggest difference is that entrepreneurs often feel stifled within the confines of the corporate structure and usually seek smaller, start-up opportunities to pursue their creative interests. Intrapreneurs, on the other hand, not only have the ability to work well within corporate walls, they know how to make the system work for them. In addition, intrapreneurs can better balance their work and personal lives by using the resources within their corporation instead of doing everything themselves.

Figure 1.1

COMMON CHARACTERISTICS OF INTRAPRENEURS AND
ENTREPRENEURS

Action-oriented

Challenge-driven

Change-oriented

Committed to the idea

Conceptual

Creative

Decision maker

Determined and driven

Feels "high" when pursuing new ideas

Feels major slump when project is over

Goal-driven

Hands-on

High standards for idea, self, others

Improvement-oriented

Innovative

Loves what he does despite the stress

Manages multiple tasks

Never satisfied

Optimistic

Opportunistic

Persuasive

Process-driven

Self-motivated

Visionary

Wants to make a difference

Whatever-it-takes attitude

Workaholic

Figure 1.1 *(Continued)*

DIFFERENCES BETWEEN ENTREPRENEURS AND INTRAPRENEURS

ENTREPRENEURS

Blind determination

Eats, drinks and sleeps her idea

Idea's needs come before people's needs

Impatient with others

Impatient with system

Obsessive

Prefers conceiving of and implementing idea vs. managing project

Puts idea before personal needs

Risk-taker

Status quo averse

Extremely high expectations of self and others

INTRAPRENEURS

Consensus builder

Customer-focused

Delegator

Desires financial security and stability for self

Employee-focused

Excellent communicator

Flexible (willing to modify if needed)

Growth-oriented

Leader

Manages conflict well

Motivator of others

Patient

Politically astute

Respect for authority

Sense of community and esprit de corps

Team builder

Understands culture and strategic objectives

Willing to work with system

If you enjoy being an intrapreneur, lucky you: You have the weight of a corporation behind you. If you maneuver wisely, you could have the best of all worlds:

- People to help research and develop your idea
- Financial backing to get things off the ground
- The clout to draw upon outside resources

You're an entrepreneur who doesn't have to hock the farm to try out something new.

Whether you are an intrapreneur or entrepreneur, this chapter addresses several points to help you with your ideas. First, we explore some ways to know whether a company is ready for great new ideas. As part of this, we will look at some characteristics and resources of a creative company. Second, we'll see how a company views its organization, and how this can impact the ideas it generates and what happens to those ideas. Third, we will look at how a creative company rewards and recognizes creativity. Fourth, where a company is in its life cycle often can critically influence how management treats ideas—we will see how this affects you.

Is Your Organization Ready?

If any idea is to move from concept to implementation, many factors must come together to create a vision that's shared by all the persons associated with its success. Thus, the internal environment is just as important as the external environment.

In some companies, innovation is always welcome. "Microsoft chases after zillions of new ideas, and has the money to do it," says J. Raymond Lewis, president and COO of Global Vacation Group. "They're a huge company that can operate like a small company. Not a lot of companies have the luxury of such a strategy."

Unlike traditional administrative companies where change is discouraged, entrepreneurial companies possess an innovative corporate vision and a culture that provides fertile ground for new ideas, nurturing them and allowing them to grow into large, profitable businesses. Figure 1.2 highlights the differences in the two diverse cultures:

Figure 1.2

Entrepreneurial Culture vs. Administrative Culture

Entrepreneurial Culture	*Administrative Culture*
Seeks Innovative Opportunities	Prefers Status Quo and In-the-box Thinking
Action-Oriented and Takes Risks	Seeks Minimal Change and Risk
Creative in Utilization of Varied Resources	Motivated to Control Resources
Desires Independence and Informal Structures	Creates Hierarchies and Autonomous Division
Team-focused	Territorial-focused
Shared Vision	Closed Vision

While new businesses can be glamorous to some, most companies focus on the businesses they already have. This can make it difficult to have a vibrant new product business, as noted in the following comments:

> The vast majority of people in any organization are concerned with existing businesses. They fight hard to keep resources flowing in their direction. Leaders may not grasp just how difficult it can be to branch out in a new direction, and may not have the patience to nurture new ventures. By contrast, companies that successfully pursue growth learn to overcome this inertia, and to create mechanisms that foster business development over the longer term. (*Harvard Management Update*, May 1999, Vol. 4, Number 5, *How Big Companies Grow*)

Start by looking carefully at your organization. Every organization has a personality that dictates how it functions. A corporation's personality may arise from tradition, from the leader, or simply from the business life cycle. Your company's ability to accept your new idea will be affected by these facets of its personality. You can recognize a company's personality by the people it employs, the programs it initiates, how it rewards—or punishes—risk taking.

Authors Ram Charan and Noel M. Tichy (1998) describe ways of identifying a company's "DNA," or inherent characteristics that support or undermine growth.

> ... operating mechanisms, behaviors, attitudes, and dialogues so deeply ingrained in the corporate psyche that we liken them to a genetic code.

Commenting on the DNA concept, *Harvard Management Update* (May 1999) says:

> These are the procedures that institutionalize an organization's mind set and strategies. Some companies' DNA emphasizes cost cutting, making the numbers, avoiding risk. Other companies' DNA constantly reinforces the importance of growth. The building blocks of the message can be simple. Regular meetings to review new business opportunities. Regular communications about new ventures and how they're faring. An executive development process that emphasizes time in the entrepreneurial trenches. Compensation policies that reward internal entrepreneurship.

Some companies are legendary in their support of innovation. Tom Peters, in his forward for *Innovation* by Kantor, Moss, Kao, and Wiersema (1997), related,

> At 3M, managers have adopted the 15 percent rule: 3M's folks can devote 15 percent of their time to projects of their own choosing, without seeking approval from above or even bothering to tell managers what it is they are working on! The company says that 30 percent of sales must come from products no less than four years old.

"Encouraging innovation requires a willingness to not only tolerate failure, but to learn from it," says William D. Bygrave, editor of *The Portable MBA in Entrepreneurship.*

The Creative Company

Creativity in a company does not happen because the CEO decrees it. CEOs can decree many things, but not creativity. They can, however, set the tone for a receptive environment that is not only conducive to but encourages creative efforts. At Mrs. Fields Cookies, next to customer service, their number one priority is to create an innovative culture that values the ideas of its employees. "And," says Debbi Fields, "the company must live and convey such a culture in everything it does and says, every single day. All its communications and reward systems should support and encourage new ideas from employees and customers."

For an organization to be truly creative, certain conditions and values need to be present. The following is a discussion of some of the basic ones. Depending on the business, other conditions and values may also need to be present for there to be a free flow of new ideas that are encouraged to grow to their full potential.

Trust. Most people do not think of trust too often, but they become acutely aware of it once their own trust is violated. Whether trust is broken in a personal relationship or within a company, it is one of the most painful negative experiences we encounter. Trust can be broken in less than a minute, but it can take years to rebuild.

Unfortunately, some surveys suggest that trust in companies has sunk to very low levels. These same surveys suggest that less than half of the employees in most companies trust their management. With all the layoffs and restructuring of the last two decades, lower trust is easy to understand. Also, massive mergers have often brought together different and sometimes conflicting cultures. For people caught in these clashes, trust is one of the casualties.

Since a loss of trust can be so painful, it suggests that having trust can be a powerful positive force. Trust forms the foundation on which other values and qualities can thrive. Stephen Covey

(1990) notes, "Trust is the highest form of human motivation. It brings out the very best in people."

For trust to exist you need two conditions. First, there needs to be integrity. If people are not honest with each other, trust vanishes. What makes this so tough is that many people can be honest some of the time, but not all of the time. Unfortunately, the times they are not honest is often when it is most needed. Integrity cannot be something you or your organization only practice on sunny days. If you want to build trust in your organization, you might borrow from the legal profession—"the truth, the whole truth, and nothing but the truth."

The second requirement for trust is competency. You can be totally honest with others, but if you are not competent at what you do, then people will not trust you to do certain tasks. Trust grows as skills grow. Often your skills improve faster than perceptions of your skills. It is therefore important to demonstrate your skills so that others will respect your competency and trust you to contribute in new areas.

Another important dimension of trust is trusting yourself. This often overlooked aspect of trust involves the same two requirements as when we trust others—integrity and competency. You need self-awareness and candor when looking at yourself. Know what you can do and how that is different from what you wish you could do. Recognize a natural tendency to overestimate your abilities. To counter this tendency, be humble but not to the point that you put yourself down. An ongoing personal growth program builds skills and you experience the resulting increased competency. With the right balance, you learn to trust yourself.

Why is trust so critical to creativity? Trust is the glue that holds an organization together and the lubrication that empowers strong interpersonal relationships. The creative process requires openness, and trust allows people to be open without worrying about hidden agendas. When trust is not present, fear usually is. Nothing stifles creativity (and most positive actions) as much as fear. This is not to say that creativity does not exist when negative conditions prevail. Creative ideas do emerge in these conditions, but the consistency, quality, and quantity of ideas is well below the levels of a trusting organization.

Win-win. the second condition that supports and stimulates creativity is when there is a spirit of win-win in an organization.

This is in sharp contrast to the win-lose attitude that prevails in many companies today. Win-lose is a product of fostering unhealthy competition within a company. Competition can occur in many dimensions. There is competition for power and rewards within a department, between departments, and across divisions. In most cases, a sense of the greater good of the organization moderates the desire to win at the expense of another. As a result, most actions are motivated by a mix of perspectives—what is good for me or my group plus a dash of what is good for others and the company.

A win-win culture consciously searches for solutions that are in the best interests of everyone affected by a decision and action. It requires a higher level of compassion and understanding than exists in win-lose cultures.

What makes win-win so conducive to high levels of creativity is the lack of power struggles, which kill ideas before their potential is known. Instead, people recognize and respect the expertise of others. They eagerly seek out diverse perspectives and embrace divergent thinking. They share needs and conditions affecting their department or division.

They look for the creative solutions that are synergistic. This word is overused and misunderstood, largely because organizations attempt to realize the potential of synergy in a win-lose environment. The power of synergy is unleashed within a win-win culture.

While you generate more new ideas in a win-win culture, the real power of win-win is seen in the stages following the birth of an idea. Fewer ideas are prematurely killed by jealousy and the "not invented here" syndrome. Instead, in the early stages, creative ideas are built upon by a variety of creative minds. Initial ideas become stronger and have the opportunity to flourish. Certainly, a time comes when an idea needs critical evaluation, but the evaluation is done when much more of an idea's potential is known.

Trust and a win-win attitude provide the foundation for an organizational culture that supports the free flow and development of new ideas. In addition, a company needs structures to support a creative environment. You saw an important one earlier—3M's encouragement to use part of each day to work on one's own ideas and projects.

Increasing Creativity

You also need the insight into how higher levels of creativity are generated. While you cannot push a button to start creativity, there are many things you can do to generate a high volume of quality ideas. Five of the important ones are:

1. Visual stimulation—If you sat down with a pad of paper to brainstorm vacation ideas, you might fill one page with ideas. Now add many travel brochures to the process and the number of ideas will probably more than double. Visual stimulation dramatically increases the number of ideas you generate versus the old fashioned "brain drain" approach. Depending on the project, you can visit a production site, look at competitive products, or review commercials by other brands with similar communication goals. These are only a few examples. Develop the visual stimulation ideas that are right for your project.

2. Mixed Brains—Adding mixed brains to the creative process takes the development of new ideas to an even higher level than visual stimulation. Mixed brains refers to adding people with different backgrounds and ways of thinking (sometimes very different) to the creative process. In our vacation ideas example, if you now added both travel experts and world travelers, the list of ideas would again double in length. In an organization, mixed brains can refer to having an off-site creative session with people from various functions—marketing, consumer research, finance, production, and sales, for example. In some instances, you may want to add even more mixed brains since all of these people work for the organization. You can add consumers of the product and people who

are creative but have little connection with the product—musicians, artists, advertising creatives, for example. And don't forget suppliers and distributors. Not only are you mutually dependent upon one another for success, but they have a great awareness of what others in your industry are doing.

3. Concentration—To function at higher creative levels, do not be distracted by irrelevant ideas and activities. People describe being in the creative zone (a time of peak creativity) as a state of profound calmness and clear focus. Anyone who has tried meditating can attest to how difficult it can be at times to calm the mind. Certain conditions foster a calm mind—being in nature and reading an inspiring book works for many people. This is one reason why so many highly productive creative sessions involve going off-site to a soothing, natural setting. The type of concentration conducive to creativity is not a forced one. Rather, it requires almost no effort.

4. Fun—Reflect on the times you have been most productive and creative. Many people describe experiences where they were having fun. While they might have been working, it felt like play. It was a joyous, even exuberant experience. You can bring fun into the creative process by bringing games and toys to liven up the process. Do not be afraid to awaken that inner child who loves to have fun. When you do, you connect with an energy that is highly supportive of peak levels of creativity.

5. Suspend Judgment—For creative ideas to flow, you need to completely exclude judgment from the process. Judging ideas as they flow—"that's a bad idea"—shuts down the flow of ideas. All kinds of judging need to be forbidden, including looks that express displeasure. Instead of reacting with judgment, get people to react by building on the ideas of others—"and you could also. . . ."

Many companies use these tools at an annual or semiannual off-site creative day or two. But since these tools are so powerful, a creative company needs to search out ways to bring them into the everyday operations. There are several ways companies can do this:

1. Focus Groups—One way of bringing mixed brains into the company's on-going creative process is through focus groups. (Fo-

cus groups are a form of consumer research where consumers are recruited to come to a location where a moderator leads them through a pre-set agenda.) In focus groups, you have the opportunity to share creative ideas with consumers. You can also give them some tools, like visual stimulation, and ask them to build a new idea or modify one you share with them.

2. Outside Companies—The world can start to look very static viewed only from your singular perch. Regularly visit other companies to get ideas. Suppliers are a natural source of ideas. They are aware of new developments and challenges that have real or potential impact on your business. By mixing together your needs and their perspectives, you will be surprised how creative the session can be. The same is true when you visit customers. These business owners see your product or service very differently. Again, when you mix together diverse views with an eye towards developing creative, win-win solutions, areas that were challenges often leap forward to the solution stage.

3. Outside World—Go beyond the world of customers and suppliers. Go to trade shows that may not seem to be directly related. For example, go to a Comdex trade show where you can see the latest technology for a wide range of electronic products.

4. Inside World—Look for opportunities in your company to have regular and spontaneous creative sessions. When you encounter a problem or a situation where you would like to explore multiple options, identify a pool of people you can call on with short notice to engage in creative problem solving. Be sure to make it fun and utilize the other factors that contribute to high levels of creativity. Many corporations utilize this process regularly to flush out solutions to a problem or inefficient process. Once a situation is identified, a cross-functional team is assigned with representatives from such areas as legal, marketing, operations, human resources, finance, and other pertinent areas to brainstorm possible solutions. These people are brought together to identify the best solution and develop a preliminary proposal for approval. Once basic approval is given the okay to proceed, a more formal team is usually established to fully develop and research the idea.

If you believe you have to be born creative to be creative, then you have a belief that limits both your creative resources and possibly your own creativity. Science has not determined that you either have or do not have a certain creative gene.

Everyone can be creative. It is a skill like any other, and, as a result, it can be learned and developed with experience. Yes, some people are more creative, just as some people are better basketball players or sales managers. But the important point to realize is that everyone is creative to some degree and can help you develop the ideas that propel your business forward.

It is also important to remember that most of the best ideas are not unique; they have evolved from an existing situation or product in an attempt to make it better. What better way to generate ideas than to look at what you or your department does on a regular basis? What could be done more efficiently to save time and money? Chances are, you have already thought of many small ideas and implemented them in your own routine to make what you do easier and more effective. While you may not consider these ideas highly innovative or creative, they are. Any idea which changes things for the better instantly qualifies as innovative and creative. They don't have to save hundreds of thousands of dollars to be successful.

You take a big step when you engage people in the kind of creative conditions just discussed. When people can connect with a common purpose in a fun environment, their level of unique and valuable contributions will surprise you. We all naturally desire a sense of community where we can feel valued for our contributions. Everyone has ideas and everyone can contribute; all they need is a receptive, encouraging audience. What better environment than a supportive, innovative company to bring out the best ideas to make a difference for all stakeholders?

How an Organization Impacts New Ideas

How a company organizes itself and treats its various functions and divisions has a significant impact on the number and quality of new ideas it generates.

For a long time in most companies, functions and divisions saw themselves as autonomous units. They were self-contained, left alone to perform their functional expertise. Competition for resources, including people and budget dollars, was fierce and set the stage for determining who was the most powerful. Divisions took pride in their operation and often viewed themselves as better than others within the same company and functional area. This pride produced defensiveness when another function or division attempted to influence what they did or how they did it. The defensiveness was an attempt to maintain control of their world.

This organizational behavior is the silo or bunker view of the world. The defensiveness produces reluctant cooperation in some cases and no cooperation in other cases. Regarding the latter, when a function took a silo view of the world, it could result in covert or overt opposition to what another function wanted to do. In fact, the standard response in a silo world is wariness of another function's requests of you.

This prevalent organizational view is one of the greatest inhibitors of creativity. Trust and openness are low when the silo mentality exists. The low level of trust comes from a lack of understanding about other functions, and from concerns about the integrity of other managers. These concerns are usually not based on solid experience, but rather they stem from a lack of understanding that comes from isolation from other functions. In the silo organizational world, one typically finds very low levels of interaction between functions. They do not socialize or work jointly on business projects except in restricted situations. For example, when another function makes a request they may say, "Send me the request in writing," instead of meeting with the other function.

The degree to which a silo mentality rules in a company varies. It usually exists to some degree. For many business managers, the previous discussion will strike a familiar cord. Silos inhibit creativity by stifling openness, trust, and understanding. The lack of understanding that exists prevents other functions from appreciating the competency of other managers.

In a silo company, ideas trickle forth and many of them die a premature death. Similarly, formal employee suggestion systems that were so popular in the past primarily encouraged individuals or small cohesive teams to submit ideas. Cross-functional teams were not encouraged unless out of necessity. Because the reward systems typically paid out a percentage of earnings from a successful idea, many people preferred to operate in a vacuum. As a result, few large ideas were successfully approved or implemented because they required cross-functional support and people were not willing to participate unless it benefited them directly.

Teamwork and Creativity

Throughout the 1980s and 1990s, companies recognized the negative effects of silo management. This recognition contributed to the emergence of cross-functional business teams. Such teams brought people from all across the organization together in one room—in many companies, for the first time.

While cross-functional teams were a big step forward in breaking down the silo system, they were not a magic wand that made silos go away. Dropping integrated teams into a strong silo culture can bring a team to a crunching halt or cause it to merely limp along.

Teams also exist in companies for a wide variety of purposes. They can be permanent teams. For example, ongoing brand teams have representation from all functions involved in a business. Often their task is managing the execution of annual plans and delivering the brand's annual profit forecast. Teams also exist to manage short-term projects. For example, there may be a team to manage the new production system for a product improvement. It starts after management agrees to the plan and ends when the new production process has completed testing and is fully operational. Again, it is composed of the decision makers critical to the implementation of the project.

As noted, cross-functional teams are not a panacea for all the troubles of the silo system. But they can allow an organization to take a big step forward towards speeding up the quality and quantity of ideas. Experience over the last two decades has taught us several lessons on how to have a highly productive team. The following is a brief discussion of some of those lessons.

First, a team needs a strong and clear charter from a manager who will be the sponsor and, when necessary, the coach for the team. A team charter clearly outlines the team's purpose, responsibilities, and authority. It is a carefully crafted document that usually is one page or less. The charter dictates the initial membership of the team, as well as the functions and level of each team member within the organization.

Once the charter is issued, the next step for the sponsoring manager is to recruit the right people for the team. The membership criteria usually dictate the people who will be on the team. When there are options, the sponsor works with the functional manager to select the best person. One challenge today's managers face is the proliferation of teams, and recruiting the best person for a new team can be a challenge because of previous commitments.

Often the first step for a new team is an orientation and alignment meeting. To get a fast start, teams often recruit a trained facilitator to join them for this first session and sometimes to act as an ongoing process consultant. Going off-site for an all-day, informal session often provides the proper environment for people to introduce themselves and begin the important bonding process necessary for a top-performing team. The informal atmosphere contributes to breaking down the barriers characteristic of a silo system. A team should use this initial session to great advantage. How successfully the members of the team bond during this session will dictate the success of the team over the initial stages of the team's effort.

Several challenges can confront a team in the early stages. Some people question whether they are the right person for the team. This feeling is often prompted by an already busy schedule that leaves no room for another team or project. The team sponsor along with the person's functional manager may have to personally convince the person about his importance to the team.

Other people question the project. They do not understand it fully and what they do understand they do not like. Again, it may require the team sponsor and functional manager to convince the person about the importance of the project.

Another early team problem can be deciding on leadership. The team sponsor often names the leader, but sometimes the team chooses a leader. In either case, those who are not chosen as leader can be resentful and work against the leader's efforts. Two approaches tend to work in this situation. First, the team sponsor can share her reasons for choosing the leader. Along with this, she can suggest that the leader meet one-on-one with the resentful team member. Often, when a personal relationship is established the problem subsides. Another approach is to recognize the member's leadership interest and channel it to a leadership role on the team.

These initial steps need to be taken or the hoped-for benefits from the team will only be theoretical. When a company uses teams, it does not mean the automatic end of the idea-stifling silo system. In fact, silos are very difficult to stamp out. Some companies that have supported teams for decades still have silos.

Virtually any level of team development in a company breaks down barriers to some degree. Every step forward you take in removing the barriers of a silo system increases the flow and development of new ideas.

A second step some companies have taken to increase the flow of ideas is to become a learning company. A company that values learning has systems and processes that enable people to learn from each other and from sources outside the company. The purpose of this learning is to spawn new ideas that will improve operational or profit-generating results.

Companies like General Electric convene regular meetings of senior managers with the sole purpose of sharing what they have learned since the last meeting. These high level meetings can be very stimulating. Often, they are followed by divisional meetings where the managers determine how the learnings of other groups can benefit them. This practical and action-oriented approach ensures that learnings move from concept to action with maximum bottom-line impact.

Some companies make learning an everyday practice. They set up intranet forums for sharing ideas and support weekly e-mail newsletters that disseminate the best ideas of the week across a company's divisions.

Learning companies also look outside the company for new insights and ideas. They do not rely on the occasional passing along of information. Rather, they have people and systems designed to collect information about competitors and any developments related to their businesses. They even look beyond the United States to examine international developments.

A learning company is one that values new ideas and knows how to generate them. It knows that learnings are great sources of new ideas. It recognizes the contributors for their efforts in the development and implementation of ideas. More importantly, for companies like Nielsen Media Research, it is a way of life. New ideas and improvements are expected and encouraged, and people feel honored to be a part of a new idea team.

Another approach to opening up the flow of ideas in your company is the open book approach. Jack Stack and John Case, who have shared open book management success stories in their books, have been champions of this approach to managing. At its heart is a company that shares all of its financial data with its employees. Employees use this data to evaluate how the company and a division are performing. They also use it to set goals and track progress.

While open book management is effective at involving people at every level in the heart of a company's operations, it is also a big trust builder. A company opens up and trusts all its employees, not just top managers, with important and potentially sensitive data. As we saw earlier, when trust is high, creativity can be high. In open book companies, the sharing of financial information often produces many ideas from employees about how to improve operations. As a result, many companies that have adopted the open book approach have seen dramatic improvements.

Corporate and entrepreneurial America has discovered the power of teams, innovative learnings, and opening their books. As opposed to the silo system, many more new ideas are generated, developed, and implemented. At the heart of these approaches is creating the conditions conducive to creativity.

Rewarding Creativity

A company can say it wants new ideas—what company doesn't? But it is another thing to foster a culture and system that support the creation of those ideas.

If a company wants high levels of creativity to be a consistent part of its operations, and not limited to the occasional off-site session, then it also needs a system of rewards and recognition. This can take all forms that are appropriate to the company and personnel.

Some companies have annual black-tie dinners where they present awards for various categories of creativity. Other companies have weekly or monthly informal beer blasts where awards are for fun and outrageous categories of creativity. Yet others post success stories throughout their communication vehicles: bulletin boards, e-mails, newsletters, annual report to shareholders, or recognition by the president or CEO at a major managers' meeting. Regardless of the medium, recognition counts and employees love it.

It is not important what form the rewards and recognition take, but that they need to be treated in a manner that is valued by others. In many companies, they are the only public awards presented by the company. When they are this important, people take note and are motivated by them.

In consumer packaged-goods companies, like Procter & Gamble, television advertising is critical to the success of many brands. P&G annually honors the best advertising campaigns of the year as measured by business results. It is the only such honors program. The top managers (mostly from the New York and Chicago agencies) are all present in Cincinnati for the evening gala. Managers from all advertising departments are also present when the best campaign for the year is shown and the story of its creation shared with everyone.

You can reward creativity in all functions, not just the ones traditionally seen as creative. Production teams have increasingly become very creative in their solutions to long-term problems. They have found that when you pool the thinking of the people who actually do the work, you find powerful, simple, and efficient solutions. Creativity in teams has been a major driving force to reshaping production systems in a diverse group of businesses.

Scientists in research and development also benefit from an environment where creativity is encouraged, nurtured, and rewarded. While dedicated to science, they can use it to seek creative ways of improving their products.

While some people might skip a heartbeat if they knew their finance managers were being creative, it is now considered a highly prized skill. Today, there are more potential solutions to traditional financial problems. Finding the right solution or the right combination of solutions is often a highly creative undertaking.

In virtually all departments and functions, there are opportunities to encourage creativity and reward it when it happens. Handled properly, these opportunities can have a broad impact. For example, a company can focus on its creative results in press releases and its annual report. The group of managers responsible for the idea usually enjoys recognition in newspapers by both the company and their community.

The Business Life Cycle

A company's position in the business life cycle might affect its readiness for new ideas as well. A corporation's mentality and culture change as it moves from the new venture stage (the early years) through growth and maturity.

In the beginning, a firm is, by necessity, more entrepreneurial and risk-taking. Young companies are likely to be opportunity-driven because they're jumping into the fray against established competitors or fickle consumers. It could be a very simple matter for an employee to gain approval for a new idea at this stage of the game.

In the early stages, a company has very few established structures. It also does not have departments for individual functions, or if there are departments, they are very loosely configured. For example, the finance and marketing managers might share adjoining desks.

Policies are also very informal and flexible. They are implemented as the need arises. The company's actions are limited solely by the judgment and values of the owners.

During this period, trust and creativity must be high if the company is going to make it to the next stage. Challenges needing solution arise daily. How good the company's owners and employees are at finding these solutions will determine if the company survives this stage.

Many companies do not survive this stage. While there are many reasons (lack of planning, skills, and financing, for example), the inability to generate new ideas to address the expected and unexpected is a major contributor.

While entrepreneurs often find it difficult to pause in the mad rush of operations, they need to if they are not generating the number of quality ideas they need to succeed. The indicators that they need to pause can be excruciatingly obvious, such as a loss of customers and the failure to attract new ones.

One of the challenges an entrepreneur faces at this stage is finding a way to be more than a one-person show. If she is quick to judge others' ideas and always insists on doing things her way, then she will not have the new ideas she needs, unless she is exceptionally creative herself. Since most owners are not that talented, they need to examine their operations to find ways to encourage and support the flow of ideas from others in the company and from trusted advisors outside the company. The flow of ideas at this stage determines when and if the company will graduate to the next stage.

As a company grows and attempts to create market share and name recognition, it usually remains open to new concepts. At some point, however, every firm faces a dilemma: The organization grows beyond the abilities of the founders, and must find a way to continue to grow. This is the time when a company usually becomes more control oriented, more administrative, and more reliant upon specialized skills and functions in order to manage its success. Many companies fail at this point because they can't navigate the transition. The founders may find it difficult to relinquish control.

The desire to control usually means the owners do not trust others to make decisions. As we have seen, when trust is low, it chokes off the flow of ideas. This desire to control and lack of trust are common in many companies, even some large ones. The larger ones seem to survive either because of the brilliance of the owners or because of a deep, talented group of managers. Other companies that are not so fortunate struggle and often fail at this stage.

When a company reaches a certain size, the owners realize that they cannot do it all themselves. They face a crucial decision. Do they bring in more outside talent to do their bidding or do they hire leaders who will be coequals? If they make the former decision, the flow of new ideas may initially increase only to drop when people recognize the only ideas that count are those that come from the owners.

If they make the latter decision, they often face a tough transition. The owners are accustomed to doing it all. Can they move meaningful power to another leader? If they can, the flow of new ideas will increase, sometimes dramatically. If they cannot, the company is likely to take a big step backwards. The recently hired leader will struggle for power (he thought it was promised) and eventually lose, often after a bitter and debilitating battle.

Original owners can bring new, professional managers into a company and let them be true leaders that prosper. One of the best recent examples is Dell Computers. Michael Dell founded the company and was very successful in a very crowded field of non-IBM suppliers. But he reached a point where he knew he needed help if he was going to take the company to the next level.

He created the office of the chief executive officer. Michael is one of the three people in this office. He brought in Kevin Rollins from Bain & Co. Kevin had previously been a consultant to Dell

Computers. He is now vice chairman. Michael also brought in Morton Topfer from Motorola's Land Mobile Products, where he had been division president. He is a vice chairman at Dell now.

Dell's success since bringing this team together is extraordinary. Dell is now number two in the industry and the fastest growing company. It pioneered the direct-to-consumer approach that does not rely on retailers. It has also led the way by selling computers on the Internet. It currently sells $18 million worth of merchandise a day from its Internet site—*www.dell.com.* Its business model has many innovative aspects that Michael has credited his fellow managers with contributing.

In this regard, Dell is a model for how to make the transition to a company where the founder's talents are powerfully supplemented with the talents and ideas of others.

Finally, either a company reinvents itself through the entrepreneurial spirit or it stagnates. This is the point at which we often hear the term "corporate reengineering."

If a company is to succeed long term, it must make a transition from a strictly entrepreneurial style to a balance of entrepreneurial and growth characteristics. Another way of saying it is, innovate or die. To ensure ongoing health, a company must address how it:

A.   Delegates responsibility and authority—As we saw earlier, without delegation the owner/entrepreneur becomes the only source of ideas. The vast majority of companies do not have a Bill Gates or Ernest Gallo as their founder. Those companies that delegate responsibility wisely generate more ideas.

B.   Hires to the entrepreneur's weaknesses and shortcomings—When a company adds talented managers, its first priority is not hiring people with the same skills as the owner. If the owner is highly creative, its first hires should be administrative, sales, or finance managers.

C.   Shares the glory and rewards of the business—This is similar to delegating. If the owner takes all the credit personally, he is likely to have disgruntled managers who will leave in most cases.

D. Keeps its focus on customers: who they are and what they want—This is one of the most important challenges companies face. When a company becomes enamored with itself, it can think that it is smarter than the consumer. Instead of letting the consumer tell it what is needed, the company tells the consumer what she should want. This is a critical and often terminal mistake that a surprising number of companies make. The company that is always customer-driven gets many powerful ideas from those customers about how to improve its business.

You can see that a company's position in the life cycle dictates what type of projects it will pursue.

Sometimes a firm will change direction entirely in order to continue on a growth path. In its 1999 round-up of 500 top companies, *Fortune* magazine cites major direction shifts in several significant U.S. players: DuPont switching from chemical company to the biotechnology business; IBM bolstering its equipment business with heavy-duty services; and Procter & Gamble aggressively looking for a new culture-changing product.

Less recently, Ross Johnson, former chairman of RJR Nabisco, had the wisdom to see the handwriting on the wall in the tobacco industry. He de-emphasized the traditional tobacco line and moved toward food products, using some of the same distribution outlets and channels.

ServiceMaster used its foothold in labor-intensive business services to develop a very comprehensive business and household services firm that includes, among others, pest control, lawn maintenance, and household cleaning.

Just as Mrs. Fields Cookies was hitting a comfortable, profitable point in the business life cycle, technology opened new doors, allowing it to centrally produce products and eventually franchise. Prior to this, all cookie dough was made daily from scratch in each of the stores. This was very time consuming for the employees and kept them in the "back of the house" away from their customers. After years of research and the appropriate technology, Mrs. Fields was able to create consistent, perfect cookie dough using only the finest ingredients specially blended to allow shipment all over the world.

Of course, some companies resist their position in the cycle. They can't or won't let go, or simply can't make the transition. The result can be devastating: Ford Motors initially resisted downsizing its cars to compete with the Japanese models, and suffered greatly in the process.

Companies sometimes don't recognize the need to change, or they may recognize the need but stay stuck in the mud through either bad decisions or through extreme discomfort and resistance to new ways of doing business. It's like a case of corporate schizophrenia. The company espouses change and hires bright, innovative managers, but shoots them down when they challenge the status quo. The company sees a need to make the transition, but can't bear the pain. This can be quite a confusing situation for an ambitious manager who doesn't know whether to dodge left or right.

Your job is to interpret your company's IQ (Innovation Quotient) by looking at some overt and some subtle signs:

A. Where is your company in the life cycle?—We saw earlier that a company behaves differently depending on where it is in its life cycle. This behavior can dramatically influence the quantity and quality of ideas.

B. What is your company's personality?—If the company values learning, for example, its personality is supportive of people generating new ideas. If the personality of a company is solely that of its founders, then the only real source of ideas is likely to be them.

C. Does management focus on ways to grow or ways to cut costs?—What are the current business and economic trends affecting your business? These will determine if your company is in a growth or cost-cutting mode. Either way, your company will value the generation of new ideas—if they are in tune with where your company is today and where it wants to go. Typically, entrepreneurial and innovative companies look for new revenue-producing ideas whereas more administrative, conservative companies seek more cost-cutting ideas.

D. Is your company into control or into giving people autonomy?—For most companies, this is a delicate and complex balancing act. Many factors go into creating the best balance—level of trust and expertise, degree of openness, and corporate culture, to name a few. Whatever the right balance appears to be for a company, the senior managers should tilt the balance in favor of greater autonomy. Autonomy is directly associated with higher levels of innovation.

E. Who gets promoted: the risk taker or the person who maintains the status quo?—This is an often-overlooked but very powerful signal in companies. If the company says it values new, innovative ideas but does not reward those who lead the way, then it will not be long before innovation dries up.

The clues are there. Look at them to ascertain whether or not your company is in a position to be receptive to your new idea.

Key Learning Points

1. Examine your company's readiness and receptivity to new ideas. If there are low levels of trust and toleration for failure, your company probably experiences low creativity also.

2. The kind of organization a company has can hinder or encourage the generation of new ideas. A company that has functions operating within silos does not experience the creativity that comes from cross-functional teams, a learning orientation, and a strong sense of openness about the most important company facts.

3. Rewarding creativity is necessary if you want to encourage new ideas and set the bar for how big you want those ideas to be.

4. Where a company is in the business life cycle defines the kinds of challenges it faces in creating an idea-friendly environment. It also defines the kinds of ideas a company most likely needs.

CHAPTER 2

Educate Yourself

"Upon this point, a page of history is worth a volume of logic."

Oliver Wendell Holmes

The best way to prepare to launch a new idea is to become a know-it-all. It is essential to be an expert on your subject, to understand all the factors that could affect your idea's success. This means educating yourself about conditions inside (and outside) your company.

Educating yourself needs to be both open-ended and focused. The education needs to be open-ended to provide the freedom necessary to explore unexpected leads. If you knew what you were going to learn beforehand, you would not need to educate yourself. Success at this stage is often a direct result of how open-minded you are. If you enter the education process with even some preconceptions, you are likely to miss important learnings. Preconceptions have a way of limiting your vision to what you already know.

Maybe the single biggest step you can take to open your mind is to adopt a spirit of adventure and fun about learning new things. If you fear learning new information because it might undermine your idea, then you will miss major insights. These insights often make the difference between a good idea and a great one.

These same learnings which you may now fear often become the breakthroughs that later sell the idea. So welcome learning even when at first it seems to be bad news. There is good news in everything you learn, if only your vision is broad and clear enough to see it.

Take what might be the worst possible thing you could learn— your idea has already been done and is patented very tightly by another company. At this point you may be devastated. By looking for the positive in this learning you might see:

- How a joint venture with the company holding the patent could be an even bigger idea
- How you can use the learnings and experience from working on this project to benefit your company in other ways
- How much time you now have for other projects that are also very promising

When you want to see the benefits, you will see them. This attitude is crucial to your success at this early stage.

Focus also helps the education process. There is a vast amount of information available today on virtually any subject. You can get so caught up in the research and discovery phase that you lose perspective and fail to initiate action. This is one reason many ideas never make it to implementation.

How do you bring focus and not inadvertently become close-minded? It requires a compromise between maintaining initial areas of inquiry and staying open to new opportunities that present themselves. Setting the initial areas usually happens by following traditional areas of inquiry as well as exploring intriguing new leads or developments. For example, the latter could be emerging technologies that might have a future application in your business. No one else has thought about the connection but you want to take a closer look.

After the initial areas of inquiry are established and the education process has begun, you will run into the unexpected. Treat this as a gift and you will learn from it. When encountering the unexpected, be intrigued and curious. Follow new leads until your judgment tells you either you need to learn much more or that you know enough. This judgment will be easy if you have a positive attitude about the education process.

Done right, the education process greatly enhances the probability of success. Look at education as the foundation to the building process. If your understandings and learnings are not solid at this stage, then at minimum you will waste considerable time and more likely you will make weak recommendations that, if implemented, will have a higher-than-necessary probability of failure.

The costs of failure are always more than financial and can involve impaired careers and a damaged public image. Both will affect your ability to develop and implement critical new ideas in the future.

The education process also has the benefit of getting you on a par with senior management—the decision makers. This is especially true for the broader areas of education, like taking a world and international view. Senior management lives in a broader world and your ability to understand and move about in their world will influence their decision-making process.

To set your idea on firm ground, you'll have to do a lot of homework, make observations, and come to some conclusions about whether conditions in the market, and in your company, are favorable to launch your idea. Your first step, then, is to research your idea from all standpoints.

In general, you'll need to start by getting background information about these topics:

- Your company's strategy and goals
- General business and economic conditions
- Your industry
- Your market
- Your idea

This information will help you form some opinions about the overall climate and how your idea might fare given current conditions. As you become more convinced of its potential, you can delve deeper into specifics that will ultimately become part of a formal proposal or business plan. Everything you discover will contribute to your idea's potential for success.

It may seem a bit overwhelming to go about collecting such extensive information without even knowing if the idea will gain approval. But the process of educating yourself is a necessary one. To sell an idea you must be sold on it yourself. If your idea is truly viable, this process will help you become sold. That doesn't mean simply being enthusiastic or even passionate about your brainchild. It means knowing that there truly is a market for it. "You must show others in the organization that your idea is really important and that you are totally committed to doing whatever it takes. Stress the benefits to the organization as a whole. If you are not perceived to be totally committed, no one else will be." says G. Richard Shell of Wharton School of Business.

This chapter describes generally some areas you can explore that will make you more knowledgeable and better able to evaluate your idea's long-term potential.

Your Company's Strategy and Goals

Many companies attempt to capture their personality in mission statements, vision statements, operating principles, values, or other formal descriptions of how they do business. For public companies, you'll also find cultural road signs in some obvious places like the company's annual report, the letter from the chairman, or management's discussion and analysis (often called the MDA).

There is great variability in company mission statements, vision statements, and value statements. They include companies that have such things because they feel it is what good companies do. This kind of effort lacks an understanding of the mission statement's power and these managers quickly file the statements, which is an indication of their ineffectiveness.

If you are in a company that handles mission statements this way, you face a tough challenge. The thinking captured by these kinds of statements, when enthusiastically embraced, provides important insights into the culture of a company. When the statements do not exist or exist in name only, then you are left to fill in the blanks about the culture, which can be a very difficult process.

While difficult, it is worth the effort of trying to develop a proxy for these statements. In a public company, a review of annual reports for recurring themes is often productive. In a private company, understanding the values articulated by its founders often provides valuable clues and insights about the company's culture.

In companies that embrace the process of developing vision, mission, and value statements, you have very valuable information to guide your education process. But be cautious—determine if the formal statement accurately reflects current thinking. Often when one of the statements is more than five years old, informal addendums exist in the minds of top leaders.

The second caution is to carefully explore the meaning of key words in a statement. As we know from other communication processes, words can have many meanings. Even when there is basic agreement on a word's meaning, there can be important nuances you need to understand.

Lastly, a company that frequently publicizes its statements is especially likely to respond to ideas that help them deliver on their statements. The frequent publicity indicates that top managers are strongly committed. This commitment usually makes them highly responsive to ideas that deliver on the promises inherent in these statements.

While mission statements are, by design, broad, they're supposed to deliver a short, punchy message about the company's heart and soul. Intel's mission statement says it wants to "Do a great job for our customers, employees, and stockholders by being the preeminent building block supplier to the computing industry." The word "preeminent" leaves nothing to the imagination; they intend to be number one.

In some companies, you will not find mission or vision statements. This tends to happen in small- and medium-size companies, but there are many large companies without effective statements. A special effort to determine the unofficial vision and mission of the stakeholders of the company is often required in smaller companies owned by an entrepreneur or partnership. These stakeholders usually hold personal mission and vision statements that should exist in written form, but often are just in their heads. It is worth the effort to interview them to determine how they see their vision and mission. It may be one of the most valuable parts of your education process.

Mission and Vision Statements

In many mission and vision statements there is no specific mention of measures or objectives. Even where there are no specific numbers, there often are key words that signal some level of measurable achievement. Some examples are:

- *Excellent* or *Excellence*—These are common words in statements and you need to understand how the authors define excellence. It is not safe to assume that it means 100 percent. For example, a baseball player might define "hitting excellence" as hitting safely 30 percent of the time (a .300 batting average).

- *Most, leading,* or *highest*—Some vision statements call for the highest level of achievement in a measure. For example, the vision may call for achieving the highest market share. Depending on the product, this can vary from 10 percent for some products to 50 percent for others. If you are going to use this information to motivate others about your idea, then you need to know where you are now and how far you need to progress to achieve the goal.

Sometimes an annual report can provide useful insights that will help you sell your idea. For example, Intel's 1998 Annual Report said, "Our segmentation strategy is designed to allow us to participate profitably in various segments of the computing market and to pursue new growth opportunities in the high-end server and workstation market segments." With this statement you want to know more about what is considered profitable, what are the segments, and what is the higher end of the market. Propose an idea that supports one of these areas and you'll greatly increase your probability of success.

The emphasis on innovation almost goes without saying in the technology industry. But airlines aren't known for their creativity. No wonder we know Southwest Airlines for its somewhat unusual—and refreshing—service. The Southwest mission statement is not exactly mainstream; it includes the noncorporate words "warmth" and "friendliness." An employee orientation video revealed what the company values as well: employees who are happy to be on stage, performing over-the-top routines to let new employees know what kind of company they've joined.

ResortQuest International, only recently gone public, says it wants to develop "trusting relationships with our customers so we may serve them for a lifetime." The 1998 annual report delineates strategies such as acquiring properties in new resort locations, delivering consistent quality, and creating operational and cost-saving synergies. As a researcher, when you embrace this information, it shapes both your idea and the later selling of it.

Ronald Terry, retired chairman and CEO of First Tennessee National Corporation, explains that although mission statements won't give you real insight into specific directions for an idea, they do communicate whether creativity and innovation are important to the company's culture.

This, of course, assumes that the company is actually living its mission statement. In some cases, it's obvious. When Promus Hotels says it is committed to guest satisfaction, a 100 percent Satisfaction Guarantee backs it up.

Delta Beverage Group, a Pepsi-Cola bottler, states that it wants to provide "a more secure future which leads to mutually beneficial results for our families." Pick up the company newsletter and you'll find employees retiring after forty-five years, saying they've stayed because Delta helped them educate their kids. They say they'd do it all over again.

When companies walk their talk, it shows. Truly international companies teach employees other languages, have their business cards printed on both sides in two languages, and implement other procedures that speak clearly about their international commitment.

General Electric's mission statement hinges on just three words—"Boundaryless (in all our behavior); speed (in everything we do); stretch (in every target we set)." When you have one this clear, you are blessed with quality direction. More importantly, General Electric walks its talk.

Even if your company welcomes innovation, it has a filtering process to determine which innovations will move it closer to its goals. You will have to prove that your idea fits your company's business strategy. That doesn't mean it must be in the exact same business; diversification is worthwhile. But whatever you do should fit with what your company hopes to achieve long term. Of course, business strategies change over time, so it's critical to recognize patterns and anticipate when the tide will turn.

Recently, Microsoft had to do just that. Steve Ballmer, president, abandoned the company's outdated motto crafted in 1975 which read, "A computer on every desk and in every home." To reflect rapidly changing technology and mediums, he designed a new vision statement which reads, "Empower people through great software anytime, any place, and on any device" (Bank and Clark, July 23, 1999).

John D. Rockefeller, named Entrepreneur of the Century by *Inc.* magazine, essentially invented the modern corporation. In 1863,

Rockefeller began "dabbling in oil refining." Eventually he bought pipelines, refineries, and tank cars, using tank wagons to sell kerosene to stores across the country, all staffed by his own employees. Standard Oil became the first modern corporation, controlling every transaction through the new concepts of horizontal and vertical integration.

Check out this more modern-day story of changing strategies. Back in the 1970s, Holiday Inn founder Kemmons Wilson revolutionized the lodging industry by "inventing" the first hotel chain. He then set out to acquire a myriad of businesses that would supply goods and services in support of hotels. Since hotels needed drapery, it made sense to manufacture drapery. And since they needed cabinets and tables, why not manufacture them, too? What about meat packing? Hotel restaurants needed meat. And since travelers get to hotels on buses and steamships, perhaps the company could run a bus and steamship line so it could deliver its own guests. By the late 70s, the company had an assortment of approximately forty businesses. This horizontal integration strategy was followed by Holiday Inns for a number of years.

In the late 70s and early 80s, however, new Holiday Inn management divested those forty businesses and concentrated on providing lodging for travelers.

Different Times, Different Strategies

How can you know whether your idea fits your company's current business strategy? First, understand your company's goals. In many corporations these are widely publicized in employee communications such as orientation materials or newsletters and in shareholder documents such as quarterly or annual reports.

In their book, *The Discipline of Market Leaders*, Michael Treacy and Fred Wiersema (1997) talk about Intel:

The urge to innovate, to create breakthrough products is deep, almost uncontrollable at Intel. The company shelled out about $1.1 billion on R&D in 1994, and another $2.4 billion in capital spending to deliver on CEO Andy Grove's commitment: To make "the fastest chips in the newest applications." The company takes huge risks, swinging for a home run with each product. When one engineering team chalks up a win, another sets out to knock the legs out from under it with a better product. Birth and death, innovation and obsolescence are part of the daily life at Intel. .

You need to know whether your company wants home runs or singles—it makes a big difference in both the development of your idea and how you sell it.

If your company is not committed to product innovation, then an idea for a radical new product line may not be a good fit.

What is your company's leadership goal? Does it want to be a leader in innovation or a follower? For a number of years, Avis carved a niche for itself as number two to Hertz. While some companies have a goal of being the first to offer new products or services, others make a habit of letting others do the research and development, then jumping in when the market has been established and the bugs have been worked out. Know your company's goals. Does your company have a tradition of being the first on the market with new products?

Is your company a growth company or a company that wants to maintain the status quo? This makes a huge difference in how you approach your idea. "In entrenched companies, management frequently looks for a reason to say 'no,' because it's easier and cheaper than saying 'yes,'" according to Ray Lewis, president and COO of Global Vacation Group. "Saying 'yes' involves risk, and requires work. In companies where that's the case, entrepreneurial people have to find ways to make it safe for management to give the go ahead."

General Business and Economic Conditions

If you decide your idea is in sync with your company's plans, you're ready to assess whether the overall business conditions are right. Timing can be everything. A phenomenal idea may be positively or negatively affected by business and economic conditions on a local, regional, national, or international basis.

For example, if the country is in the middle of a recession, how many people will really buy a product that's extremely expensive and considered a luxury item? It may be hard for you to gain approval for a new high-end product or service. At the same time, you may stand an excellent chance of gaining approval for an idea that will save your company money or better yet, a product that promises to save customers money.

The value of exploring general business conditions varies by type of product or service. For example, general business conditions are less important in evaluating new toothpaste benefits and more important in evaluating products requiring capital spending.

For necessity products like toothpaste and bar soaps, sales are not very dependent on recession or boom economic times. They are more affected by longer-term trends on commodity ingredient prices, and these tend to be influenced by general economic conditions. Consequently, an investigation of general business conditions has its benefits even for products like these.

Beyond necessity products, general business conditions can have a modest to significant impact on a new business idea. If it is a product requiring capital spending by a customer, interest rate trends affect cost and payout requirements for the new idea. All discretionary budget items are subject to varying degrees of general economic trend influence.

A note of caution—if general business trends are down, it does not mean your idea is in trouble. Many new ideas prosper in tough economic times, especially ones that help consumers become more efficient and productive. Plus, what is down now may rise later.

Key Factors

Different things affect every company's revenues and sales. Some are indirect, such as the economy's growth rate, interest rates, unemployment, inflation, and so on. For example, if you're in the real estate business, movements in interest rates are very important to you. When rates are high, people don't buy as much, and your business may suffer. By the same token, if you rent apartments, those same rising interest rates that stunt home sales may stimulate rentals.

Therefore, it's important to know:

- Which factors are important to your business
- What variables affect your company's sales
- What information you can gather to stay current about those particular variables
- How they affect your company positively or negatively

Business publications such as *The Wall Street Journal, Barron's, Fortune,* and *Forbes* are all good sources for getting a feel for the national and international climate. Business publications are most accessible on the Internet. The old way of finding articles through the local library and a guide that summarizes magazine articles still works. Unfortunately, it is very slow and relatively difficult to find what you want.

Most business publications have Web sites where past articles can be retrieved. These sites usually contain search engine functions that allow you to search past articles for your key words and then rank the relevant articles in one or more ways. The search engines vary in power and some have a section on search tips—use this section to refine your searches. Knowing the type of search capabilities enables you to quickly find the relevant information available from the magazine.

The following is a listing of some of the more powerful and useful magazine sites on the Internet. A note of caution—magazine Web sites are dynamic and may have changed since this 1999 status was written. The good news is that the changes usually result in better, more powerful sites.

- *Fortune* (*cgi.pathfinder.com/fortune*)—From this page you can access the archive of previous issues from 1995 to present. You can search by key words and limit your search to specific dates. The relevancy of the word or words in the article determines the rank of the search results. A brief summary is provided with each result. You can register to have your purchases charged to your credit card. The Northern

Lights search engine handles these transactions. You can also access the *Fortune 500* list for no charge.

■ *Fast Company* (*www.fastcompany.com/homepage*)—This rapidly growing business magazine allows you to search its archives from the first prototype issue to the current one. You can do a key word or natural language search—a very nice feature. Again, search result ranking is by relevancy of the search words. You can retrieve the articles for no charge.

■ *New York Times* (*www.nytimes.com*)—You can access their archives from the home page. You need to register as a user but the registration is free. As a registered user, you have access to 365 days of back issues and the Encyclopedia Britannica Online. The search provides a brief summary of the story, but to obtain the full story requires a purchase of about $2.50 per article.

■ *The Wall Street Journal* Interactive (*www.wsj.com*)—You can access their archives from the home page. There is an annual registration fee. Searching headlines and article summaries are free, but to print out a complete copy of an article requires a fee of $2.50.

■ *Inc.* (*www.inc.com*)—This search function provides great flexibility to explore all issues or just parts of issues and then rank results by relevancy or date. This magazine has wonderful stories about small- and medium-size businesses. The retrieved issues are free.

■ *Business Week* (*www.businessweek.com*)—You can easily search back issues since 1995 from their search page. To retrieve articles you need to be a subscriber to this service. You can subscribe for a single article (about $2) or other options ranging up to an annual rate for unlimited access (about $20).

Other magazines and newspapers are also accessible from a variety of other sites that cover many sources. In some cases there are hundreds of searchable magazines and newspapers at a site. In most cases, these sites charge for searching and retrieving information. Some of the better sites are:

- Northern Lights Special Collection (*www.nothernlight.com/ pubsearch.html*)—According to *PC Magazine,* this is the best search engine for over 5,400 magazines and newspapers. You can search just the publications from this site or go to the home page (*www.northernlight.com*) and search both the Internet and the publications at the same time. You are provided a brief summary of the article and if you are interested, you can then purchase it. Once you register you can order an article with one click. Some independent evaluators rank this site as the number-one search site.

- Electric Library (*www.elibrary.com*)—You need to become a registered user at this site. You can enroll for a month at a time and retrieve unlimited articles. You can also enroll for a free thirty-day trial. This site is a favorite of schools. They have books, magazines, maps, newspapers, newswires, transcripts (radio, TV, and government), and pictures that you can search. For example, you can search everything from the complete works of Shakespeare to the transcripts of specific government committee meetings.

- CompuServe—CompuServe is an Internet and information service like AOL (which owns them). It is one of the most resource-rich services. The resource section (accessed from the home page) provides numerous helpful databases. Many of them are located in the "General Resources" section. Some of these are free while others have small charges. CompuServe also has many forums on a wide range of topics. You can review previous messages on topics of interest or post your own message and have members reply with suggestions. You can subscribe to CompuServe Classic and 200. The latter has an AOL feel since CompuServe is now owned by them.

Annual business round-ups provide pithy summaries of the previous year's effect on business, as well as outlooks for the coming year. Here's an excerpt from the *Fortune 500*: "Margins are under considerable pressure due to an almost complete lack of pricing power, intense global competition, low capacity usage, tight labor conditions, and general deflationary pressures." Quite a bit of food for thought in just one sentence.

The *Fortune 500* issue also provides valuable economic and industry perspectives—much of the information in these issues often leads to additional research.

Newsletters published about your industry are full of good information. Again, the Internet can help you to find these newsletters.

Every industry has associations and publications specifically for people who work in the field. These associations are good sources for trends and predictions about where the industry is headed and what factors will affect the future. Trade associations gather information from members, conduct surveys, and do special studies related to opportunities and other topics of interest to their members. Many association publications' December or January issues feature outlook articles.

Industry associations often have Web sites to which even nonmembers can subscribe. It may also be worth a phone call to the public relations office, or directly to the president of a trade association, to talk informally about the industry and to ask for suggestions of other good information sources.

Trade shows always feature speakers discussing the future of the industry. If you're lucky enough to have the right timing, you may find a meeting that coincides with your research schedule.

Some of the broad magazine and newspaper Web sites, like Northern Lights, also have publications focused on particular industries. Northern Lights even has a search capability that allows you to quickly focus on particular industries and types of products.

The U.S. government also has a wealth of information that can be helpful in your research. One of the best search resources is again from Northern Lights, which has a search engine that focuses on government periodicals, reports, and a wide range of resources. This is the major nongovernment search function for people needing to obtain information about agencies, departments, or legislative and executive actions.

Local business conditions may be important to your plan, too. And don't assume that local conditions mirror the nationwide climate; some areas experience unique economic downturns or upturns. Local information can be more difficult to tap into depending on your area. Again, the Internet can be one of your best resources to find local information.

Many local newspapers maintain a Web site where you can search and retrieve past articles. In addition, more television stations are building Web sites where you can search past news stories. Government agencies at the national and state level often publish economic data for cities and regions. For example, the United States Department of Labor cost of living index is available in considerable detail at the regional level for many areas.

For instance, in 1999 a U.S. housing boom boosted sales for building supply companies. The *Palm Beach Post* (3/23/99) said, "Thanks to a nationwide building boom, supplies of many constructions basics . . . are increasingly hard to come by. Getting drywall can take a month, and it can cost more too." But while the housing boom was driving profits for some areas, things were not so rosy for people who lived in communities with a high concentration of steel mill employees. Competition from foreign mills cost many communities their jobs.

International issues can affect your company whether it does business internationally or not. A financial crisis in Asia, for example, weighed heavily on U.S. farmers who depend heavily on exports.

Your Industry

For many businesses, your industry is different from your market. For example, your industry could be computers, but if your product is the Palm Pilot, your specific market will be the small, hand-held portion of the computer industry. Remember that you can segment an industry on several dimensions, each worthy of investigation.

In the computer business, you can segment the industry based on the size and power of the unit. This range includes units like mainframes, servers, workstations, desktops, laptops, and down to the hand-held. Each segment is large and dynamic.

But the industry can also be segmented by method of distribution. For example, there are computers sold at retail stores, like Compaq and IBM, and those you buy direct from the manufacturer, like Dell and Gateway. Looking at the computer industry from this perspective provides valuable insights that might be missed if you only looked at it by the size and power of the computer.

> Like cats, the microprocessor chips made by Intel Corp. are blessed with nine lives—or so Intel claims in its recent advertisements. In a graphic display, the ad shows Intel's third-generation 386 chip as having exhausted all nine of its lives; it shows the fourth generation 486 processor with two lives left; only the Pentium processor, Intel's newest and fastest microprocessor, still has all nine lives ahead of it. What the ad leaves out is mention of the Intel engineers who have been working since long before the Pentium chip was released to design the successor chip that will put even this fast cat down. . . . (Treacy and Wiersema, 1997)

Had you been in the computer industry a few years back, you certainly would not have wanted to spearhead a project to improve the 486 computer when the far-advanced Pentium (and its grandchildren!) was already on the horizon.

Whereas general economic conditions have more of an indirect effect, particular industry conditions can have a direct impact on your plan.

Some of the industry-related issues you'll want to investigate are:

- Technological picture—What are the uncertainties and promising directions?
- Industry growth—Is the industry gaining or losing ground? Has there been a boom, and is there about to be a downturn, or vice versa?
- Barriers to entry—Can you take advantage of economies of scale? Can you compete with existing competitors' brand

identity and loyalty? What are the capital requirements? What is the expected reaction to new entrants in the market?
■ Distribution—Who are the suppliers and distributors, and are they reliable?
■ Consumer—What is the profile of the buyer?

To get a good picture of your industry, review economic census information about competing firms: how many compete, how many employees they have, what have been the trends over the past few years. There are numerous books and publications which compile information by industry, as well as encyclopedias and survey reports that list companies and their performance. Look first at public companies, then at private ones.

What key trends have been taking place in the industry, and what are industry-wide results? Are industry sales up or down, and what are the annual growth rates?

You almost always need an international perspective on your industry. As many industries have discovered, what is happening internationally today critically shapes the industry of tomorrow.

Maybe the best-known example is the car industry. At one time, the Japanese car industry was inconsequential in the United States. It took only a gas shortage and a growing consumer interest in quality to springboard the Japanese car companies into industry leaders in the United States. In the 1970s and even the 1980s it was difficult to imagine that a Japanese car company would have the best selling luxury car in the United States, but that is what Toyota's Lexus is today.

How does the industry measure its results? In other words, what are the common financial factors, such as gross profit margin, operating expense ratios, and net profit margin?

Industries usually go through stages. In the beginning, one company often leads the way. Then high levels of innovation and new companies follow. If it is an industry with significant potential, it can take decades for this potential to unfold.

The computer industry is a good example. We are in the midst of a continuing expansion—no one can predict how large this industry might grow to be. Eventually, an industry will reach mature status, which is a time where growth is flat or equal to the rate of population growth. Innovation subsides and the new ideas are mostly modifications to features that have existed for some time. Industries also can begin a period of decline, which may go through several stages. Clearly, it is important to know where your industry is and where it is likely to go. Do not be discouraged about your idea because the industry is in a declining stage. Often the highest profitability is achieved in this stage.

Financial analysts track public companies, and some specialize in industries. Check the analyst who follows yours. If you have a full service broker, ask for her reports. If you use a discount broker, then consult his Web site to determine what reports he has on the companies in your industry.

What if your concept is in an area that's outside your realm of expertise? For example, suppose you're an accounting manager with a brainstorm about a new training technique. Once again, an analyst or subject matter expert can help. Ask friends or colleagues in the field to steer you to the right associations, or try the library or the Internet to locate potential contacts.

Maybe the single most important perspective you need in researching your industry is determining the customer or consumer dynamics. The investigation starts with the basics, questions like who are they demographically and how many of them are there. More important in some cases than the raw numbers are the trends. If yours is a growing industry, who are the new consumers discovering your products and how are they similar to or different from your standard customers?

Demographics are important, but you will need to dig deeper for the insights that help you determine the potential power of your idea. Consumer attitudes and reasons for buying often provide the critical clues about the potential for your idea. Sometimes you find that consumers of the same product have very different reasons for buying it.

For example, through its research, the wine industry found that it had several types of consumers. One type of consumer was very clear that they would never buy an advertised wine brand. They loved discovering a new winery and then sharing the wine with friends. They loved learning about the nuances of wine and could often describe in detail such things as where the best grapes are grown, the optimal production process, and details about the winery history. These same people describe the taste of a wine in elaborate terms—a hint of apricot, a dash of vanilla, with a strong note of cherry on the finish, for example.

They also identified another type of consumer—one that could not be more different. This type would only buy an advertised brand of wine. They wanted the safety cues in a social situation that an advertised brand gave them. They did not have the time or interest to learn about the lore of wine. When they described the taste of their favorite wine, they would say something like, "It's good, not too sweet."

Obviously if you were in this industry, it would be very important to understand about the differences between consumer attitudes. In this case, the marketing plan for your idea would be very different for the two types of consumers.

In almost every industry, you can discover that there are consumer segments that want different benefits and buy for different reasons. Unless your industry association conducts this type of research, the only way you can obtain it is through customized research.

To get the most value from this type of research, you need to conduct it more than once. Often the most important thing to learn is the changing trends.

For example, in the wine industry, the people who would never buy an advertised brand were an increasing segment. While they were relatively small in number, they were growing rapidly and bought the most expensive wines. This made them a valuable segment for wineries to focus on. If the industry only had a one-time snapshot of this segment, it might have dismissed them as too small today to focus on. Instead, with years of this type of research, it saw a steady rise in both the number of this type of consumer and their per capita consumption.

Industry Data

Depending on your industry, the amount of available data may be measured by the pound. The challenge is identifying the important numbers, which vary by industry. In most industries, the following numbers are important:

- Size—In most cases, the size of an industry is important. The size influences your predicted sales based on the share you expect.

- Trends—The fact that an industry is growing, flat, or declining usually is critically important to how your idea will be viewed by senior management. The trend data is used to make projections of future sales and to suggest future industry dynamics, like the entry or exit of other companies in the industry.

- Profitability—Current industry profit margins and their future prospects are critical pieces of data. Within this there are two important components—prices and costs. For example, if your new technology can dramatically lower costs while prices appear to be steady, then the profits from your idea will be very attractive.

Your Market, Your Company, and Your Competition

Typically this is the portion of your research where the data multiplies. This can overwhelm even the best researcher and analyst. While vast amounts of data are involved in this stage, you will most likely emerge with two or three key insights that will determine how well your idea will perform.

There are three areas of investigation, explored individually but not unrelated to one another.

The first is your market, which is the portion of an industry where your idea will compete. In the computer industry, for example, your idea may compete in the laptop market. Your market includes everything from making to selling your product.

The second area that you want to educate yourself about is your company. We already discussed this with the exploration of your company's culture, vision, mission, and values. But as you will discover, it is much more than that.

Lastly, you want to educate yourself about your competition. It is amazing how often this is overlooked during the education process. You should know your competition almost as well as you know your own company.

Your Market—The Power of Knowing Who and What

Not every idea represents an opportunity. To be viable, an idea must have a market: a group of willing consumers with buying power. It's not enough to envision something you would use; would anyone else use it?

Take the typewriter as an example. Until the computer overtook our lives, the typewriter was standard in every office, and, fairly often, in people's homes. Yet the typewriter took about fifty years from its invention to be seen as a useful tool.

Henry Mill, around 1714, invented early versions of writing machines. Mark Twain, in fact, bought the first Remington in 1874, and he was, apparently, just about the only person to appreciate its benefits. From its introduction until the early 1880s, only 5,000 were sold. However, by 1888, Remington was selling 1,500 each month.

You probably don't have twelve years to wait for the public to appreciate your idea. Define your market on the front end to determine how big it is. Ask yourself, "Is this market limited to local opportunities, or could it extend to the national or even international arena?"

In some cases, your idea may be in response to a market need. For instance, Internet banking was clearly a result of consumer demand. The Hampton Inn hotel concept, a limited facility hotel primarily for business travelers, was also a market-driven opportunity.

In other cases you may actually be creating a market, in which case an education process is a prerequisite. Microwave ovens took a number of years to catch on because consumers had to be convinced of their value and their safety.

Today, even with the Internet growing in scope and popularity, consumers are wary of banking and conducting other financial transactions online. Any idea that eliminates consumer concerns and is easy to use will appeal to this market.

Clarence Saunders, founder of Piggly Wiggly food stores, originally found no market for his supermarket concept. Today it is a multistate success.

FedEx did find a market for its combination mail delivery/guaranteed overnight service. It found the consumer need for fast and reliable delivery was powerful when there was a high level of dissatisfaction with the U. S. Postal Service.

And Bank of America, now owned by Nations Bank, pioneered the credit card business. When it first started, it was met with some skepticism and resistance—hard to believe in today's world of broad-based acceptance.

Perhaps your idea is the next McDonald's!

These are just a few examples of why it is important to understand your market. As you set out to understand your market, there are a few critical areas for you to understand. How much you need to learn depends on what is right for your idea. An expert in consumer research can help you make these decisions.

First, you need to understand your consumers—the people who you hope will use your product. We touched on this in the previous section on understanding your industry. At this stage you want to dig even deeper. You want to understand what benefits people want from their product. You quickly find that different people want different things.

For example, in the beer market some people insist that they determine the brand they purchase based on taste. Within this group, some people purchase a beer for its very light taste. Coors Light has a very loyal following because of its light, unassuming taste. Another group wants a deep, rich taste in their beer. These people might consider Coors Light bland and uninteresting. People who want a robust taste often purchase one of the hundreds of microbrew brands. There are other groups of consumers for whom different taste characteristics are important.

If your market is beer, you should not stop learning about these consumers at this stage. You need to dig deeper. For example, do the reasons they express for buying suggest a certain profile? Does this profile match their actual behavior? Often people will tell you one thing in the course of research but act differently. Where behavior and attitudes do not match, it suggests there is another factor that really controls their purchase behavior.

This could lead you to identify large groups of consumers who choose their beer brand for reasons that have nothing to do with taste. There is a large group of consumers whose primary reason for buying is that they identify with the image of a brand.

For example, some people love the Bud Man image. Some forms of research will have difficulty detecting this, but more sophisticated forms of consumer research will not. Other people love the image of a microbrew brand. Research often finds that consumers who buy for image-related reasons often reject their brand in blind taste testing—where they taste their product unaware of the brand.

In this brief discussion, we have only touched on the depths you need to go to in order to understand the consumer part of your market. In consumer research, many available tools help the investigator develop a clear understanding of his consumer. The tools are both quantitative and qualitative.

Qualitative Research

Extensive qualitative research, such as focus groups and one-on-one consumer research, often precedes quantitative research. One of the most important determinations in qualitative research is understanding consumer language about products and brands.

For example, in the beer market, there is a taste language unique to the beverage. If you do not understand the language, the questions you ask in later quantitative research will not be understandable or relevant to consumers. If you do not have the right language, consumers will still try to answer the questions in quantitative research. Unfortunately, the answers need to be treated with great caution, and may even be misleading or worthless if they are not in the consumer's context.

When doing qualitative research you need to resist the urge to draw quantitative conclusions. When you have an idea and all ten people in a focus group love the idea, it can be difficult to resist the urge to say that 100 percent of consumers loved the idea in consumer research. But resist you must. The problems far outweigh the time saved. A few key problems are:

- It is the opinion of a few people in one or a few cities. It is not the sample size or diversity necessary for quantitative research.

- People often are not candid in group research like focus groups. Instead of expressing their honest opinions, they often alter their expressions to draw a favorable response from others in the group.

- If products are used in the focus groups, it is not the environment where a consumer is accustomed to using products. One of the advantages of quantitative research is that products are used in their typical environment.

As useful as research can be, you need to be careful extending research findings across cultures. Mrs. Fields Cookies found that its most successful marketing tool for bringing in customers in the United States—passing out free samples outside the store—proved to be a total disaster in Tokyo. Not only did people in Tokyo not take the offered samples, they crossed the street to avoid them!

What they later learned was that the Asian cultures do not support eating food in public while walking down the street. They quickly wrapped each sample in gold paper tied with a ribbon, and once again offered the samples. Not only did people take the samples, but Mrs. Fields Cookies eventually opened thirty-five stores across the Pacific Rim due to the demand!

Mrs. Fields experienced another unanticipated marketing issue regarding pricing. In the United States, its stores often held promotions where, for example, if you bought three cookies, you would receive one free. However, in certain countries in the Pacific Rim, it realized that particular numbers held a cultural significance: Some numbers are lucky and bring good fortune, others have a negative connotation or meaning. Local management determined which numbers were acceptable in setting prices and promotions, and which numbers should be avoided.

Qualitative Data

While qualitative research should be devoid of numeric conclusions, there are some key numbers you need to know that will help you sell your idea:

- Scope—How extensive was your qualitative research? Did you just do one night of focus groups or did you do five nights in five carefully chosen cities? The key numbers here include the number of nights and consumers talked to in the groups.

- Breadth—How many concepts or ideas did you share with consumers? How many of them changed, if any, during the course of the research?

- Nonnumber numbers—It is inappropriate and misleading to state numeric conclusions (53.5 percent of consumers liked the idea), but it is fair to give a numeric sense of the outcome. Thus, words like "many," "most," "some," and "little" are appropriate to give management a sense of the response.

Quantitative Research

Quantitative research collects data that is representative of a national sample of your consumers. The amount of data you collect during quantitative research can be overwhelming. The researcher's job is to find one or two gems—those pieces of data that indicate whether your idea is a good or bad one.

The researcher has many forms of validated research methods at his disposal. The first challenge is knowing the strengths and weaknesses of these different methods. As valuable as consumer research can be, there are some crucial elements of your idea that it may not reliably measure:

Price—Research generally is not effective in evaluating whether the price you want to sell a product for is the right one. The major challenge is that consumers do not have to spend their money in the research so it is not a realistic situation. There are research methods that can provide guidance about the right price, but only selling the product in the market will provide the answers you need.

Imagination—Asking consumers to imagine a new product usually results in vague and confusing results. Even if the results appear to point clearly in one direction, do not rely on them 100 percent when making important decisions. For reliable results, give consumers the real product. You can, however, provide consumers a clear, complete concept to evaluate. While this may be only words or words and pictures, it often provides valuable guidance. The research remains valuable only if the actual product delivers on the promise of the concept.

If you are not a professional researcher, you need to use one to structure new research and evaluate old research. It is crucial to use an expert in planning new research because of the importance of how you ask a question. Questions need to be asked very objectively, using proven answering methods—scales and key words, for example.

Evaluate previously conducted research with care. Often you may want to evaluate a sub-group of the research.

For example, you may want to look at the reactions of only the people between 20 and 29 years old in a piece of research done among people 20–65 years old. A frequent caution with evaluating sub-groups is that the number of people may be too small to provide reliable data. Frequently in one-time studies, a sample size of 100–150 people will provide a nationally representative sample. When this is the case, it can be difficult to obtain sub-groups large enough to evaluate. If you want to conduct new research, know beforehand if sub-group evaluation is important. If it is, then increase the sample size so that there will be enough people in the sub-groups.

These cautions should not dissuade you from using quantita-tive research on your idea. Most major companies use research be-fore an idea becomes a product and hits the market. Some of the important answers research provides are:

How well consumers like the major benefits of your product—Giving consumers an actual product sample and allowing them to use it in their daily context provides some of the most valuable in-formation. This research is even more valuable when consumers also try a competitive product and evaluate it the same way they evaluate yours.

What benefits are most important to consumers—Knowing what benefits consumers want most in a type of product is crucial to evaluating an idea. If your idea provides a benefit that ranks low on consumers' lists of importance, you may be wasting your time. If it is truly not important to consumers, then even a major im-provement will create a yawn.

For example, a company once touted the medals it won in com-petition with other products. When the advertising failed to gener-ate much of a response, the company conducted research to find out why. It discovered that consumers ranked "winning medals" as the twenty-fourth most important benefit they wanted from their product. When a benefit is ranked outside of the top two or three, the benefit is likely to appeal to a limited number of users. Some-times in a widely used product category, an idea with narrow ap-peal can still represent millions of consumers.

How consumers use your product—It is dangerous to assume that everyone uses your product the way you intend. When you conduct basic habits and practices research, you will be surprised by the diversity of use your product receives—who, where, when, and why. This research is especially valuable when it is conducted every few years so that trends in usage are evaluated. These trends often spark new ideas and applications for your product.

Preliminary market appeal—Concept research can signal the level of interest consumers will have for your new idea. This research is also most valuable when the results can be compared to other concepts that either failed or succeeded in the market.

Rough volume estimates—Several companies sell research that provides a rough volume estimate, plus approximately 20 percent. The reliability of this research varies by product category and the quality of the inputs.

For example, the assumptions you make about the level of distribution and television advertising critically influences the estimate you receive. If you fail to reach your distribution target in the designated time, or if the advertising is not effective, then your estimate may be of little value. Some companies have enough experience with this type of research that if certain minimum scores are not achieved then they will not proceed to a test market.

Quantitative Data

What data from your research is most important to your idea depends upon what product or category of products your idea fits into. In most cases, data from quantitative research is most valuable when it is compared to other projects that were eventually marketed. With this caveat, there are certain measures that often are very important to a project.

Overall rating—In research, consumers rate an idea on a five-, seven-, or nine-point scale. On a five-point scale, the number of responses in the highest rating are most important. For seven- or nine-point scales, you want to pay attention to the responses in the two highest ratings. Even when considering the top two, the highest rating is still very important.

Purchase Intent—When consumers are asked on a five- or seven-point scale to indicate their intent to purchase, you should evaluate the scores as you do the overall rating. An important word of caution—do not use the percentage of people saying they would purchase the product to create a volume estimate. Indications of purchase intent only measure relative enthusiasm and interest in the idea.

Positive and Negative Ratios—The ratio of things people like to the things people dislike can be an important measure of an idea's strength. For example, if 75 percent of people like something about your idea and 50 percent dislike something, then your ratio of likes to dislikes is 1.5:1. Depending on the product this may be a good ratio, but often a 2:1 like to dislike ratio is desirable. In fact, you want dislikes to be as low as possible. When they are higher than 25–33 percent, they provide clues as to how you can improve your idea.

Key Benefit Scores—When you know the top reasons people buy a product, you want to know how well your idea scores on those reasons. For example, if fresh fruit taste is one of the key reasons people buy a beverage, then you will want very high scores on this characteristic. While this varies by product type, you usually want 50 percent or more of people to rank your "fresh fruit taste" as excellent or very good.

Your Company

You may think that you know your company well and that additional education is not necessary. Before you decide this, visit other departments and ask for their help in your research.

Departments inside your company can be very helpful in defining the scope of a new venture. Remember, however, that everyone is busy; be sensitive to others' priorities as you request assistance, and try to give adequate lead time to allow them flexibility in fulfilling your request.

Lisa Albanese, business development advisor at a major corporation, offers one very good piece of advice before soliciting input from other departments. She says,

> Try to understand as much as you can about the various functions outside your area in order to establish credibility. Research everything you can about finance, marketing, operations, etc., so you will understand what they are telling you. That way, you will also ask more appropriate, intelligent questions, using everyone's time more effectively.

If you don't already have strong internal relationships, seek out someone in an area that's pivotal to your project, such as finance or marketing. Pick a person who has a good reputation, and who seems to have the respect and confidence of senior management. Is there someone who has been instrumental in another successful project? Solicit that person's assistance. Ask her to be on your research team, and build your network from there.

To get the best results from your network, let your sources help define what's important to the project. Give them an overview, acknowledge their expertise, and ask them for counsel on what numbers and information are relevant. Let them help you determine the ripple effects of your idea, both positive and negative, and what steps might help to mitigate any problems. This is a way to begin building ownership for your idea, a factor that can make or break it down the road.

A side benefit to the process is that you'll be giving a heads-up to departments that will be affected once your idea is approved. They'll have time to plan their own changes to support your plan.

You want to know where your company has advantages and the strength of these advantages. Probe any patents your company holds that might relate to your idea. Be careful—just because your company has a patent does not mean that a competitor could not match your idea some other way. At the very least, a patent related to your idea would probably slow another company down if it tried to respond to your initiative.

Some companies have advantages that are difficult to measure. For example, a sales organization may believe it is the best, but how can this be determined? If your company has access to channels of distribution that a competitor does not have, then this may be a meaningful advantage.

Financial resources also can be an advantage. It is important to understand the financial condition of both your company and your competitors. Determining everyone's debt levels and available cash can be important.

If your company has exclusivity agreements with other companies, this may be a meaningful advantage. For example, if you have an exclusivity agreement with a supplier of a key part (for which they may have a patent) or ingredient that is critical to your idea, this may provide an important edge.

As important as advantages are, you also need to know where you have disadvantages versus other companies.

Your Competition

In an existing market, you'll need to know as much as possible about the competition. What are its strengths and weaknesses? Are its customers' satisfied with the existing product or service? And how will it react to more competition?

You may be amazed at how much you can discover about your competitor. At the end of your investigation, you may know them better than you know your own company.

Companies frequently learn more about their competitors by putting a talented person on special assignment to discover all he can about them. This "special agent's" efforts often include:

Public Data—There are exceptionally rich resources available for information on most companies. Start by collecting all of the company's published data—annual reports, Web sites, and press releases. Many companies make all of this available at their Web site or you can contact their public relations office. The next step is conducting a search of magazine and newspaper stories. Again, Internet search capabilities can help you collect most of these stories in a couple of hours.

Next, contact your company's broker to get published analytical reports on the competitors. They can also help you obtain public SEC reports that are not widely available. The library often has the Value Line service, which has extensive data on most publicly traded companies. When you have collected all of this, the challenge becomes understanding the companies' strategies, strengths, and weaknesses.

Service Data—Through service companies like Nielsen Media Research, you can purchase data from companies that sell their products in retail stores. You can determine the level of retailer support: number of ads and displays, pricing, out-of-stock levels, distribution by size and type, and share of various market segments and product categories. You can also obtain information from services about the level of marketing support. For example, services collect information on the number of television and radio advertising spots. With the help of a media company, you can calculate advertising costs, which can be an important part of calculating profitability. Financial service companies like Dun & Bradstreet are also excellent sources of information.

Personal Investigation—Most companies offer tours of production facilities. Tour competitive facilities with an expert from production at your company. Go with your sales managers to call on major customers to discover what they know about competitor policies and initiatives. Are your competitors liked? Where can you find an opening to gain an advantage with distributors or end sellers, like retailers? You can also get a sense of the size of their sales organization, which may be an important cost component. Talk with your raw material suppliers—in many cases they also supply your competitors.

Vendors and suppliers have a different perspective on your business. They undoubtedly serve others in the same industry, which gives them a broader view of issues. These outsiders' perspectives can frequently make you aware of roadblocks you might not otherwise identify. For example, several years ago paper industry sales reps predicted a 30 percent increase in paper costs a year in advance. Such information would have been immensely important to you had you been considering expanding into the publishing industry. Without breaching confidentiality agreements, learn all you can about how they make their products and what their costs are.

With a resourceful attitude, you will discover additional sources of data unique to your industry and competitors.

Remember, the goal is not just to collect data. Rather, you want to synthesize the data to learn the company's strategy, profitability, new product ideas, and areas of advantage and disadvantage versus your company. When you have this information, you can better evaluate your idea.

For example, if you discover that a competitor has advantages you do not have relative to your idea, or that you would be entering your competitor's core business, you may want to reconsider your idea. This competitor might put up a very strong defense to your attempt to enter one of its core businesses. The result might be erosion of market profitability and ultimately the failure of your attempt to gain business at the competitor's expense.

Figure 2.1 provides a good format for organizing and analyzing data about your competitors.

Figure 2.1

Checking Out the Competition

* How many firms compete?
* Are there a few dominant firms and many "mom and pops"?
* What is the financial strength of the major players?
* Do competitors enjoy any distinct location advantages?
* Are there brand names that give competitors an edge?
* What is the consumer's perception of the service?
* What type of distribution channel is the customer accustomed to?
* How is the product or service sold, i.e., catalogue, retail, Internet, door-to-door?
* Is the competitor satisfied with its current position?
* Where is the competitor most vulnerable? Financially? R&D? Distribution?
* What businesses will the competitor defend vigorously?

Competitor Data

While the numbers that are most important to your idea may be somewhat unique, there are important numbers regarding your competition that almost all projects need.

Profitability—By following the steps outlined above, you can develop accurate estimates of a competitor's costs and selling prices.

Trends and Size—The sales data from Nielsen Media Research and other services is an excellent source of volume and share trend data. Often data for multiple channels is available which can represent over 50 percent of a competitor's volume. That is enough of a sample to make reasonably accurate estimates. With size and profitability information, you can estimate total dollar profits.

Vision and Goals—Often the information you collect about a competitor's vision and goals do not have specific numbers. But it often has phrases like "being the market leader" that suggest the approximate position they hope to achieve. Often the failure to mention some of their businesses suggests these businesses are secondary priorities. This can be important information for your idea.

Synthesizing and Concluding

By this point you have reviewed an awful lot of data. All of it is helpful to some degree, but there are a few critical learnings, maybe only one or two, that help you shape and mold your idea into a really great one. Now that you have looked at your market, company, and competitors, it is time to look for interrelationships between the points you have learned.

Two examples help illustrate how valuable this process can be:

1. You find the market you are interested in is growing rapidly now and looks like it will continue for at least a couple more years. Your company has the expertise to make a better-performing product than the number one and two brands on the market today. You also discover that the company that makes the number one brand is very committed to the market out of the many it competes in today. It made its number one brand in this market the centerpiece of its most recent annual report. It indicated that research and development spending was up over 50 percent on the business and that the company made other investments in the brand. This is a strong cautionary note. You know it would vigorously defend against the introduction of your idea. This puts a premium on ensuring that

your improvement is exceptionally strong and that there are adequate defenses, like patents, to prevent the number one brand from quickly duplicating your effort.

2. Your education process discovers that the market you are interested in has flattened out and is showing signs of a possible decline in future years. Two secondary market share brands have pulled back marketing effort, which may be a prelude to dropping out altogether. Your brand is number two in the market and has increased its market share for the last three years. Your investigation of your number one competitor revealed it significantly changed the components of its product and moved assembly to offshore. This lowered costs by about 20 percent while increasing selling prices about 4 percent per year. Net, the number one competitor doubled its profit margin in the last three years.

This information provides you the encouragement you need to undertake a marketing initiative to turn your idea into the number one brand. By making similar cost improvements in your brand, you increase the potential investment funds. In addition, while other companies are pulling back you can build on the momentum you already have to take the number one position.

In both examples, what was learned about your market, company, and competitors is brought together. Weaving the learnings together creates an integrated view of your idea that fully acknowledges current realities. This is a powerful stage where a few key insights shape both your idea and the direction in which you take it.

Your Idea

As much as you may want to believe your idea is unique, it's possible that someone thought of it before. That could be good news or bad news. The good news is that it may still be a viable idea, and you can go to school on what contributed to its success or failure: timing, marketing, capitalization, risk, or perhaps other factors.

In your research, you may find that someone has tried an idea very similar to yours, but you believe that there are significant differences in your version. Treat this as good news because you now have the opportunity to "go to school" on a previous effort.

Immediately launch into a learning mode. Collect every available piece of data. If the product is sold in retail stores, you can probably buy data to determine a wide range of useful information—sales pattern, pricing, retailer support, distribution, and other useful input. You can obtain this information for any test markets and regional and national expansions.

If the company advertises, you can have an agency search several services for copies of print or television ads. Ads often signal the company's thinking about why consumers would purchase the product. Ask your sales department about its insights and maybe it can collect retailer insights about the product. If possible, purchase a sample of the product. Use it yourself and have your research and production managers evaluate the idea.

It does not matter at this stage whether the similar idea succeeded or failed. What some people consider failures turn out to be great learning opportunities for others. Disposable diapers, Procter & Gamble's largest-volume business today, "failed" in test market ten times before it was expanded nationally.

Look for similar ideas in other product categories. If your idea is an improvement to an existing product, for example, look for products in any business that tried to do this. See if you can determine introductory elements that seemed to work and those that did not seem to work. Look at packaging and all forms of communication to consumers or end users of the product. What seemed to be the most effective form of communicating the benefits of the product improvement?

We hear a lot about ideas that work: Southwest Airlines, Post-It Notes, Microsoft Windows. But what about the ideas that languished in market research and never got off the ground? Or, worse yet, were implemented and fizzled out before they even got started?

Other failures never achieve enough significance to even be a blip on the marketing calendar. It's best to know as much history as possible before you waltz into your CEO expounding the benefits of something that should never see the light of day.

As you consider your idea, there are often special considerations. Two of the most common are:

1. Businesses Outside Your Field—Getting into a business that's new to your company, even if it is in the same general industry, is a little like running a start-up: high risk. You do not necessarily have the experience and expertise that helped you succeed in your current businesses.

Recognize this as a challenge. As you move forward with your idea you will need a plan to address how these shortfalls will be dealt with. Some alternatives are: hiring consultants with relevant experience, hiring new managers from similar businesses, or acquiring a company already in the type of business you want to enter. Information is for sale from a host of companies that specialize in market research, economic forecasting, and other complex topics. There may be substantial fees for such services. Typically, before investing in a consulting agreement, you'll want to get preliminary approval from management. Be sure that the idea is one they believe worthy of this kind of expenditure. When the last alternative is pursued, you must rely upon the expertise of the other company's existing management. Plans for retaining those managers will be essential to your overall success.

What synergies exist with your current business? Are there ways to shorten the learning curve? These are just a few of the questions you need to ask when your idea involves entering a business outside your current field of experience. The general advice is to proceed with caution. The right attitude is critical. You need to assume there are major things you do not know. Develop a never-ending desire to learn and when you think you know it all, be prepared to learn some more.

2. Regulated Businesses—Aviation, banking, and other government-regulated industries carry their own peculiar risks, because regulations can always change. Regulations also impose a heavy administrative and legal expense that is more than most unregulated businesses. In fact, some businesses that aren't regulated

today could be tomorrow, for example, the tobacco industry. Who could have predicted that advertising would be outlawed?

First Tennessee National Corporation experienced the effects of changes in regulatory requirements with First Express, a product that eventually became highly successful after a slightly challenging start. Prior to 1980, the Federal Reserve was not allowed to subsidize their activities in the check-clearing business. The Banking Act of 1980, however, required the Federal Reserve to fully cost and to charge for their check-clearing services. This provided an opportunity for commercial banks to compete with the Federal Reserve and First Tennessee seized that opportunity. By partnering with FedEx and anticipating that the Fed would lose its competitive position, the company began First Express.

Environmental issues have taken their toll on many a business, with provisions for emissions hitting manufacturers of a wide array of products.

So, in any business that's regulated, things can change without warning. Stay on top of developments and depend on experts to help you understand what could be on the horizon in the next five years.

To help you navigate this situation you need help—consultants and lawyers—which can be expensive. Be sure to factor this into your estimates and plans.

Supposedly, a good attorney never asks a witness a question without knowing what the answer will be. With proper preparation, you will be in a better position to competently answer any questions about your idea, and will have substantial backup material to support it.

What Type of Idea Is It?

Determining the type of idea you have helps to point your education process in the right direction.

An innovation is more than an invention. Management expert Peter Drucker (1985) says that "Innovation is the specific function of entrepreneurship . . . it is the means by which the entrepreneur creates new wealth-producing resources or endows existing resources with enhanced potential for creating wealth."

Some innovations are radical, involving new products or new markets, while others are less radical, involving minor changes or extensions of existing businesses.

Several specific types of innovation deserve brief definition. First, an invention is something completely new. Thomas Edison's light bulb and the Wright brothers' airplane are good examples

Second, a product modification is usually an improvement in one of a product's benefits. The "new and improved" announcements you see on products are usually examples of this.

Third, a product extension is when an existing product is sold for new uses. This usually involves introducing, sometimes in modified form, a product to a new group of consumers or users as a replacement for an existing product. Coca-Cola has tried numerous times to convince people that its Diet Coke and Coke products make good coffee replacements. This attempt to extend their usage into a new consumption occasion has not met with much success. McDonald's has been much more successful extending itself into the breakfast business although it is still a secondary segment for them.

Fourth, an expansion is similar but usually involves the distribution function. For example, at one time someone had the idea to expand Coke into Japan. Expansion of well known brands into new markets has been a major source of growth for most international companies throughout the 1980s and 1990s.

Fifth, forming alliances with other companies has been a major business-building approach for years. Reviewing Microsoft's press releases over the last couple of years reveals a wide range of alliances the company has formed with hardware manufacturers, software providers, and consumer products.

Sixth, mergers and acquisitions like Citibank and Travelers and Smith Barney have become significant ways to build businesses in an international business environment where size and breadth of services becomes critical to long-term success. Mergers and acquisitions enable companies to offer a fuller range of products to the customer base of each organization. The information you will need for your idea varies by type of innovation. For example:

Invention—The legal department is often quickly involved with an invention to determine if it can be patented and to ensure that confidentiality agreements protect the company's interests. You often need to learn about the engineering and technical aspects of your idea more than with other kinds of innovation.

Modification—This type of innovation can require many of the same perspectives but usually to a lesser degree. This type of idea often puts a premium on excellent consumer research—do consumers want your modification and, if so, is there enough of an improvement to make consumers want to switch from a competitive product.

Extension—The learning curve for a product extension can be a broad one. You usually need to learn about a new group of users or consumers, or an environment that is different from what you are used to. The learning can involve going back to basics as McDonald's found out when it first undertook a serious effort to increase its share of the breakfast business. Almost anyone whose idea has involved extending a current product into new uses tells stories of how much more difficult it was than they expected.

Expansion—The education process can also be arduous if your idea is to expand an existing product into a new market. Just ask Kodak about its multiple attempts over two-plus decades to build a business in Japan versus Fuji.

Alliances—The skills used to learn about a competitor outlined above are useful here. You need to learn as much as possible about a potential alliance partner—are their perceived strengths real and defensible, for example.

Mergers and acquisitions—The education process is even more critical in a merger or acquisition than in an alliance. If you are the acquiring company, you will need to live with the good, the bad, and the ugly. The depth and breadth of learning about another company is never deeper than in this type of innovation.

Exactly what information you need also rests on factors such as whether the project is intended to generate revenue, save money, or improve your culture. Naturally, the numbers will be a critical part of what you're presenting, but there is quite a bit of other information that's necessary to develop an effective plan.

All plans should include information about the background of the project and projected results. For certain types of projects, you'll need additional data:

- Projects that produce revenue: You will need heavily market-related and sales information.

- Projects that save money: What expenses will you cut? Where will savings come from and how long will it take to recognize them? What will the effect be? If you cut ten positions and save $1 million, what will the impact be?

- Projects that improve quality: While many quality issues are subjective, you can measure related factors such as customer satisfaction ratings, number of complaints, or employee satisfaction levels.

- Product improvements: Will you improve the product by redesigning it, or by using a new production process, or will you tighten production standards? What will the trade-off be? What percent of mistakes are you willing to live with? How will it affect customers?

- Service improvements: How many man-hours will it take to achieve the improvement? What's the trade-off? Will it reduce service in another area, or will it require additional labor hours? What training will be required? How will it affect customers?

- Employee-related improvements: What critical business issues will it address (declining quality, customer complaints, etc.)? How will it contribute to future efforts to attract or retain employees? How will you measure progress?

Startup Ventures—Often a Special Case

When you're proposing to expand or modify an existing business you will already have comprehensive information about the marketplace and the track record of the business; this is the foundation for predicting growth. With a start-up venture, however, you'll have to make a lot of educated guesses about the potential for success.

Start-ups require well-grounded market analysis that will convince executives to take a risk on an unknown market.

Idea Life Cycle

Regardless of the type and magnitude of your idea, you must realize that every idea has a lifespan and will eventually be modified or die. This is not to say that your idea was not a good idea; in fact, all ideas must eventually evolve to keep abreast of changing times. Therefore, not only should you plan for the birth of your idea, but also its death. Betsy Williams, VP of human resources at Nielsen Media Research explains, "Your goal should not be limited to just getting your idea launched—that only offers short-term value to a company. To provide long-term value to a company, an idea and its processes must continually be evaluated and modified to stay current."

Final Checking

So far we have covered a lot of ground in a relatively short time. It is now time for a thought-provoking checklist of questions frequently encountered along the path of educating yourself. Use this list to stimulate your thinking and feel free to add to it those questions that will make you prepared to know if you have a good idea or a really great idea.

Marketing and Sales

- What is the market for this product? Is it growing?
- What segments are growing the most/least?
- Have there been any recent changes in the market?
- Where are the customers and how will we reach them?
- How will we sell the product or service?
- Is this product in response to customer needs or will we have to educate them?

- Who is the target audience for the idea and why? Are there enough of them to make this a worthwhile idea?
- Are there existing outlets or distribution channels?
- Will we have to advertise?
- Do we have a well-founded, compelling message for consumers?
- What will a marketing program cost?
- How should we price the product?
- Should we test market? What is our greatest learning need?
- How long will it take to generate sales?
- What sales should we project?
- What will the pattern of sales be? How long is the sales cycle?
- What share can we expect to earn, and how long will it take?
- How will competitors respond?
- Can we maintain a timing advantage? Can competitors quickly replicate our idea?

Market Research

- What existing research can we draw upon?
- Will we need to do original research? How long will it take and what will it cost?
- How reliable are the research tools that can provide information about my major questions?
- Who will conduct the research?
- Will this project require market testing?
- How much lead time will we need to conduct any studies?
- Is it actionable or simply nice-to-know research?
- When the product or service is in place, how will we measure customer satisfaction?
- How often should we measure progress?

Operations or Production (if applicable)

- Will we make this product, or should we contract out? What would it cost? How would we control production quality?
- What equipment will be required to produce this product?
- Do we have the equipment?

- Will our existing facilities need to be revamped?
- Will we have to buy or lease equipment? How long will it take to get it?
- How much will these things cost?
- Do we have existing vendors for the supplies we'll need?
- Can we get supplies at a reasonable time and cost?
- Can our current employees be trained to operate the new equipment?
- How many employees will be required?
- How will we monitor and ensure quality?

Information Technology (IT)

- Is this project in keeping with current IT trends?
- What technology would be required to support this new idea?
- Will we need to buy or lease new hardware?
- Do we have the staff to develop and implement it?
- What technical support would we have to provide, and for how long?
- How many other areas will we need to interface with, and can we do that cost-effectively? How long will it take?
- Are our vendors and customers equipped to handle this project? What will it cost?

Human Resources

- What staff resources will be required to support the operation?
- Should we consider outsourcing?
- Are those resources on staff now and can they do this?
- Where would we need to recruit from?
- How will we reward, recognize, motivate, and retain employees?
- What wages and benefits will be required?
- What training is necessary and who will do it?
- How soon will we need to hire staff?

- How long will it take?
- Will we need outside resources? What will they cost?
- Will there be negative consequences to the organization as a result, such as elimination of positions, lowered morale, and so on?
- Can we absorb existing employees into other company areas?
- What type of outplacement program will we need? What would the timing and cost be?

Legal

- Are there legal restrictions or requirements for this idea?
- Should it be operated as a separate company or as a division of the existing corporation?
- Are there legal considerations before or after it's implemented?
- What will it cost to prepare legal documentation?

Communications or Public Relations

- Will there be positive consequences for the community? How can we take advantage of this?
- Will there be negative consequences for the community? How can we offset or minimize bad press?
- When and how will we communicate information to employees, customers, shareholders, and other stakeholders?

Accounting and Finance

Accounting and finance should be your last stop for information, because you'll need to take with you a summary of all the information you've gathered. By now you should be able to give the finance and accounting management a clear overview of your project and its scope, including costs.

Ask your financial sources to review your information about costs, savings, etc., and to help you decide what economic assumptions are valid. They can also guide you in what ratios are important to management, such as earnings per share and internal rate of return. They can help you develop a projected balance sheet, income statement, and cash flow statement, and help you develop comparisons or translate your numbers into measurements that are meaningful to your industry or company. For example, the hotel industry commonly describes revenue per available room; banks use return on assets; insurance agencies cite commission revenue per employee. Any project developed for those industries should be expressed in terms of their own applicable measurements.

With their assistance, you can determine how much working capital you'll need and can suggest how the project will be funded.

A question to ask your financial analyst is, "Will we need any special controls for this venture?" Let him help you define an audit trail for the project.

Key Learning Points

1. You must be thoroughly knowledgeable in all areas that impact your idea in order to convince others of its value. You may be surprised how much you can learn.
2. Assess your company's philosophy and readiness to accept your idea. Its vision and mission statements provide valuable clues.
3. Vast amounts of data are either free or available at a low cost on the Internet. You can learn about general economic conditions, your industry, markets, and competitors, and about international developments that can impact your idea.
4. Original research, usually with customers, is often the most useful and persuasive research you will do.
5. The most challenging part of the education process is synthesizing and drawing conclusions from the data. Anyone can collect data; it takes careful analysis and experience to draw insights that make a difference.

CHAPTER 3

Building a Business Case

"It usually takes more than three weeks to prepare a
good impromptu speech."

Mark Twain

If you've made it through the research phase and you're still
convinced your idea is sound, it's time to take the next step: Look at
your idea from an objective point of view. Try to see it as others would.

This is when you "build a business case." That is, you think your
idea through logically and back it up with the facts and figures to
prove it's a viable opportunity. Following this process will not only
reinforce your own belief in the idea, but it will also help you organize your information in a way that gets others just as excited.

In this chapter, you will learn the first steps necessary to develop your idea into a presentation to management for approval.

You will also learn about the kinds of financial numbers you may need in your presentation. Understanding what measures you will need to take is important before you begin to assemble the details of your plan.

When you have completed this preparation, you are ready to construct your proposal for management. This chapter puts a spotlight on the business plan, but also discusses other approaches major companies use to review and approve new ideas.

Taking the First Steps

When Peters and Waterman, authors of *In Search of Excellence*, were conducting their interviews at 3M, they were astonished that proposals for a new product rarely exceeded five pages. When asked about it, a vice president said, "We consider a coherent sentence to be an acceptable first draft for a new-product plan" (Hay, 1998).

Perhaps the key words there are "first draft." Ultimately, you will create a formal document known as a business plan, which could amount to 100 pages or more with all the backup detail.

The first steps depend on the practices within your company. In some instances, the first step is the full blown business plan just mentioned. In others, like at Procter & Gamble, it can be a "Basis for Interest" document. This outlines the rough parameters of your idea in one or two very well constructed pages. It essentially says to management, "If we could do this, would you be interested?"

Before you put pen to paper, however, it is important that you have identified in the education phase who the key people are that will be affected by your idea. G. Richard Shell, director of the Wharton Executive Negotiation Workshop and author of *Bargaining for Advantage: Negotiation Strategies for Reasonable People* (1999), stresses the absolute importance in building a coalition of support of your idea even at the early development stages. He says, "Once you have the seed of an idea, you must begin to plow the ground very carefully and methodically, talking to people, getting them interested and involved, and gaining their support."

He goes on to say,

> Be a good listener. Find out what others are interested in. Is your idea in their best interest? Don't give away too much too soon. Share you idea bit by bit as it relates to their interests. Let them help evolve the idea and share ownership. Get as much information and support as possible, even before you approach your boss, unless you are sure he or she is an immediate ally.

Is Anyone Interested?

Once you feel you've gained sufficient preliminary interest and support, albeit very informally, it is time to use the information you have gathered and proceed further in the inquiry process. The next step would be to schedule an appointment with your boss to discuss the idea and determine any additional front-end issues that might be of concern to senior management.

At this point, you might consider sending a document to the appropriate senior management that simply says, "We are thinking of doing _____. We think it is right because _____. The benefits of this are _____. If you agree, we will forward a formal proposal _____."

In a little more detail, the outline might be:

1. What you want to do—test higher levels of advertising, for example.
2. Why you are interested—the current advertising is working and might work harder at higher levels, for example.
3. What would be involved—the approximate cost of a test market and noting if the money is within current budgets or would require a supplemental request, for example.
4. Next steps and timing if there is an interest—management would have a formal proposal within two months, for example.

This approach can save you time because management has the opportunity to express initial concerns or questions. This helps you focus your work when you develop the extensive business plan. This approach is particularly helpful in advance of a new budget year. If you want to include the initial development costs of your idea in next year's budget, agreement to a preliminary interest document can often trigger that action.

The risk of this approach is that management might disagree with you. At the preliminary interest stage, you are not armed with your best case. For example, the product improvement is in the early development stages and you are unable to demonstrate how good it is. If it is not agreed to, it makes your job tougher in some regards, especially if you cannot get development work budgeted. The good news from an initial rejection is that you have a clearer idea of the issues you face and how strongly management feels.

Lisa Albanese, Business Development Advisor for a large international corporation, says that when such an initial rejection occurs, you must go back, research their concerns, and redefine the situation until all the key players understand the benefit to the corporation.

In other companies, there may be very informal first steps for a new idea that allow you to preview an idea and get some early management input. You may have an observation and go to your boss for initial input and feedback before pursuing any type of solution. At some companies, once an idea has been given an initial thumbs up by your boss, a cross-functional team with representatives from such areas as legal, finance, marketing, operations, and other impacted areas is put together to brainstorm solutions to the idea. Those solutions are explored with the best solution presented to key management for approval.

Some companies, instead of using a preliminary interest document, hold a meeting with verbal presentations and discussions. Search out opportunities in your company to have an informal presentation of your idea.

At this stage, you alert management to your purpose. You need to be clear that the project is not yet at the formal presentation stage. On the other hand, you need to have a clear, in-depth understanding of the major points that you believe should interest management in the idea. The education process discussed in Chapter 2 should be very valuable at this stage.

Before you embark on developing a full-blown plan, preview your idea by writing an informal summary of key points that you've researched, featuring a sentence or two in response to the questions in Figure 3.1:

Figure 3.1

Planning Questions

1. What is the product or service that will be sold?
2. How does it differ from other similar products or services?
3. If it's the same as an existing product, what's your edge?
4. Can you produce or deliver it less expensively or can it expand into new markets?
5. Who are the customers, and why will they buy? Does it require educating customers?
6. Does it represent a change in buying habits?
7. Is the market large or limited? Is it growing or declining? Is it complicated to produce or explain? Is it a regulated product or service?
8. Who will run the operation?
9. Does your existing management have expertise in this business, or will you have to recruit management?
10. How much money will it take to start up? How much to keep it going?
11. How long will it take to get underway and to reach the break-even point?

When you're satisfied that you have solid answers to these questions, you're ready to move on to the next steps: conducting more detailed research if necessary, making projections, and writing the business plan.

Every great idea needs a business plan in some form. Why? Because by practicing the discipline of creating a business plan, you give yourself a leg up on success in two ways:

First, it forces you to think through your idea, and to evaluate it in terms of its value to the company and its potential earning or saving power.

Second, by following the structure of the business plan, you can be more confident in answering management's key questions.

What Approvals Are Required?

Before you get too far into the business plan process, determine what approvals you will need. Knowing this often determines the kind of numbers you need in the plan. While some measures are common to most business plans, there are always unique perspectives that a manager wants to see to evaluate a proposal. These unique needs usually relate to his or her background. For example, a manager with a financial background will often look in greater depth at financial measures than a manager with a marketing background. Knowing this, you should be sure to include the data the approving manager prefers. Your plan will vary depending upon what type of project you're recommending and what level of approval it requires. Does your plan require a lot of money or a little? In most businesses, different levels of operating management have limits on expenditures they can approve without getting clearance from the next level up. These limits vary from company to company.

Your selling strategy will depend on how much money your project requires to get off the ground, and on how far-reaching the consequences will be. The buy-in you need could be a simple OK from your manager, or as complicated as getting a sign-off from multiple levels of management—sometimes up to and including the CEO or the board of directors. Either way, it takes a lot of prep work to give your plan the maximum chance for success.

How you present your idea will be shaped by whose approval you need. Most big ideas in large companies go through several levels of management before they are finally approved. For example, if you are a brand manager in marketing, your idea will probably need to be approved by your department head, general manager, and maybe a senior or executive vice president. A big idea would need to go to the president, chairperson, and board.

If you are looking at a hierarchy of approval levels, your number one priority is to satisfy the first level. Without their approval, your chances of support from higher levels are low.

The first level often requires considerable detail before they will approve the plan and recommend it to their boss. Interestingly, the higher you go in the approval process, the more of an overview or summary of the proposal is presented and discussed.

What Role Do the Numbers Play?

Numbers tell a story about what you expect to happen with your concept. It is important that you know the numbers associated with your project before you get too deeply into the business plan process. When you know your numbers, it dictates your next steps. They range from going back to the drawing board to racing to a computer to write your management proposal. Obviously, if your numbers fail to meet the minimum requirements for your company, you need to search for ways to reduce costs and increase revenues.

When you're working with numbers, context is everything. One million dollars in sales means something entirely different to Nike than it does to the corner grocer. Your job as the sponsor of a plan is to turn your numbers into measurements that are relevant to your company or industry. Your senior team will want to know, for example, how the performance of your idea might compare with a similar business that's already up and running. Someone in your finance department can assist you with this.

We've said that success is a numbers game, and that's true to varying degrees. In some cases, the numbers are all important: A proposal provides an acceptable return or it doesn't. End of discussion. Either a new product makes money or it doesn't. But how much does it make, and how quickly? When is the break-even point reached?

When a proposal represents an important new direction for the company, long-term gain may be far more important than short-term impact. The actual numbers may not count as much when the nonmonetary aspects (real or perceived value) of the project are significant.

For example, work and family programs, virtual office arrangements, and on-site childcare actually create expense, but the payback in ability to recruit or retain employees might outweigh the costs. A customer frequency program may be hard to measure in bottom-line dollars, but it might increase brand awareness or enhance customer loyalty. Perhaps the program is one that represents a cost of entry: When a bank's competitors, for example, are all offering online banking, management may give the go-ahead to enter this arena even if current financial projections do not support it.

And, of course, there's always the project that simply turns someone on. One particularly large-scale project we recall was launched not because of the numbers, but in spite of them; it was a favorite child of a division president. Numbers mean different things to different people, and may mean more or less at different times. A sexual harassment training program might not have been worth $100,000 to a company in 1980, but it would have great worth in 1999, following a multimillion-dollar lawsuit. Determine what you believe the outcome is for your idea, and build your case to support it. Stress the result that is in support of your company's goals. And let the numbers speak for themselves.

Numbers: On the Mark or in the Ballpark

Business plans—or project proposals—are just that: proposals. Because they involve things that haven't happened yet, they're based on a lot of estimates. Management expects that results will vary, and in a broad sense a project that shows a 15 percent return on investment is not considered much different from one that shows a 13 percent or a 17 percent return. Expected results should fall within a certain acceptable range; management expects some degree of variance in real world results.

Numbers can be viewed absolutely—standing alone—or in comparison with other numbers. Usually, management wants to use a yardstick that indicates the project's degree of potential as it compares with other successful or failed projects. If the numbers can be so variable, or if they won't be the deciding factor in a project's fate, why bother with them at all? For several reasons. Making the calculations demonstrates your discipline in organizing assumptions and plans. The calculations indicate if the project meets, exceeds, or falls short of the company's minimum acceptable level of performance, and by how much.

Paint Three Pictures

Given that projections are only estimates, should you err on the optimistic or the conservative side? Which approach will provide the greatest chance for success? Both—plus one more. You want to prepare three scenarios: worst, best, and most likely case. You will need a strong justification for all three.

Management is aware that you're making educated guesses. They want to know what is the best-case scenario, what is the worst, and what is most likely.

Both Debbi Fields of Mrs. Fields Cookies and Betsy Williams of Nielsen Media Research say they want to see a "visual" description of the idea which would include: 1) what success would look like, 2) what failure would look like (including hidden risks), and 3) a realistic timeline for monitoring progress (including the break-even point and a decision point for idea expansion or death).

It never pays to show only a glowing pro forma. Management will consider it unrealistic and lose confidence in your objectivity. James A. Thomas, founder and chairman of New South Capital Management, once asked a presenter who was painting a particularly rosy picture of his idea, "Have you ever seen a pro forma with a *negative* bottom line?" Of course, he knew the answer, but his point was well taken.

And when you've only presented the most optimistic projections, at best, your project will meet expectations and merely be a success. A better approach is to undersell and over-deliver. Take a conservative view that tells management you are aware of all the risks. That way, if the project meets expectations, it's a success; if it exceeds them, management is ecstatic . . . and you look like a genius!

Number Concepts

The amount of numbers people use to measure success is almost limitless. Naturally, some numbers are more meaningful than others. There are certainly numbers and formulas that are particularly relevant to your company, but there are also some general numbers that are universal, which you should understand. Every plan has financial implications. Although your financial advisors will help you with the calculations you need, it's important for you to understand the underlying concepts specified in Figure 3.2.

Figure 3.2

Key Concepts in the Numbers Game

1. Growth Rate
2. Balance Sheet
3. Income Statement
4. Cash Flow Statement
5. EBIT (Earnings Before Interest and Taxes) and EBITDA (Earnings Before Interest, Taxes, Depreciation, and Amortization)
6. Break-even Point
7. Payback Period
8. Discounted Cash Flow
9. Net Present Value
10. Internal Rate of Return
11. Hurdle or Threshold Rate
12. Ratios

The following section provides an overview of these terms. Be careful in using these terms because the emphasis on numbers varies from company to company and with changing circumstances. In matters of this importance, be sure to check with your finance resource to arrive at a common understanding.

Growth Rate: The growth rate is the average change in percentage terms over some defined period, taking into account the effect of compounding. It is stated as an annual rate.

Balance Sheet: This is one of the three key financial statements (see also Income Statement and Cash Flow Statement below) that indicates a company's health at a specified date. Numbers on a balance sheet are shown in three categories: assets (what the company owns), liabilities (what its obligations are), and stockholder's equity (what's left over after liabilities are subtracted from assets). Assets minus liabilities equal stockholder's equity.

Generally, for project proposals within a company, top management and the financial people will worry about what impact, if any, your proposal might have on the balance sheet. It's not something you would put in your business plan, but it is something others will take into consideration. And since they do, you should consult with your finance advisors about the impact your idea might have on the balance sheet. The "others" are most likely senior managers—if they are going to know, you need to know. You do not want hidden issues. If there are balance sheet issues you want to know of them and address them.

Income Statement: This second key financial statement includes revenues, expenses, and profit over a defined period of time, usually monthly, quarterly, and annually. The firm has an overall income statement. Your project will have its own mini-version of an income statement that will be incorporated into the big picture. It's your particular bottom line that's important in the approval process.

Cash Flow Statement: The third key financial statement depicts cash inflow and outflow during a specific period of time, usually coinciding with the income statement period. Cash flows arise from three different activities: operations, investments, and financing.

You don't have to get all involved in the technical aspects of cash flow statements—the finance department will help with this. But you can bet the guys up front will want to know about the cash flow implications. Thus, be familiar with the concept.

The key focus is the cash flow from operations when particular projects are being considered. Cash flow considerations from investments and financing activities are generally something the "big picture" guys look at. The cash flow statement is not the same as the income statement since some income statement items do not represent actual cash items (outlays or uses) during the current time period. For example, sales are included as revenue on the income statement whether the sale was for cash or on credit. The sale for income statement purposes is revenue in each case; however, if the sale is on credit, the actual cash is received sometime later—in a subsequent period after the sale was recorded. Another example is depreciation expense. Accounting practice requires that certain assets be depreciated (expensed) over the useful life of the asset. This pro-rata expense is recorded on the income statement for each time period even though the asset may have been completely paid for at the time of initial purchase.

Awareness of the cash flow requirements for your idea can be a critical factor. For example, imagine a situation where almost all the money is spent on the idea before there are any actual results or information about how well your idea is doing.

An alternative is to spread spending out so that it is done in stages. Consider presenting to management the cash flow needs in stages. It is a means of providing checkpoints where you evaluate results to determine if you want to continue supporting the idea. The timing of the spending impacts the evaluation of the proposal using time value of money concepts described below.

EBIT and EBITDA (Earnings Before Interest and Taxes, and Earnings Before Interest, Taxes, Depreciation, and Amortization): These two measures are a special grouping of income statement items that reflect the true results of operations (EBIT), and the true cash flow from operations (EBITDA). Operating results is the measure that your project should be judged on. Interest expense is a function of how, and if, the project is financed (usually a decision made by the finance department) and is independent of the merits of the project itself. Taxes represent an outside factor that has nothing to do with the operation itself. Management will view the pre-tax results and worry about the taxes as part of the big picture.

Break Even: This is the level of production or sales at which revenue equals cost. There are two types of costs: fixed and variable. Fixed costs are those that do not vary with the volume of business in the short term, such as rent, insurance, mortgage, or executive salaries. Variable costs are those directly related to the volume of business, such as raw materials, production labor, or delivery expense. On a per-unit basis, the fixed costs decline as volume rises, because you're spreading the overhead over more units. Variable costs rise or fall with volume. The break-even point is that volume level where the total costs per unit equal the selling price per unit.

Payback Period: This is the length of time required to recover the initial investment in the project. Management wants to know, "How soon do I get my money back?" This is one of the simplest and most common criteria in evaluating the merits of proposals. To determine the payback period is a simple calculation that requires adding up the net bottom line cash flow year by year until the sum equals the initial outlay. Generally, the quicker the payback, the better.

Since this number is so critical, you will want to know what criteria your company's managers want before they will approve a project. Be careful because the criteria can vary by division and by type of project. The latter is important for some companies because some projects are riskier than others, and the time frame for producing a favorable bottom line depends on the nature of the investment. Many projects are acceptable even when good results take longer. Discounted cash flow analysis is a more comprehensive method of measuring the merits of a project.

If you find your payback period is longer than the company typically approves, consider three actions. First, reexamine your spending to find the dollars that are working least hard for the project. Consider reducing total spending and what effect that has on your payback period.

Second, look harder at your revenue projections—is it reasonable to promise a higher number or are there ways to improve revenue with efficient additions to the plan? Delayed spending or accelerated revenue lead to improved discounted cash flow results.

Third, if reduced spending or higher revenue are not right for the project, examine your argument to management about why they should make an exception for this project. For example, success might improve the company's image and credibility with the public or stakeholders. It is difficult to put a value on this benefit, but it could be meaningful enough to tip the scales in a close call.

Discounted Cash Flow (DCF): These are calculations for evaluating projects using the time value of money. There are two DCF techniques: net present value and internal rate of return. Both methods are more complex than figuring the payback period, but they are more comprehensive and accurate measures of the true investment merits of a project.

Net Present Value (NPV): This method evaluates a project's worth, taking into account the time value of money. It compares the timing of cash flows and the firm's threshold, or required rate of return (see below). The future net cash flows from a project are discounted back to the time when the project began, and compared with the original investment. If the NPV is greater than the original investment, the project is financially acceptable.

Internal Rate of Return (IRR). This is similar to NPV. The two come to the same decision in different ways. In the case of NPV, we take future cash flows and discount back using the appropriate hurdle rate; then, we compare the dollar amount of the NPV with the original investment. In the case of the IRR, we use the same cash flows and the same original investment amount and solve for the implied internal interest rate. If the rate that equates the two is greater than the hurdle rate, the project is acceptable. Then, why do it two ways? Some members of the approval committee like one, others like the other.

Hurdle or Threshold Rate: This is the required rate of return for a project to be acceptable from a financial standpoint. The rate is different for each company. It consists of two elements, both related to the firm's cost of capital. First, it relates to the opportunity cost of money, the rate that the company could earn from alternative investments; secondly, it relates to the risk perception of the project and the firm itself. This is something you get from the finance department, but it is good information to know.

How do you know how risky your project is? This is an important but tough question to answer precisely. One way of looking at risk is to look at two evaluative points:

1. Are you trying to do something the company has not done before? If so, then risk tends to be high. For example, if you are the first company brand to recommend expanding into Europe, risk will tend to be high. If you are the third or fourth brand to expand, then there is a proven distribution and sales system. Risk is lower.

2. How reliable is your pre-testing research? We discussed this somewhat in Chapter Two. For example, most volume-estimating research makes a volume estimate that is approximately 20 percent accurate. If you need volume near the top end of the 20 percent, then you have more risk than a project that can be a winner at almost 20 percent less than the volume estimate. If you have test marketed an idea, do not assume risk is low. Competitors often react very differently when something is expanded nationally. Therefore, their test market reaction may not be an accurate barometer of what to expect.

What's Important to Management: Ratios

To a very limited degree, numbers stand alone. Tell a manager you can generate $10 million in revenues and it will probably buy you attention. But more often, numbers are important only when they're put in context. This is where ratios become important.

Ratios compare one number with another. They are used to compare different aspects of a business with others in the same industry. They also make internal comparisons over time within the business. Since ratios can be very important, the next section covers them in greater detail. As an example, a ratio makes it possible to compare the results of your local pizza parlor with the results of IBM, even though the two organizations are very different in size, industry, and essentially all other factors. Using a ratio, you can judge which is more profitable, in a relative sense.

Financial ratios are used for a variety of purposes, chiefly to:

1. Measure the performance and health of a particular firm at a given point in time.
2. Gauge and measure the performance of a firm over a period of time.
3. Compare the performance and health of a firm with others at some point in time.
4. Track the trends in performance over time.
5. Make projections of line items in a financial statement based on historical ratios.

Figure 3.3 shows six categories of widely used ratios and what they measure. This is only a limited list. Within each category there

Figure 3.3

Most Frequently Used Ratios

Name	Calculation	What it Measures
1. Liquidity Ratios: (Ability to meet financial obligations)		
Current ratio	Current assets/ Current liabilities	Cash and liquid assets available to cover short-term obligations
Quick ratio	Cash, Liquid assets, & Accounts receivables/ Current liabilities	Cash, other liquid assets, and receivables available to cover short-term obligations without reliance on inventories

Figure 3.3 *(Continued)*

Most Frequently Used Ratios

Name	Calculation	What it Measures
Cash ratio	Cash & Liquid assets/ Current liabilities	Cash available to cover short-term debt

2. Profit Ratios: (Ability to earn satisfactory profit and return on investment)

Name	Calculation	What it Measures
Gross profit margin	Sales - Cost of sales/ Sales	Percent of each dollar of sales left after direct cost associated with producing the sales
Operating margin	Operating income/ Sales	Percent of sales left after all costs except interest and taxes
Net profit margin	Net income/Sales	Net profit after all costs as percent of sales
Return on assets	Net income/Total assets	How well total assets under control of the firm are utilized to generate net profit
Return on equity	Net income/ Stockholder equity	Profit as percent of equity investment
Return on investment	a. Net income/ Stockholder Equity b. Net income/Assets c. Net income/ Project Assets	How much the subject investment generates in net profit as a percent of investment

Figure 3.3 *(Continued)*

Most Frequently Used Ratios

Name	Calculation	What it Measures
3. Debt Ratios: (Compares debt relative to size—a measure of leverage)		
Total debt (Leverage ratio)	Total debt/Total assets	Amount of debt used in relation to assets employed
Debt-to-equity	Total debt/Total equity	Amount of assets creditors provide per each $ of equity the stockholders provide
Interest coverage	Earnings before interest and taxes/ Interest expense	How many times a company can cover its interest obligations out of earnings
4. Market Ratios: (Comparisons against market values)		
Price earnings (PE)	Market price of stock/ Annual earnings per share (multiple)	How much investors are willing to pay for one year of earnings. More growth and more stability command higher multiples
Dividend yield	Dividend per share/ Stock price	Percent return each year relative to investment in the stock

Figure 3.3 *(Continued)*

Most Frequently Used Ratios

Name	Calculation	What it Measures
Payout ratio	Total common stock dividends/Net profit	Percent of profit paid out in dividends

5. Activity Ratios: (Various internal measures for management of certain assets)

Name	Calculation	What it Measures
Sales-to-assets (asset turn)	Sales/Total assets	How well total assets are utilized in generating sales
Inventory turnover	Cost of goods sold/ Average inventory	Rate at which inventory is used
Inventory turn-days	Number of days in period x Inventory/ Cost of sales	Average number of days of inventory on hand
Accounts receivable turnover	Credit sales/Accounts receivable	Rate at which accounts receivables are being collected on annual basis
Accounts payable turnover	Purchases/ Accounts payable	Rate at which accounts payable are being paid.

6. Income Statement Ratios: Each item on income statement is compared to sales. These are useful in preparing budgets, developing pro formas and comparing with other firms in same industry.

are other ratios. That's because different companies consider different ratios to be important.

Here's an example of how a ratio can work. Suppose you own a company that earns $1 million this year. You spend $250,000 on advertising. Your advertising to sales ratio is 1 to 4. For every $4 you earn, you're spending $1 to advertise your product. Next year you make $2 million, but you manage to hold your advertising costs to $250,000. Now your ratio is 1 to 8. You're definitely improving your advertising performance.

Another way to use the ratio is to compare your company with your competitors, or with your industry. If the industry average ratio is 1 to 2, you're definitely doing better than the industry. But if the industry average is 1 to 10, you're falling short.

There is an infinite number of ratios that you could use, but some are more meaningful than others. The previous chart shows the ratios that are traditionally used by corporations.

"Don't be afraid to ask to be educated," says Ken Glass, president of First Tennessee Bank Corporation. "Before you prepare your report, you should ask what's important to the senior management group and be ready to present information with that at the forefront. And don't be hesitant to ask questions or admit that you do not have all the answers. If someone enters a presentation thinking they have all the answers, they may not have asked all the right questions."

Companies use financial ratios to help them evaluate how they're doing. Ratios allow them to compare things, and to make judgments and decisions on those comparisons.

In general, companies use financial ratios to measure performance or a company's position either at one time or over a period of time; to compare one company or item with another; or to make projections for the future.

For example, comparing the gross profits of Domino's Pizza with the profits of your neighborhood Pizza De Love-it doesn't make any sense. It doesn't tell you anything worthwhile.

On the other hand, you can calculate the *ratio* of profit to equity for IBM compared with the *ratio* of profit to equity for Pizza De Love-it. Those ratios will tell you how each is doing relative to its size and to the other. In other words, if IBM has a net profit margin of 20 percent, and the pizza palace's is 25 percent, the pizza palace is actually doing better (for its size) than IBM.

The Elements of a Business Plan

Now that we've covered some key business concepts, you're ready to begin preparing your plan. There are several ways your idea can be presented to senior management for approval. We will focus on the business plan because it is the most extensive way of presenting your idea.

Many companies use less extensive ways of presenting and evaluating major ideas. For example, for decades Procter & Gamble (among others) has insisted that even the most complex business proposals be limited to a few pages. In many cases, these companies encourage limiting it to three pages with a few attachments. This limited space forces the writer of the proposal to be disciplined and focused on the factors critical for management to make a decision. The writing of a recommendation has become an art in companies like this.

Other companies operate without any written form of proposal. They evaluate a proposal entirely via personal presentations. The presentations include printed materials to help management evaluate the idea. The benefit of this approach is that management can have a dialogue, which often brings perspective not present in a written document. For example, they can evaluate the confidence and abilities of the team presenting the idea.

However the idea is presented, there are usually great similarities in the thinking and use of key numbers. Again, our primary focus is on the business plan format because it is so comprehensive. There are a number of business plan formats, but they vary only slightly.

Every business plan is different, since the subject matter is always unique, i.e., some form of innovation. However, most plans must include certain types of information. It is up to the innovator to mold the specifics of his idea around the framework of the general outline. Figure 3.4 shows the outline of a typical business plan.

Figure 3.4

Business Plan Outline

1. Executive Summary
2. Description of Your Idea
   a. Type of business
   b. Complete list of products and services
   c. How is it unique and is the uniqueness important?
   d. Basis for growth potential
3. Research, Design, and Development
   a. Technical expertise necessary and where you will get it
   b. Research costs and timing, plus the role it plays in the decision-making process
   c. Marketing and competition
   d. Who are the potential customers and how many of them are there?
   e. Competitors—strengths and weaknesses relative to your idea
   f. Promotion plans and budgets
   g. What market share do you estimate and where will it come from?
   h. Basis for pricing
   i. Advertising plan, including strategy, execution, and media details
4. Technical, Legal, and Regulatory
   a. Legal agreement
   b. Patents involved, if any
   c. Plans to implement new technology
5. Financial
   a. Amount of funding
   b. Timing and source of funding
   c. Appropriate return measures

Figure 3.4 *(Continued)*

6. Risks and Reward
   a. Risks and basis for them
   b. Alternatives to manage risks
   c. Outcome scenarios—risks and rewards of each
7. Management
   a. Who will manage and what qualifications do they possess?
   b. Staffing—numbers, costs, availability, and sources
   c. Licenses and permits needed
   d. Special help needed—costs and potential issues
8. Supporting Documentation

At this stage, you want to outline the plan and develop a rough draft.

Experience suggests that the steps you take in the outline and rough draft stages of a business plan are critical in shaping the final proposal. Sometimes the champion of an idea feels her idea is so strong that she does not have to spend much time on the business plan. She thinks, "The idea will sell itself." In truth, very few ideas sell themselves. Your idea will only be a great idea if you first convince others that it is great. So, invest the quantity and quality of time necessary to make the business plan as good as or better than your idea.

Making Your Point

While a business plan is extensive, there usually is only one key point that you want to make—you want commitment to your idea and a plan to bring it to life. You cannot let this point get lost in the one hundred or so pages a business plan can include.

As we said, there are infinite ways to measure success, and you want to select the ones with the most impact. What will management want to know about your project? That's what you should present. The type of project you're recommending will determine what information is important. For example, if you intend to introduce a new product to the market, projected market share will be a key measurement. While the effect on the profit forecast is important, it often is a secondary concern in the recommendation to management. There are several sections in the typical business plan. Each is briefly discussed below.

Executive Overview

The shortest but most important part of your plan is the overview. It summarizes the key points of your proposal. It should deliver a first impression with punch, because it may be the only document senior management reads about your concept.

The overview should provide information that's sufficient for management to decide to either ask for a more in-depth review by the financial department or send your idea to the recycle bin. Your executive overview can gain you conditional approval, subject to the numbers working out favorably.

In a few (usually five or fewer) pages you must pique their interest and make them want to know more about your concept. According to Lawrence Ladove, CEO and chairman of Ladove Inc., an international skin and hair care research, development, and manufacturing facility, "All any senior manager wants to know boils down to just three things: 1) How much will it cost? 2) How much will we make? and 3) When will we get our money back? The rest is all supporting data."

In reality, however, the executive overview will contain a description of about five important sections.

What the Project Is

This important section also clearly states what you want from management. This section should be 100 percent free of ambiguity. It should be simple and clear. The opening sentences are especially critical. Do not be surprised if you must rewrite these several times.

For example, the opening of this section might say:

This seeks agreement for $20 million in incremental marketing support and $12 million in capital within current budgets for the national launch of Brand A's CQ formula for the "cleaner and fresher clothes" product improvement. Agreement to a July 2000 introduction will contribute 32 million incremental cases and $9 million in incremental profit for the current fiscal year.

The manager reading this immediately knows the requested funding, the brand and nature of the initiative, the timing, and the benefits from the effort in the current financial year. Importantly, he knows that $20 million is not in current budgets, which can be a major concern in some cases.

In your project description, share with the manager the most important reasons this project makes sense. If you only factually describe the project, it leaves him with an empty, incomplete feeling. He is familiar with the kind of project you are proposing in most instances, and probably has some understanding of the project from previous briefings. Once you give a clear description of the project, he immediately wants to know why you believe he should approve it.

A caution about describing the project—do not mix execution in with what you want to do in the early stages of this section. In the first paragraph, you want the reader to know exactly what you want him to do. There are probably some things in the plan that you do not need his agreement to. For example, you need this manager's agreement to the incremental marketing support but you need another manager's agreement to the specific television advertising campaign you want to use. If this is the case, then do not include mention of the ad campaign in the early parts of this section. It will be important later in the presentation, but you want the initial focus to be on the project description and why it should be approved.

In about five pages of a business plan, you should communicate considerable information. Resist the urge to tell the reader all you know about your idea. This is only an overview. It is a balancing act—you need to provide the reader enough information to agree with your proposal, but not so much that you overwhelm and confuse him. Put yourself into his chair and determine what would be essential for you to make a decision or, at minimum, be positively inclined.

As discussed earlier, you want to take a step beyond mere project description in this section. You want the manager to know the basis for recommending that the project move forward to the next stage. In the above example, the manager will want to know about Brand A's product improvement. What makes it so good that the manager should be willing to spend the requested $32 million? In this case, the writer would consider consumer research and test market results.

The consumer testing that demonstrates the efficacy of the product is often crucial in a consumer-driven company. Provide the most important research finding, not the inner details of the research. For example, "The CQ formula was preferred by Brand A and competitive users in a paired-comparison, blind, in-home test." This gives the reader important information—competitive users notice the improvement and prefer it to their current product.

A second key point is that test market results support the promised incremental volume and profit. Again, an overview is needed, not all the details. For example, "The test market produced a 22 percent volume gain in the first year and only a 17 percent volume increase is needed to produce the incremental 32 million cases."

The reader will also want similar assurances that the incremental profit is reasonable. When the manager knows what you want and that it is reasonable based on reliable testing and evaluation, you have taken big steps towards securing his agreement.

How This New Venture Fits into the Corporate Vision

You can take the next step forward by demonstrating how the project fits the corporate vision. Before addressing the vision, make sure you fully understand it.

Is the vision important to management? Look for evidence in annual reports and company newsletters. If it is stated clearly, and reaffirmed by the company's current practices, then proceed. If it is not reaffirmed, be direct and ask your management what is the primary focus of the company today. Even when you have the right words, be sure you have a clear understanding of the key words.

With this, demonstrate how your idea fits the corporate vision. Sometimes you can make a very direct connection with your project—"The Brand A CQ project reestablishes Brand A as the preeminent leader of its category and thus achieves the market leadership position called for in our corporate vision. The initiative achieves both market share and benefit leadership in the category."

Visions are intended to be relevant for many years. Another way to connect to the vision is to demonstrate where the current proposal fits into the brand's longer-term effort to fully realize the company vision. Often a brand has multiple projects underway. Each project plays a role in elevating the brand's share and profits.

For example, there may be product improvements, like the one in the example, that improve the level of an important benefit the brand delivers. There may be other projects in the pipeline that take the same benefit to even higher levels or improve another benefit consumers want. Other projects may reduce costs or seek to advertise the brand's emerging ability to deliver superior benefits to consumers.

Other times, you need to make a more indirect connection. It may be difficult to find a direct, literal connection between your project and the vision. When this is the case, connect yourself to some key words in the vision statement. Words like "leadership" and "excellence" are frequently used in vision statements. In this case, you might write, "The Brand A CQ formula enables the brand to again deliver the highest level of the most important benefit consumers want from a product in this category. By moving from parity with other brands in the category to superiority, the brand delivers the excellence called for by the vision."

There will be times when it feels like a stretch to connect your project with the vision. If the product improvement merely brings the brand to up to par for delivery of an important consumer benefit, then you may need to position this effort as part of a longer-term effort to regain excellence.

In other cases, the project may appear to be contrary to the vision. This frequently happens when the business you are working on is not in the mainstream for the company. In other cases, it may not be on the list of businesses the company sees as important to its future. In this case, the company may not envision any effort on your brand. Do not despair. In a business like this, you can sometimes help the overall vision by making your brand more profitable. Then the increased profits can be used to fund the important businesses included in the vision. This harvest strategy can often play an important role in generating the funds necessary for overall company profitability.

Whatever your degree of connection to the vision, it is very beneficial to make it as strong as possible. The senior managers whose approval you need are often the people in the company who are held responsible by stakeholders with delivering the vision.

Cost/Benefit Analysis: What Benefits/Risks Do You Expect?

Earlier parts of this chapter have already addressed these points in some detail. In the overview, you want to provide the most important dimensions of benefit and risk that the approving manager wants to see.

You do not want to share with him every dimension of financial benefit—there are other sections where this can be covered. In addition, on the most important dimensions you probably do not need to tell him everything that can be said about the measure or measures you have chosen to focus on.

In some companies, the most important financial dimension is the profit forecast for a brand or business. Typically, a business reports monthly to senior management about how well it is doing versus the current year forecast. In addition to the current fiscal year profit forecast, there is usually an agreed-upon profit forecast for one to five or more fiscal years.

In the previously shared example for Brand A's CQ formula, the writer of the proposal shared the impact to the current year's profit forecast for the brand—". . . $9 million in incremental profit. . . ."

Depending on the company, approving manager, and idea, there may be another dimension of benefit you want to include in the overview. For example, an idea to improve profitability by reducing inventory levels might include other dimensions in the overview—total profit increase, the increased returns, the reduced number of days supply, and the amount of capital freed up from the reduction, including the one-time benefit from the reduction. There are other types of ideas where different financial measures become important enough to include in the overview.

The overview also wants to address the subject of risk. In an earlier section, we suggested that profitability from an idea be viewed from three perspectives—best, worst, and most likely. Depending on the nature of the project, you may want to address these only in summary fashion—"The most likely profit outcome is an incremental $9 million this fiscal year. On the downside, the result is break-even and on the upside the incremental profit is $12 million." You may leave the explanation of calculation method to other sections that follow the overview. In cases where the volatility is great or there is little testing or quantitative support for the idea, then a more detailed explanation may be called for. In both cases, you may need to address in detail the range for the approving manager if you expect him to become favorably disposed to your idea from the overview alone.

When working on this section be aware of an attitude that many approving managers have—the person proposing the idea is more inclined to see the positives and is reluctant to fully and honestly address the downsides and risks. If you can convince the manager that you have honestly and objectively done due diligence, you will quickly build confidence and credibility.

Some of the hardest risks for a proposing manager to see are:

1. The manager's creative idea will not work. When you are the creator of an idea, new packaging for example, it is very difficult to imagine it might not be effective. The lesson is to recognize this bias and to seek the objective counsel of trusted and skilled advisors. Listen fully to his feedback—not just the good stuff. If he doubts the power of the idea, treat

the feedback as a gift. Learn from it and make your initial idea even stronger.

2. Consumer research's conclusions are not 100 percent reliable. When a manager receives a positive research score, he is inclined to interpret the score as gospel—the consumer has spoken. It is good but not perfect news. The manager needs to recognize how many times good scores have not resulted in good business results. While it is true that few ideas with poor scores do well, it is not true that good scores alone are an accurate predictor of marketplace results. Research does not measure such things as the price you charge, competitor reactions, and sales execution.

3. Test market results are not 100 percent reliable. Many of the same cautions about consumer research apply to test markets. Managers need to be wary of test market results. Often sales execution in a test market is much better than you receive on national expansion. Competitors may use the lead time provided by the test market to develop better ways of responding to your idea when it expands nationally. It is not unusual for a competitor to test different response programs in your different test markets. It may eventually use a response that is different from any it tested. Separately, you may learn from a test market and incorporate your learnings into a different plan when you expand. While you certainly view your changes as "improvements," they are often untested and capable of reducing results.

Often a company has a base of experience with ideas that it can use to evaluate risk. Consult this database to determine the range of expectations you might realize. If you conducted several test markets, you may use the best and worse market results to calculate your range.

Ultimately, assigning risk is not an exact science. This should not prevent you from providing the approving manager a knowledgeable risk assessment. Even the most benign-sounding ideas involve risk.

Just talk to the computer systems manager who said the purchase of a highly tested and market-leading accounting software program would be an easy transition. Many of these have turned into nightmares because the recommending manager did not fully assess the problems that might occur. Importantly, because they did not assess problems, they did not develop backup plans. When they discover a problem, most of the damage occurs between the time the problem is discovered and the time when the backup plan is implemented. If the risk assessment had been more thorough with a backup plan in place, damage might have been minimal.

Many managers resist a thorough risk analysis because they fear the downside might scare the approving manager so much he might not approve the idea. Most senior managers have enough experience to know that risks are very real. As the recommending manager, you will have to live with any approved idea.

Failure to conduct an excellent risk analysis probably means you will be unprepared for the glitches and bumps in the road that will occur. At a minimum, your price will be elevated levels of stress. The problems may be so severe as to cause major profit shortfall. Whatever level of problems, if you are not prepared, your career and business will suffer.

After you have addressed the major financial measures in the overview, it may be appropriate to provide a top line of other important financial measures that are presented in more depth. You can present these in a bullet point summary. For example, consider presenting the following points:

■ How it will affect key performance measurements such as earnings per share. If your project is big enough to affect the total company's results, then provide a rough estimate of its impact. It will be rough because you may not be aware of important factors.

■ The amount and timing of funding. This can be a critical point when significant spending straddles two or more fiscal years or is all in one year. Senior management sometimes faces tight fiscal years and years in which it has greater flexibility. Knowing this flexibility can help you position and adjust your request.

■ Your sources of funding (internal or external). If you are financing your needs totally within the profit forecast for your business or brand, then it is usually easier for management to agree with you. If you are expecting other corporate sources to fund your idea, then it usually increases the degree of difficulty you face in gaining agreement from senior management.

■ Internal Rate of Return (IRR). This is an important number in most companies and deserves particular attention. Regardless of the project, the internal rate of return compares the investment with the potential risk and reward. Typically, the higher the IRR the greater the potential for reward, therefore a company is more tolerant of risk. Do not hide it in later, more detailed sections. Remember, if senior management needs certain numbers to make a decision, then provide them in the overview. Details on how the number was developed and a more in-depth discussion can be presented in later sections.

After you've outlined the pertinent points that will capture management's attention, you'll provide more detailed information on the following subjects.

Background and Need

This section is where your extensive research comes into play. Describe the situations you envision that support a need for your project. Be careful in this section. The goal is not to impress management with how much work you have done. If you succumb to this temptation, you will just dump a bunch of data into a plan. It will be left to the reader to ferret out what is important.

Use this section to make the one to three key points the manager needs to know. If there is only one point to make, feel comfortable limiting it to that. The manager reading the report will appreciate and respect your discipline and keen insight.

The points you want to make here may include:

Economic and Business Conditions

Resist making this a national economic projection, which may not have much relevancy to your project. It is more likely that a narrow economic or business measure is important. If you are running a bar soap business, the tallow business, mundane and uninteresting to most people, can be critical to you. In this case, you may want to focus on cattle projections and potential international factors influencing supplies and costs.

Market Conditions

This may be the section where focusing is the greatest challenge because you know so much about your market. Share only the insights that are important to evaluating the strength of your idea. For example, if it is a service business, look broadly at who is providing the service today and who might provide it in the future. The stock brokerage business is seeing its business change almost overnight in historical terms. For decades, there was a limited number of large, established businesses providing its service. In a few years, the online trading services have made a large impact by offering greater convenience, faster service, and lower rates. As you look at your market conditions, be sure to widen your vision beyond the traditional definitions and methods of providing a service.

Competition

In a similar regard, look widely at who your current and future competitors are. Provide perspective to management that truly helps them evaluate your idea. If you have information that a current competitor is researching new ideas that, if successful, would directly threaten your business, then provide all the detail and support you can. When you have an important point, make it completely and persuasively.

Industry Outlook

This can involve making predictions, which is an inherently risky undertaking. Take the same approach that you took when you estimated profitability. Present management with a range of predicted outcomes, including conservative, optimistic, and most-likely projections. Have a strong basis for each. In cases where your conservative projection threatens the viability of your idea, acknowledge this. Share with management how you propose handling this risk. It might include checkpoints in the project. If the checkpoints suggest the conservative projections are materializing, you may have a contingency plan where spending is reduced.

Implementation Plan Overview

This section is where you include important information about how the idea will be executed. While agreement to most ideas hinges on the bigger picture, like consistency with the vision and profitability, some ideas that meet these requirements fail on executional details. The failure can sometimes be temporary as you make revisions, but sometimes the failure can be final. Management looks for thoroughness in a presentation. Use this section to impress them with your ability to take something from the idea stage to reality. Your creativity is as needed in this stage as it is during the initial development of the idea. In this section, consider some of the following points, but do not feel limited by them:

Describe what the product is, and how you will actually produce and sell it. In some cases, this may not be worthy of extensive comments. In other cases it may be. For example, perhaps your company manufactures all of its own products, but you are proposing contract manufacturing for this idea. This can raise quality assurance issues for the production department.

If the idea involves new production processes, you may need to convince management that this can be done on the timing you propose. Any time execution of your idea depends on something new, you need to address how this works. Always have a contingency plan in case it doesn't.

Describe how the project will be organized, where it will report, if it overlaps other areas or requires support from them, who will carry the ball internally, and any other details that will help management envision your plan in action. Organizational issues in some companies can cripple an otherwise great idea. When implementation requires the full and enthusiastic support of other departments, the "not invented here" syndrome can cause a good idea to die of neglect or worse. You want the full and public commitment of other departments. You can do this by giving the other departments the right of approval of all plans involving their organization. Often having other department heads initial or sign sections involving them helps convince senior management of the achievability of your plan.

Don't forget to include specific timelines for project milestones and accountabilities. Schedule regular review sessions to monitor progress, and to assess the need to change or alter the project's direction. As mentioned in Chapter 2, every idea has its own life cycle and will eventually be modified to stay current or die. Without specific timelines and accountabilities, every idea has the potential to die before ever being implemented.

Who It Will Affect

Most projects affect one or several groups of people. Delineate the ones your project will touch and explain how they will be affected positively or negatively. Here are some examples.

Employees: Adding a new product might result in a need to reorganize a division or add jobs. Any reorganization can extend normal timelines by as little as 25 percent to a doubling of the time it takes to accomplish a task. While eventually the reorganization can produce superior productivity and quality, you are better off assuming there will be delays and challenges from reorganization.

Improved technology could eliminate jobs. This could trigger union issues in some instances. Even where there is not a union issue, there are likely to be severance and outplacement costs that need to be considered. Often the people left behind after technology eliminates the jobs of others are less productive for a period. They need to master the new technology, and they may experience lower morale depending on how the layoffs were handled.

A state-of-the-art plant could increase safety. So far, you have addressed potential challenges, but you may have an idea that provides a significant and immediate upside in key operational areas, like safety. In stating its benefits, again be conservative. Over the long term, you will be better off by underpromising and overdelivering.

Customers: Visible changes need close scrutiny. Any time customers see changes that you are making there is the opportunity for problems. Even a major customer *improvement*, not properly explained or understood, can be interpreted negatively. Often management asks many questions any time they see this potential. As a result, you can help your cause by anticipating this and addressing potential concerns at length.

Customers might experience increased service, or decreased wait time. The value of this may be difficult to estimate, but in most cases it is a significant plus.

Shareholders: Project operating costs could reduce shareholders' quarterly dividends. If your project does this, you will need a very strong argument for your idea. Most publicly held companies are very sensitive to quarterly earnings. One of the best methods of selling an idea with this impact is to ensure it has a strong link to the company's vision. Also, demonstrate the longer-term impact. The impact on quarterly earnings may be limited to one quarter if spending, like television advertising, is concentrated in that quarter.

Adding a new product line could create better long-term stock-growth potential. Many times companies are willing to take a one-year hit to earnings if the future is bright. One of the most striking examples of a company willing to suffer initial losses as an investment in the future is Amazon.com. This company has built very large e-commerce revenues. The profits, they claim, will come later. Despite this, the stock market has rewarded the company with a very high stock valuation.

Qualitative Benefits

Einstein said, "Not everything that can be counted counts, and not everything that counts can be counted." Your project may offer an integral or peripheral benefit that has nothing to do with generating income or reducing costs. Some qualitative factors you might consider are how the project adds to your company's:

Positive Image

For publicly held companies image can be very important. Shareholders tend to value companies with bright future prospects higher than ones with a flat earnings future. If your idea helps the company appear to be rejuvenated or continue a proud tradition of innovation, then the positive image from your idea could be very valuable.

Long-Term Health

Predicting the future is always a challenge. If your idea involves patented ideas that elevate your product above the competition, then the long-term health of that business may be a substantial benefit. It can be even stronger if the superior product can command a higher price.

Compliance with Government Standards

Many lines of business are regulated by governmental agencies. Find out if your proposal has any unusual or special regulatory issues, and be prepared to discuss them.

Employee Morale

One of the least appreciated benefits of a dynamic idea is its impact on employee morale. Employees love working for a winner and a company with a bright future. Improved morale is difficult for many companies to measure, but the financial benefits are seen in reduced turnover. In some jobs, the hiring and training costs for a new individual equal the annual salary for the position.

Ability to Recruit

In a tight job market, dynamic new businesses can be a magnet for top talent. In a similar manner, a company with a tradition of innovation also tends to recruit people more easily. As a result, if your idea is innovative and publicity is warranted, consider a public relations plan as part of your recommendation.

Although in many cases these contributions may be intangible, quantify expected results whenever possible. The value of lower turnover has already been touched on. While estimating the value of higher morale and easier recruiting is difficult, you can put rough measures on them. For example, provide an estimate of the savings of a turnover rate that drops from 12 percent today to 8 percent a year from now. You can estimate the number of people who would not leave at the lower rate. Then, with human resource's assistance, provide an estimated savings. While the savings calculation will not be included in financial calculations like the rate of return and pay-off period, they can be the icing on your cake.

Putting the Numbers in Your Plan

Armed with relevant financial performance information, ratios, and projections, you can build a convincing argument for your idea. As always, keep things simple. Don't overkill with too many figures when just a few key numbers can sell your plan. Use key measurements in your executive overview and put the detail in your appendices.

Organize your plan so the critical numbers are easy to find. Don't bury crucial information in your appendices. The most important data should be in your executive overview. Once people are hooked with the prospect of positive numbers, the rest of the sell will be a lot easier.

Charts and graphs can be a very effective way of presenting information, even in the early stages of gaining support and buy-in from others. Computers have made it much easier to compile and present data in creative ways at all stages of idea development. There are a variety of visuals that will give your business plan more impact:

- pie charts
- bar charts
- line graphs
- flow charts
- organization charts
- spreadsheets

Certain types of charts effectively display measurement, particularly comparisons. The converse is also true: Some types of charts are extremely ineffective for certain types of information. Before you choose your visuals, review Chapter 6 for details about how to use color, typefaces, and other elements of design to make your presentation more powerful. More important, that chapter describes how to avoid visual disasters.

When you're using your company's most frequently used ratios, it will be obvious how the numbers compare with acceptable standards. If your company has different standards by division and type of project, then compare your financial numbers to the correct standard.

If you don't believe management can envision how the project will play out, compare your idea with an existing successful project or service. In making this comparison, look for opportunities to note what you learned that helped you make your idea stronger.

Backup Information

The actual narrative description and key financial information in your business plan may be concise, but you will need significant backup information to support your plan. The final document may be quite long—even 50 or 100 pages.

Adequate and appropriate documentation increases your plan's credibility. It also allows the person reviewing your information to have detailed support at hand. You want him to have whatever information he needs to make a decision.

Consider including whatever backup information you believe may help support your case. For example, include copies of market research studies, newspaper articles, competitive information, resumes of key players, and so on.

Refining the Plan

When you're completely satisfied with your plan, run through it with an associate or two whom you trust. They can play devil's advocate and offer constructive suggestions. Undoubtedly you are more convinced than anyone of your plan's value, but remember, you have the benefit of reams of background material and research, many hours of thinking it through, and perhaps months of plan-development experience. An outsider will unquestionably see things through more objective eyes, possibly reading things more clearly than you can.

This late in the game, it may be tempting to skip this step. Don't. You owe it to yourself to tweak things one last time for the big "What if."

Even people who are experienced at pitching an idea often forget to anticipate key questions. In our experience, the most often overlooked and most important of these is the big "What if."

1. What if it takes longer than you think it will?
2. What if it costs more?
3. What if sales fall short of projections?
4. What if the market changes?
5. What can go wrong? What are the hidden risks?

Despite our best plans, things sometimes do change, go wrong, or take a different turn than we expected. Although they may not be included in the written business plan document, the truly well-laid plan anticipates each possibility and includes optimistic, pessimistic, and realistic answers to these big "What if" questions. Management will want to know specifically how and when to exit the project, and how to limit losses. Be prepared to address these questions, and have alternative plans ready to discuss if needed.

Debbi Fields offers one final piece of advice: "Great ideas need a dedicated quarterback. The existing business continues but must constantly evaluate not what it did, but what it can do better to serve its customers, shareholders, and company members. New ideas and strategies are the lifeline of any business." "And," Debbi Fields adds in a postscript, "Everyone told me that soft, chewy cookies would never sell. You just never know until you try!"

Key Learning Points

1. Before you get too far, determine if there is interest in your idea and if it can fulfill the promise you see in it.
2. Explore the range of results your idea could achieve. Best and

worst case along with most-likely case establish a range of expectations.

3. Even if you are not a financial wizard, it is critical for you to understand some fundamental financial measures. You need to understand the concept of each measure and its strengths and weaknesses. Your finance support group can be counted on to accurately compute the numbers.

4. Your idea is captured in a business plan. This essential document provides both a summary and details of why people should invest in the idea. The tone is authoritative, credible, and inspiring.

5. While a business plan, at 80–100 pages, is one way of presenting your idea, it is not the only way. The options run the range from verbal presentations to written presentations that are limited to about three pages for even the most complex proposals. Regardless of which approach is right for your company, the degree of preparation and the thinking are very similar in all the options.

CHAPTER 4

Gaining Allies

"If anything goes wrong, I did it. If anything goes semi-good, we did it. If anything goes real good, then you did it. That's all it takes to get people to win football games."

Paul "Bear" Bryant, former Alabama football coach

Selling Is Not Just a Numbers Game

As the sponsor of a brainstorm, you *will* have to deliver the numbers. And not just any numbers. Optimism is great, but a rose-colored sales projection won't be sufficient to convince management to pour money into an untested venture. They'll want to know all the numbers traditionally associated with a business plan, including figures that define your market, your competition, initial investment cost, projected revenues, and all the factors that will contribute to—or hinder—your success. In fact, Ken Glass of First Tennessee Corporation said, "It all boils down to three things: research, risk, and return."

As important as they are, however, numbers alone are usually not enough to move a project from idea to implementation. More than one idea with great profit potential has been scrapped. Why? Often, it's because the author of the plan didn't do enough advance selling.

"The numbers are simply the first step," says Brandt Wright, vice president for Baptist Memorial Health Care Corporation. "Numbers are the easy part. They have less to do with a project's success than people."

In a corporation, birthing a new product, service, or business is a team effort. Putting together a plan requires input from many sources, and implementation generally requires some level of cooperation by a wide range of functional areas. Tom Peters (1999) says, "If you're in charge of a project, you ought to think like the general manager of an NBA franchise: You've got to fill twelve chairs with the hottest people you can draft."

The Center for Creative Leadership conducted a survey of more than sixty executives, and subsequently published a report entitled, "A Look at Derailment Today." The executives noted reasons that fast-trackers fail, and two stood out: being difficult to work with and failing to "lead in a team-centered way" (Leslie and Van Velsor, 1996). Positive traits such as being assertive and taking the initiative are the qualities that make people stand out. But those same traits can stymie people when they reach the executive level, where teamwork is vital.

Orchestrating such a team event requires finesse. It also requires an ability to share not only the work, but also ownership and credit. Even John D. Rockefeller, whose reputation is that of the hard-driving tycoon, ran his company by committees and consensus (*Inc. MAGAZINE*, "20 Years: The Entrepreneurial Decades," Entrepreneur of the Century, p. 159).

And, as one executive said, "It's good to get a lot of people on the boat. That way, if it starts to go down, you've got a lot of people paddling with you."

The broader base of support an idea has, the better its chances for success. Thus, what you do *before* the presentation is much more important than what you do *in* the presentation. In fact, if you've done your homework, selling as you go, by the time you formally deliver your idea to management it should already be sold. The presentation is just the wrap up: time to make a good impression, answer questions, and get management to sign on the dotted line.

Lots of footwork? You bet. But if your idea is worth the flip chart it's written on, the footwork will pay off.

Know the Process

In any organization there are formal and informal networks of approval. And while there are lots of roads to take, some are quicker than others. Clearly, it pays to understand the process in your company, so you can either take the fastest path. . .or at least deliberately choose the slower one. In some companies, several options exist depending on the nature of the project. In others, all projects follow the same formal path, but informal paths, if there are any, vary usually by the personal style of the leader of the business unit.

In an earlier chapter, we discussed the importance of knowing whose approval you would need for your idea. In this chapter, we build on this to recognize the allies you need to eventually sell your idea.

Take a few minutes to map out the process you want your idea to go through. Do the formal and informal paths together so you can see where they intersect and what time-sequencing you need. When you have a preliminary cut, share it with others who are working on the project with you. They will have some additions or subtractions that could make the difference between selling and not selling your idea.

Too often managers forget this step and proceed on instinct or business as usual. An investment of a few hours in this process can pay big dividends during the selling of the project. When you complete this process, your confidence rises. You can clearly see the path ahead of you, though it may (and probably will) change over time. For example, you will learn things that dictate involving fewer or more people, especially in the informal part of the process. That is good since it means that you are learning as you go and incorporating learnings quickly into your plan.

Methods of Achieving Buy-In

There are a variety of other ways to achieve buy-in from your associates. The first rule is "no surprises." People want to be informed in advance of things that will affect them. Surprises tend to quickly undermine trust. As we saw earlier, trust is the glue that holds things together. Since it is so important, you need to be sure that you have zero tolerance for surprises among your allies.

And participation usually leads to some level of buy-in because people want the projects they're associated with to succeed. Remember, buy-in is different from formal approval. When you seek buy-in, you are looking for valuable input to improve your idea and for supporters who will stand up with you to help sell it. In some companies, you need to have buy-in from specific people before management will agree to your idea. For example, if you are citing consumer research findings in your recommendation, you may need a senior consumer research manager to sign off on your written description of the findings. This sign off may be literal—an initial on the written recommendation.

There are four major ways of achieving buy-in to your project: 1) ask for input, 2) offer joint ownership, 3) share credit, and 4) use a consultant.

"Talk to people the idea would impact on the front end" says Betsy Williams of Nielsen Media Research. "Gather their ideas and make their ideas better. Keep them involved and informed. Remember that production people always want to be involved from the beginning."

Before you actually ask someone for her input, make a couple of points clear. First, share with her that you may or may not directly use her thoughts. Nonetheless, you find most of the time that you learn valuable information just by gathering input. Often you use it in a management presentation to help sell the idea.

Second, you want this to be an ongoing dialogue. Often people reflect on the idea and a day or two later have new thoughts. You want the person to feel free to share these with you as soon as possible.

G. Richard Shell, author of *Bargaining for Advantage* (1999), says to "always remember one major underlying principle: People tend to avoid doing things unless it is in their best interest. Therefore, you must demonstrate or create the perception that your idea *is* in their best interest." He goes on to say,

> If you can get an executive to sponsor or champion your idea, all the better. But remember, while a few people will help you just to be nice and because you have a good idea, most people that really get behind your idea will do so because it may enhance their career or benefit their department significantly. This happens all the way to the top of the organization.

When you ask for input, be prepared for a wide range of potential responses and know what you will do with the full range of possibilities. At times, the response could be very negative. If a person suggests the project should not be approved, you need an immediate plan or you will have someone working very hard to derail your efforts.

With negative input, it is an opportunity to seek a win-win solution. Attitude is critical at this stage. If you fight the input instead of learning from it, you may create a tenacious opponent instead of a valuable ally. If you can find a win-win solution, you may create your most valuable ally.

This can be difficult, but "bad news" often has a silver lining. Sometimes it is an element of the idea you completely overlooked. While hearing this might feel like negative input, if your attitude is right, you will have a much stronger idea after you make constructive use of the information.

What about the situation where despite your best efforts you cannot find a win-win solution? You are stronger for having re-

ceived the input because you now know in detail how opponents of
the idea are thinking. Keep a record of their concerns as you encounter them. Look for patterns. You may find in the pattern a relevant concern that you dismissed at first. With this information,
you can plan to address objections later in the process.

Barbara Garner, manager of organizational effectiveness for a
large international corporation stressed that whenever an idea may
have a negative impact within a company, it is always best to have
a strong leader to help minimize that impact. This leader should be
someone who can clearly communicate the reasons and benefits to
the corporation as a whole, and should be someone employees
trust and respect.

Many times the input you receive may sound like mixed news.
There are some aspects of the idea that people like, and some they
dislike. There will be times when you agree and incorporate the
thinking into your presentation. There also will be times when the
input seems irrelevant and not very helpful. In these times, recall
what Laurence J. Peter, author of *The Peter Principle* (1996) said,
"You don't need to take a person's advice to make him feel good—
just ask for it."

If you've studied any how-to books to learn skills in the area of
politics, psychology, negotiating, selling, or the like, you're probably familiar with the technique of making someone think your idea
was theirs. That's a sure way to gain support. "This is especially effective when discussing your idea with your boss in order to gain
her support," says Ronald Terry, retired chairman and CEO of First
Tennessee Corporation. So, how can you turn an idea around to be
someone else's?

Solicit the key person's input. Take your idea to another person
for discussion, setting forth bite-size pieces of your plan and leading the other person to the conclusions that you believe are in-
evitable. Try suggesting that there is a problem to be solved, and
guide the discussion toward the solution you know is best. You
must be very careful not to be manipulative. You must be up front
about your purpose.

Feed back words you've heard someone use. When we hear our

own words, we know the other person has been listening. It makes us believe we speak the same language, and, by inference, that we share an understanding of the situation. Language is important here and as you share, ensure that key words have common meanings.

Regardless of the outcome, you are better off when you receive the input of knowledgeable people. But be careful. You can take asking for input too far and by doing so either slow your project down or grind it to a halt. Seek input from people who are knowledgeable and connected in some meaningful way to the idea. Make sure it is input from sources you respect. It should also be input that you can cite and call on if needed.

Offering joint ownership can double the selling horsepower for your idea. It can be tempting to want sole recognition for a fabulous idea, but don't be deceived into thinking that you won't get credit if you share ownership. Linking your department with another strong entity can both make the idea stronger and significantly increase the likelihood that it will be approved and implemented.

Be careful in your choice of a joint owner or owners. He needs to make the idea stronger. For example, politicians often use joint ownership on a bill to signal bipartisan support. They also use cosponsors to signal the degree of support an idea has. On popular bills, it is not unusual to see twenty cosponsors.

When you look for a joint owner, look for some natural combinations. For example, if the idea is a product improvement that utilizes a new, patented manufacturing process, marketing and manufacturing might be ideal joint owners. These two knowledgeable owners probably make the recommendation much stronger.

What do joint owners do? They bring combined resources, mostly financial and human, to the task of researching and preparing the recommendation. Importantly, the two owners have different insights into how to sell an idea and contacts that can make the case stronger. For example, the two managers could seek a wider variety of input to strengthen the idea. Joint owners balance each other out in areas of need. One of the joint owners might have a strong personal relationship with one of the necessary approving managers. This connection could provide insights that would generally be inaccessible to an idea with only one owner.

Sharing credit for an idea is an excellent way of building support for it. Even if it's not appropriate or necessary to share ownership with another person or area, it's still smart to share credit in a visible way.

In truth, few ideas are entirely the work of one person. Certainly there can be an inventor or founder associated with an idea, but in most cases there are people who have made significant contributions along the way. These contributions can be substantial. For example, you have an idea for a product improvement and another person suggests a unique new packaging idea to help signal the improvement. While the improvement is the central point, the packaging idea takes it to a higher level and the person who contributed deserves credit.

As you seek input, you will get ideas that you incorporate either totally or in part. Give people credit for their contributions. It is the right thing to do.

It also helps you sell your idea. When you give people credit, they often move from supporter to enthusiastic supporter. The difference can be important. For example, they might assist in the presentation to management. By taking responsibility for a significant portion of the presentation, they allow you to focus on other areas. In most cases, you also get a stronger presentation.

These supporters may ultimately be members of your idea team who can help fully develop the idea from a cross-functional perspective. Each of these persons will also have allies, and the broader the coalition of support, the better.

Giving credit to others also impresses management. They see that several people invested effort in the idea. And as we saw in joint ownership, when someone is an active participant in selling the idea, you have the strongest form of an ally.

Use a consultant when you need independent expertise. He can bring a breadth of perspective that you cannot get from within the company. This can be especially helpful if your company has limited experience with an idea. To have a consultant as an ally say,

"This worked successfully for (company) when they. . ." (with supporting data) can give your idea a big boost.

But be careful—using an outside expert can be a plus or a minus, depending upon your company's philosophy. Some companies routinely solicit input or validation by an "objective" third party. In this case you want to choose carefully from a long list of potential consultants. The two most valuable characteristics in a consultant are unique expertise and credibility.

This can be a tough choice, and you may need some help, especially if you have not used consultants before. Start your search by determining which consultants the company has already used that have relevant expertise. Determine how happy the other clients had been. Your search may end with this step. If it does not, look for recommendations from industry and association sources. If you still do not have who you need, there are consultants who can help you find consultants.

Other companies frown on the use of consultants as an unnecessary expense. And many people do not have the authority to hire consultants until an idea has received preliminary approval. At that point, senior management may recommend bringing someone in. You'll have to judge whether a consultant can add credibility to your project. If this is an unmovable obstacle in your company, there are alternatives. For example, consultants love to write articles. In your research, look for consultant articles you can include in your business plan to support your idea.

Sometimes a joint owner knows a consultant who is especially credible with management. With the aid of that joint owner, approach senior management requesting an exception to company policy. If granted, it could be a major contribution.

When you have your allies, you need to remember a very important next step—keep them in the loop about the status of the project. When you solicit someone's input and plan to use it, follow-up with her. Let her know what you did with her input.

What do you do if you used little or none of her input? If you used a little, still keep her in the loop. As you share more about the project, she may have more ideas to share with you.

If you did not use any of her input, you need to make a judgment call. For example, if you have found the person's input valuable in the past, maybe she was distracted or too busy when you initially approached her. If you keep her up to date, maybe she will have thoughts that will help further down the road.

You can keep people in the loop in a variety of ways. The easiest and least expensive is e-mail. While most e-mail is rather plain, if you are in company that has a common software platform, like Microsoft Office, you can send out some snazzy newsletters. Microsoft Publisher is an excellent program, and you can include pictures and attractive graphic themes. If e-mail does not work for you then use another mail system—interoffice or USPS.

You can also use meetings to keep people up to date. Once you have put together your idea team, these meetings are important to convey information, dictate changes, and make reassignments. Whenever possible, present the information with enthusiasm and a little flair. You want your allies to be positive and motivated to continue helping.

Understanding Hidden Goals

Despite all your detective work, you won't always be able to discover where people stand on things, or what their needs or goals are. Signs aren't always clear, and people do have hidden agendas.

Gabarro and Kotter (1993) described one situation in which a newly hired vice president of marketing accepted the challenge of turning a sagging division around. Given free reign by the president, he quickly identified the problem and adopted a plan to fix it. He braced for negative financial results short term, anticipating that the strategy would deliver great long-term improvements. The president, however, wasn't content to wait. He quickly took control of the situation and made decisions that resulted in the same disastrous results as before the vice president took over. Soon, both were fired.

What the new vice president had not known until it was too late was that improving marketing and sales had been only one of the president's goals. His most immediate goal had been to make the company more profitable—quickly.

Nor had the new vice president known that his boss was invested in this short term priority for personal as well as business reasons. The president had been a strong advocate of the acquisition within the parent company, and his personal credibility was at stake.

The vice president made three basic errors. He took information supplied to him at face value, he made assumptions in areas where he had no information, and—what was most damaging— he never actively tried to clarify what his boss's objectives were.

Unfortunately, there are too many stories like this. It underscores the need to be as good at preparing to sell your idea as you were at inventing it. If you do not have the expertise to sell an idea, you will be handicapped unless you get help from people who know their way through the maze.

Make Your Plan Sell Itself

Think of your research as a form of "reconnaissance." Your internal research is not simply a fact-finding mission, it's also a selling function. If you have done excellent research, you have made a big down payment on helping your idea sell itself.

By recruiting allies, you take the next big step forward. Allies can help you perform many valuable tasks critical to the selling of your idea. The following is a discussion of some of those areas where joint owners, input providers, consultants, and people with whom you are sharing credit can help.

Identify Obstacles

From the limited scope of your area it may be impossible to see all the factors that may affect your plan, or to anticipate all the things that could go wrong. You may assume that something would be simple to accomplish when, in fact, it could be quite difficult. For example, during a reorganization of a customer service department, employees asked that a certain information field be added to the customer information page on their software. It seemed a simple request but, in fact, it required numerous links with other elements of the software. What appeared to be a minimal alteration was a major technological project.

This example underscores the biggest problem many inventors of ideas have—a blindness to obstacles and challenges. Even when they can acknowledge that these obstacles exist, they tend to minimize their importance. If you are the champion of the project, you need to recognize this natural bias and work to neutralize it. The biggest neutralizer is the right attitude. You need to be humble in recognizing that there is much you do not know, and eager to use learnings to make your plan better. Finally, you cannot be a glory hog who is unwilling for others to get some credit for helping.

Those who assist you often bring a fresh, less invested attitude that produces a more objective evaluation of obstacles. The ultimate helpful attitude is "obstacles are my friends." When an obstacle is an enemy, it is something you fight to eliminate; it is a threat and there is little thought of its positive qualities. The same obstacle when viewed as a friend becomes powerfully positive. When you ask, "What can you teach me about how to make this idea better?" your perspective opens to learning. When you incorporate learning into a better plan, the obstacle disappears in most cases.

Educate and Recruit People

Education is an important part of the selling process. By talking to multiple sources you'll lay the groundwork for approval by building constituencies. Involvement engenders support; thus, your research process can kill two birds with one stone. If you've gotten others excited, they will most likely help you sell your idea to others.

Educating and recruiting people are different from soliciting input, although you are likely to receive input from the process. Your goal is to inform and motivate people. Their help is often needed to prepare the idea for management review. This includes additional research and learning which is more in-depth than your first round of investigation. Maybe you discovered an interesting lead and you now want to drill down to better understand it.

At Nielson Media Research, an initial idea team may start out with four to five key people and then grow to fifteen to twenty people as needed. These people are brought in from all applicable areas such as finance, marketing, legal, operations, production, human resources, and customer service. Eventually there may be several sub-teams that are doing research in their specific areas of expertise. Regular meetings will be held to review progress and brainstorm any changes that are needed. In the end, they may have 100 or so people involved, with the buy-in of their managers. In this case, allies are gained exponentially.

This type of educating and recruiting helps you get off to a fast start when the idea is agreed to by management. Key departments are already up to speed and are eager to begin bringing the idea to life.

An interesting group to target for educating and probing is other senior managers who are not in your approval chain. They have a unique and highly valuable perspective. They know what issues are hot with top management now. They hear the senior managers you need approval from talk about projects. From this they know what these managers tend to like and dislike. Sometimes your joint owner or consultant can help you with this valuable input.

Overcome Objections

As you speak with people in other areas, ask them what they think common objections might be. Have them play devil's advocate and help you figure out how to resolve potential problems and address objections. Even if they don't admit it, sometimes the objections they cite will actually be theirs. That's even better: Now that you know their concerns, you have an opportunity to acknowledge and respond to them either at that time or later.

This is one of the most important ways allies can help you at this stage. When you eventually make the presentation, you will receive objections, even from supporters who are simply testing the idea. Any help you receive at this stage in identifying objections puts you in a great position to prepare quality, in-depth answers.

Anticipate Questions

What will management ask? You always want to know the answers before the questions are asked. People from a variety of areas will have different perspectives and different questions. Find them out now.

Questions are not the same as objections. Often they are requests for information. If you are prepared, the flow of the discussion proceeds. If you do not have the information, the entire decision-making process can be put on hold until you have it. The costs can be even higher if management believes you should have been prepared with the information.

The good news is that you will develop most of this information in your research and through seeking input from others. And most, if not all, of the information is in your business plan.

But answering questions is more than having the information. The information needs to be accessible and presentable, which we will discuss in later chapters.

Recognize People Who Will Not Get on Board

In some cases, no matter what you do, you will have detractors. It's better to know now so you won't be taken off guard. As a former corporate vice president says, "Always count the tanks before the meeting." In other words, know who will support you and who will not.

Knowing who is against the idea and why is critical intelligence. When you prepare your presentation, you build in your response. Taking a proactive stance can make the opposition's case more difficult to make. As long as you have done your research and have the data to support your idea, it will be hard to refute. However, the stronger your coalition of support and the more senior managers you have on board, the easier it will be to sell your idea.

In some instances, knowing who is against you helps you identify people you want to recruit to address their concerns. For example, if a senior manager with finance background is against your idea, recruiting a joint owner who is especially credible with him could be a big step towards diminishing the importance and power of his concerns.

Ask about Presentations

Take the opportunity to poll people about their experience presenting to the senior management team. Input from others can help you tailor your presentation to fulfill your audience's needs. They can describe what to expect and predict what members do and don't like. Be sure to ask if management has any particular hot buttons that relate specifically to their area. For instance, if a management team member is an advocate of training, you may want to stress the training element of your plan in your presentation.

Current events within the senior management team are often the most difficult to detect, so you want to be aware of topics discussed in the most recent management meetings. If you are going to be blindsided, current hot topics are a very likely source. Use all your resources to detect what these issues are. Reread management's comments with the latest quarterly earnings for clues. Revisit the last thirty day's press releases for clues, also.

If you submitted a basis-for-interest document previously, review the comments, both written and verbal, that were made in the process of gaining agreement to it.

Competition for Resources

Every new idea is automatically in competition for resources, whether for financing, people, or time. In reality, annual budget and strategic planning processes are continually in competition for resources. This goes on all the time throughout an organization, so senior management is used to making evaluations and decisions based on what's best for the company. However, Ronald Terry and Ken Glass of First Tennessee National Corporation said that what they look for in selecting projects are "how well the idea supports the company's strategy, the competence of the people developing the idea, and the long term financial and market share benefits." Ron Terry goes on to say, "Remember, it is not just *your* idea that is up against competition for resources, but everything involved in short term and long term planning."

Be realistic. There are certain facts of corporate life that have been true through the ages. When people are competing for limited resources, there's always some degree of politics involved.

As you make the rounds, remember that not everyone is interested in change. In fact, most people resist it.

The classic bureaucrat and the satisfied manager, for example, are both concerned with maintaining the status quo. Their questions typically are: How do I retain control of the resources I have? How do I keep others from affecting my ability to perform? Which projects threaten (or protect) my turf? Ideas that interest them are ones that strengthen their hold on the status quo. So they are not opposed to all new ideas. Look for a way that your idea may help achieve their objectives, even if it may be a bit of a stretch. If you are successful, you may convert a stick in the mud to a neutral position and maybe even make him a supporter.

Whether you realize it or not, your ability to get your idea implemented hinges at least to some degree on the attitudes and mind sets of those to whom it's presented. An executive described the culture in his former company: "Information was power, and if people liked you, they'd share information with you. If they didn't like you, they'd find a way to withhold it. For example, you had to ask for a report by the exact name, or request information very specifically, or else the manager would later claim, 'Oh, well, he didn't ask for that.'"

As a result, it's always best to confirm information from more than one source.

While you need to be realistic, be careful about taking this too far. If you believe your idea is very good and meets the needs of the company, then take the posture of a champion, of an advocate. Don't be afraid to be idealistic; your energy can inspire and motivate some people you might have written off as opponents or as not caring.

So far, we have talked about many people as allies and helpers. We have not yet talked about your boss, but he or she may be one of the top two or three most important potential supporters.

Get Your Boss on Board

No matter what your plan may be, the first step you must take is to run it by your boss. You're in a partnership; it's each partner's job to make the other look good.

Gaining your boss's support is not a political move; it's a means to "obtain the best possible results for you, your boss, and the company." Of course, the boss-subordinate relationship is somewhat flawed from the start, because it involves "mutual dependence between two fallible human beings" say Gabarro and Kotter (1993).

Understanding and tolerance are required on both parts, but since you are the one with an idea to sell, it behooves you to take the lead here. This person does control, at least to some degree, your visibility and image in the company, and may have more information and contacts than you do. A good boss can pave the way for an idea.

Keep in mind, too, that your activity will have a direct impact on your boss, who will be recognized (positively or negatively) based on the merit of your work. In this case, it's the trickle *up* effect. And the trickle goes beyond your corner of the world: Whoever hired your boss will also look good or bad depending on your outcome.

Selling, then, begins with your boss. Here are some questions to ask yourself:

- What is my boss trying to achieve personally and professionally? This can be difficult to determine, but with the right approach you can learn what is important to him. Often a social or after work environment is best. A common characteristic of many bosses is that they love to talk about themselves. Thus, this should not be a difficult question to answer.

- Does my boss maintain the status quo or seek innovative solutions? Again, your initial perceptions about his position may be flawed. You may interpret his feedback as not supportive of new ideas in general. The truth may be very different, especially in a company that rewards new ideas. Even if he is status-quo orientated, you can create enthusiasm for your idea by showing how it is more evolutionary than revolutionary. Even the most conservative boss can be motivated some of the time. Usually you need to take on more risk and do more of the work, especially the critical thinking.

- What immediate and long-term pressures is my boss under? Listen to your boss's complaints and you will learn about many of his pressures.

- Is the department's plate too full to handle another project? Is the timing right? If you see your boss is overwhelmed at the time you are ready to solicit her help, consider backing off. Take the next steps on your project list to keep the project moving forward. Alert your boss to the open-ended need you have to discuss the project with her. If you make it her call, when you get her attention it is likely to be more valuable than if you force your project into her day.

- Can my boss handle risk or controversy? If the answer is yes, you have no problem here. But what if it is no? Then you need to find ways to minimize risk. Consider building more alternatives into your plan. Also look for opportunities to reduce costs and increase revenues. This can make the required payout move from attractive to very attractive and reduce the project's risk. Another way to help your boss handle risk is to spread it around. Getting a quality joint owner can be a big step forward, especially if it is a highly respected person within the organization.

- Is this project a threat or an opportunity? If there is any serious threat associated with the project, you will be hard pressed to have an enthusiastic boss at your side. You can take similar steps that you took to reduce risk. Once you have neutralized the threat, make it an opportunity he can be enthusiastic about. Reinforce your links to the company's vision and current company goals. It is not enough just to eliminate the threatening aspects of the idea, you need a positive association or you will be swimming upstream.

Only by knowing the answers to these questions can you intelligently decide how to approach your boss with an idea. If you don't know your boss well enough to answer them, find someone who does. An assistant or someone who spends a lot of time with your boss can provide input.

The key will be to gain support by demonstrating how it will make your boss look good, or accomplish personal and professional goals. (A good—that is, smart—employee never outshines the boss.)

Before you show your whole hand, though, you should "read the tea leaves," says one executive. Subtly explore with your boss some potential issues, probing for sensitive spots and weighing reactions.

Projects are seldom introduced to a boss for the first time when all the work is done. If this is done to speed the project forward or to impress the boss, you may accomplish neither objective. The boss's comments may mean there has been lots of wasted work. If you have gone astray (in your boss's opinion), the boss may be concerned with the quality of your thinking. About the only time this approach works is on projects that are very similar to ones that you have previously worked on together.

In most cases, you want to share your project with him in ministages. It can be a combination of short meetings and highlighting project advances on your weekly project list. If you do not operate with a weekly project list, consider one just for your special project. You need to strike a balance here. You want to work independently and have plenty of opportunity to take ownership for the project, but you also want to benefit from your boss's input. You also want your boss to feel some ownership for the project. Strike the balance that fits your situation and do not be afraid to involve your boss in creating it.

Take the information away and digest it. Does your idea seem to fit with your boss's plans? When you've evaluated the situation, you can find a way to position what you're doing as an extension of something your boss is committed to, or as a solution to a problem. And, if you can convince him it is his idea or an extension of his thinking, all the better.

If your idea isn't met with enthusiasm, retreat and rethink your strategy. One approach is to try the project out on a small scale and measure its success. Or, you may build a coalition of support outside your immediate area, gather appropriate supportive data, and approach your boss again. You'll have positive results to present, which always makes it easier for people to say "yes." While this can be politically dangerous for you (your boss may not be pleased that you went around him), generally he will reconsider if others he respects have given their thumbs-up. It would be very important at this point to include your boss to demonstrate his renewed confidence and support.

Once you have your boss's go-ahead, keeping her informed will be crucial. The worst possible thing you can do is allow your boss to be in the embarrassing position of not knowing as much about your plans as someone outside your department. The first time that happens may be the last time your idea sees the light of day.

Another important role your boss plays when you have her support is as champion for the project. As your project moves forward to the ultimate approval level, your boss will play a critical role. In many companies, your boss may write a cover note to your business plan or recommendation. This cover note may be the first document senior managers read. You want to be sure you review it before it is sent.

A boss is also likely to be asked questions by senior managers in any discussions. You can help your boss by being sure she has the entire business plan and any additional backup information you have.

Scaling Brick Walls—The Boss Who Gets in the Way

Is your boss generally supportive or unsupportive? This is something you should know intuitively or be able to ascertain before you plunge in irreversibly.

There could be many reasons a boss won't support your idea. First, don't assume that your boss's reluctance stems from ignorance, disagreement with your concept, or lack of support for your goals. Your boss may be privy to inside information that has a bearing on what you're proposing and may not be at liberty to divulge it. Before you push ahead, it's best to seriously consider what circumstances could be at work behind the scenes.

And, as we said, there could be other legitimate reasons. If your department is under the gun for other projects, your brainstorm could be one your manager can't afford to spend time or resources on.

There is, of course, the possibility that your boss simply doesn't understand.

When you find yourself at odds with your boss, resist the urge to charge ahead. You could back yourself and your boss into a tight corner. Now is a good time to take a deep breath, pause, and collect information. You have run into something unexpected and if you are going to resolve this, you need your best listening skills.

One of Stephen Covey's seven habits of highly effective people (1990) is to first seek to understand and then to be understood. You need this spirit plus patience if you are going to secure the support of your boss.

Set aside your idealism long enough to look realistically at the possible obstacles, and ask yourself if you're willing to take the risk of moving forward. After all, your career could be at stake.

Can you pursue your idea without your manager's support? Is it smart to go outside the chain of command? This is dangerous ground. A lot depends on what type of company you work for.

Growth companies are often interested in new possibilities and encourage idea sharing regardless of the forum. In some (few) companies the chain of command is more a matter of courtesy than policy; you might get away with casually bouncing an idea off another manager and letting it grow from there.

The Gallo Winery is an interesting company in this regard. For decades, Ernest Gallo wanted to hear ideas from deep within the organization. As a result, employees could present an idea even if the boss disagreed with it. Amazingly, there were no political consequences from taking such an approach. The spirit of this carried over into meetings. In advertising and packaging meetings, very junior people were free to have very different positions than their boss, including those several levels up the hierarchy. For years under Ernest's leadership, this freedom of expression was a major positive for people in the company.

But in an organization that's highly committed to following procedures, going around the boss can be career suicide, no matter how good the idea. Managers don't appreciate people circumventing them, especially if they've already expressed lack of support for an idea. That's why scoping things out subtly in advance is a good idea; it gives you a chance to form Plan B.

The best Plan B relies on how well-connected you are and what type of support you can elicit from your network. Assemble a multidepartment team to jointly explore an idea. Take your boss to lunch and explain to her that your group has an idea it wants to run by her. Then ask for her input. You're building ownership from the start.

Worst case scenario: Your initial exploration tells you you've hit a dead end. If you're altruistic and simply want to see a good idea put in place, you can "leak" the idea to someone from another area who can champion it. Once you've taken this road, you may need to bow out of the process or take a lesser role in the idea's development. Eventually, if your boss perceives the idea to be a good thing, you may end up getting full support for involvement.

One last tip for those times when you think all hope is lost comes from a CEO who described "computer types" as people who regularly get away with ignoring the hierarchy, as if their scientific bent relieves them of the responsibility for living by the corporate rules. He explained: "They'll see me in the hall and say, 'What about this idea . . .?' If people encounter resistance, I'd say try that approach." It plants a seed that may actually grow without all the initial buy-in traditionally required.

If you're determined to make your mark, you can take your idea to someone you think can make it happen, usually your boss's superior or peer. But be prepared: There could be major career fallout from this strategy. When you're considering bucking the system, proceed with caution. If you're in an innovative environment that supports new ideas, push for all it's worth. If you're in a conservative environment and you're trying to push a dinosaur, tread carefully.

Advocates and Champions

You want an advocate at senior levels, if at all possible. Seek someone who is well-positioned and considered to be influential in the senior management team. People who have had success building their own departments or divisions are clearly more powerful than those who haven't.

Before you solicit the support of an advocate, keep in mind that any potential supporter will be weighing the answers to two questions:

- Is it worth staking my credibility on this?
- Is it worth staking my career on this?

Direct, outspoken support can be very helpful, but you can also use effective behind-the-scenes advocates who will quietly plant your idea with the right people. Most people will not take the role of visible supporter if they feel that position makes them vulnerable. When you approach potential supporters they have three choices:

- Support it
- Keep quiet
- Shoot it down

Someone who goes out on a limb for you should have something to gain, either now or later. Being an advocate can be challenging and risky. But this is nothing new. Machiavelli said, "There is nothing more difficult to take in hand, more perilous to conduct, than to take a lead in the introduction of a new order of things, because the innovation has for enemies all those who have done well under the old conditions and lukewarm defenders in those who may do well under the new."

You are looking for that rare breed—a person willing to champion your idea among the owners and leaders of a company. Your project may not have such a champion, but it can be so valuable that it deserves your best effort.

In every company there are people who support the status quo, as well as people who are what Ken Glass of First Tennessee National Corporation calls "Champions for Growth." These champions are people who regularly propose or support ideas that will move the company forward. They can be a powerful channel for putting your idea in front of management and lining up the necessary allies to win management support.

Champions for growth are generally close to the top of an organization, either formally or informally. Their reputations make them easy to identify: They're usually running growing divisions or departments. They frequently have lunch with the CEO, belong to the same club, play the same sport, or even drive the same car. Regardless of these external clues, however, it is known throughout the organization that these people have the respect and ear of the most senior managers. They are sought out for their ideas and are members of important task forces and strategy planning sessions.

You will never be able to satisfy everyone, so concentrate your sales efforts on the four or five most influential people in your organization. If those persons are sold on your plan, they will help you sell it.

Build a Network of Support

Building a network of support is all about building relationships. And relationships are about trust. Although trust can only be developed over time, you can begin to expand your foundation of allies as you explore possibilities for your project.

You've already identified people whose direct support you'll need: They're the ones you're asking for help along the way. Other allies can provide you with additional valuable information, deflect criticism you may not even know about, and talk your idea up to people you may not have access to.

How do you develop allies? Certainly, finding opportunities to socialize or work on common projects present a strong foundation for building relationships. "Personal relationships create a level of trust and confidence between people that eases anxiety and facilitates communication," says G. Richard Shell in his recent book, *Bargaining for Advantage* (1999). He goes on to say, "At the core of human relationships is a fragile interpersonal dynamic: trust. With trust, deals get done. Without it, deals are harder to negotiate, more difficult to implement, and vulnerable to changing incentives and circumstances." The secret to creating and sustaining trust in negotiations, he says, is the human behavior referred to as the "norm of reciprocity." The concept of reciprocity has been described by Dr. Alvin Gouldner (1999) as:

> Duties that people owe one another, not as human beings, or as fellow members of a group, or even as occupants of social statuses within the group, but rather because of their prior actions. We owe others certain things because of what they have previously done for us, because of the history of previous interaction we have had with them.

But there are some other simple ways to gain teammates:

- Involve yourself in task forces and projects that ensure visibility. From the first day of your employment with an organization, you should offer to participate in as many teams as possible and do the best you can. You will make numerous contacts across the organization and become known as a "doer." Offer to take on small projects or head a task force that a senior manager considers important. Look for projects and volunteer readily. Never say no, unless it is impossible for you to do it. But, remember, whenever you say yes to a project, you must do your absolute best.

- Involve people from other departments in your projects. Do not isolate yourself on this project or others. You want to have a wide network of people who know you and the good work that you do. They may not provide direct assistance on this project, but if they are asked by a decision maker outside of the process, they will put in a good word for you.

- Thank people for their help. Whenever anyone lends assistance, be quick and appropriately effusive with the thank-yous. Some people are very good at this. They have special stationery and a system to support the prompt written reinforcement of their appreciation. Send fun little gifts that will continue to motivate them such as a pack of Extra gum for going the extra mile, a Kudos candy bar to say thanks, etc. People love to receive treats, no matter how small.

- Send her a memo and send a copy to her boss. One of the most powerful compliments you can give is to send a copy of your thank you to the person's boss. You can outline the specific things she did that helped. At the end of the project, put the ultimate thank-you note outlining the details of her involvement in her personnel file.

- Mention her accomplishments to others. Go beyond letting her boss know by openly sharing your appreciation. Often a good forum is a weekly team meeting where you can share your thanks before the group.

- Acknowledge that person's involvement in the presentation meeting to senior management. Sharing the limelight with your fellow idea contributors gives you even more credibility with senior managers, letting them know that this idea is not just for your personal gain but for the good of everyone in the organization.

There may be people or departments you believe won't be affected by your plan, or who you feel can't add anything to the process. Nevertheless, think carefully before excluding anyone. Everyone wants to feel important and included. You want to build consensus for your ideas, as well as develop a network that can be mutually beneficial for future endeavors.

Who will you include in your network building activity? Select people from several groups.

Your peers—When people like and respect you, they find it easier to support you and harder to shoot you down. It makes sense then to build a widespread base of people who are on your side.

Besides, having peers in the loop can make your project more efficient. You won't have to be an expert in all disciplines or pay big bucks to go out and hire the tremendous resources it takes to pull off a new venture; you'll have almost all of them at your fingertips. With finesse you can tap those resources and get others involved. The true art is in knowing who, what, and how to ask.

Peers are also an excellent source of information. They are probably talking to management about their projects about the same time that you are. You can benefit from what they have just experienced and learned. A warning about peers is that they may see themselves as competitive with you for career progress and salary rewards. This sort of silo within a silo in some companies prevents much interchange between peers.

Even if this is present in your company, be brave. Seek out counsel in a friendly, nonthreatening manner. You will get a few nuggets of help. (Suggest this person be a joint owner or on the idea team. People who become involved no longer feel in competition.) Of course, be appreciative and send a follow-up thank-you note. You could pioneer a new, more open culture and break down a silo that is not serving anyone well.

Senior management—Who's your friend, who's your foe? When you meet with a senior manager, take along an expert from that person's department who has already bought into the idea. This gives you someone to answer technical questions and demonstrates you've already addressed any considerations for the department.

As you build your network of support, these can be some of your most helpful contacts. For example, consider meeting with a senior finance manager to review your numbers even if his approval is not needed. Since he does not need to commit, he may feel free to give you a range of helpful insights. As with others, he will be sensitive to the most recent hot topics among top management.

Movers and shakers—Opinion leaders can be your new best friends. They can spread the word for you and gain buy-in from diverse sources. Certain people influence the decision maker, either through their positions of power or because they're part of the decision maker's network of trusted friends or associates. Cultivate them.

Most movers and shakers should be people within the company for security reasons. Sometimes suppliers who have management's ear can be great additions to your network. In marketing, if the president of the advertising agency is a respected voice, then make sure she is fully and appropriately briefed on the project. She often has quality time with senior managers and is seen as being insightful about the potential of new ideas.

Does this sound self-serving or manipulative? Not if you recognize that it's a two-way street. We're simply suggesting it's easier to work with people you know than people you don't. And people who like and trust you will put you under kinder scrutiny than those who don't.

A basic part of networking wisdom is that relationships that are win-win prove to be the most productive ones. So, recognize that while you are looking for help now on your project the day will come when you can return the assistance. The old saying, "If you scratch my back, I'll scratch yours" is alive and well and not to be minimized. Be sure to reinforce this point with those who help you.

Make yourself available to people. Take the time to cultivate relationships as a give-and-take proposition, and you'll reap not only the benefits of professional success, but also personal rewards in the shape of friendships. As Franklin D. Roosevelt once said, "If you treat people right, they will treat you right—at least 90 percent of the time."

Who Gets the Credit?

If you successfully develop a network of support and gain the advocates you need for your project, you'll also share the credit with others. It's true you may not be recognized as single-handedly changing the face of your company. But you will have a successful project, and that's the best public relations you can have. People who get results are often asked to participate in other high-visibility projects, and word of your contributions will spread.

No doubt you've heard stories about a manager working diligently on a project only to have the champion be accorded responsibility for the achievement. The purpose is to get the job done, and a champion can do it. Don't worry that you won't get credit; management generally knows who won the game, no matter who carried the ball across the goal line.

"Never feel bad when the CEO takes your idea and makes it his," says Ken Glass of First Tennessee National Corporation. Instead, consider it as a moment for celebration. After all, isn't that the ultimate compliment? Your project now receives all the resources it needs and the inside track to quick management decisions when they are needed.

Key Learning Points

1. The most effective way to develop an idea is through networking, gaining allies, and building a strong cross-functional team.
2. When sharing your idea with others, listen to what they have to offer. Incorporate their thoughts as much as possible. Give them credit.
3. Be aware of who may be affected negatively. Identify them early on and begin to address how they will be affected and how this might be neutralized or mitigated.
4. Avoid going over your boss's head; rather, try to get his support and involvement early on.
5. Understand the ripple effects of your idea on the company and its stakeholders.
6. Recognize that there are limited dollars and human resources and that your idea is only one of hundreds competing for implementation.
7. Understand how change threatens status quo. Identify those that might be threatened and visit them early to address their concerns.
8. Never forget the "norm of reciprocity" in establishing relationships with others: People will always be inclined to help those who have helped them in the past. Start nurturing these relationships early and offer to help others accomplish their goals.

CHAPTER 5

Assessing Your Audience

"I made some mistakes in drama. I thought drama was when the actor cried. But drama is when the audience cries."

Frank Capra

We've decided that the biggest barrier to communication leaders face is this: They are usually more focused on what *they* want to say than on what their *audience* needs to hear. True communication occurs only when a message is sent, received, and correctly interpreted. Therefore, creating an effective presentation is a great deal more complicated than simply deciding what you want to say. More important is, what does your audience need to hear, and how do they prefer to hear it?

David Ogilvy, the advertising guru, told a story about Max Hart, the men's clothing tycoon. Hart complained to his advertising manager that he didn't like the latest campaign. "Nobody reads that much copy," he said.

The advertising manager disagreed, and made a bet with Hart. "I can write a whole newspaper page of solid type and you will read every word of it."

Hart took the bet.

The advertising manager said, "I won't have to write even a paragraph to prove my point. I'll just give you the heading: This page is all about Max Hart" (Peter Hay, *The Book of Business Anecdotes*, 1988).

In sales, we speak of WIIFM: What's In It For Me? That's the question audience members are asking throughout any sales pitch or presentation.

Imagine that you are the leader of a company that's in turmoil as a result of a major reorganization. Employees are uncertain about whether or not they'll have jobs. You call an all-employee meeting to discuss next year's corporate goals. How much attention do you think employees will pay to your message? Not much. Why? Because employees first want to know whether they'll be employed. They're not worried about the company's future; they're worried about their own.

Here's another example: How often do you receive memos from people in other departments asking you to participate in fixing a problem they're having? Do they ever explain how you will benefit, or do they usually just say what they want from it? How much more likely would you be to make it a priority if you thought you too would have something to gain?

WIIFM is just as true for a CEO as it is for any employee (Bennis and Nanus, 1997). Warren Bennis and Burt Nanus describe the leaders' struggle to retain credibility:

Leaders are being scrutinized as never before. . . . Current public sector checkpoints leave little leeway for anything but rectitude and responsibility. Valid, important, and constructive ideas have fallen prey to disclosure and criticism. . . . Deep feelings of insecurity are the norm. They are experienced by people from all belief systems and economic brackets, all spheres of influence and all levels of competency.

Carol Coletta, founder of BusinessThinkers.com, puts it succinctly: "Everyone wants to look smart when they make a decision."

In Chapter 1 we talked about aligning your idea with the company's strategy. This chapter is about aligning your idea with management's strategy, both personal and business. You have done a lot of work to get to this point. You have collected data, polished your idea, and developed a foundation of support with allies from across the organization. Resist the urge to think you know it all. This and the future stages are ones where you start using the raw materials—the information—that you have collected so far. This is where you sort out what is critical from what is just very important. It is time to start making the critical decisions that determine whether you will be successful.

Hopefully, you know by now that your success is not determined by the quality of your idea alone. In fact, the bigger your idea the harder it will be for most senior managers to agree with you. This may sound preposterous but it isn't.

This chapter is devoted to grounding your idea. Of all the points you can say about your idea, which ones will be most beneficial to decision makers? It is not what points you think are most important. It is what points are most important to the decision makers on your idea.

This is a perspective that many very good managers forget and it can be their downfall. When you master assessing your audience and targeting your message to them, you will make the actual presentation much easier and more successful.

The positioning or targeting points may be ones that you did not even consider when you started the process. You have many choices when it comes to positioning your idea. Probably only one or two of them will achieve the objective you have.

To illustrate how the best positioning may be one that you have not thought of previously, consider this perspective, "The only prize much cared for by the powerful is power. The prize of a general is not a bigger tent, but command" (Holmes, 1913). You have probably thought of profit, vision, and market share positioning, but not the power of the decision maker. Power is not the right positioning for every project, but in some form, it plays a role in many.

A major health care institution was on the brink of change, ready to break out of its nonprofit, traditional curing-patients mode and into a customer-service mode. The president hired a new vice president of marketing from outside the medical community. Having been charged with turning the organization into a more businesslike enterprise, he jumped in and began challenging the status quo. He ran immediately into a brick wall. Management wasn't really ready to make the switch, and within a year the new vice president was out the door.

Envision your proposal from your audience's perspective: What do they need to hear? And what are they ready to hear? Remember, timing is as crucial as content.

Positioning Is Everything

The word "positioning" has become an integral part of our business vocabulary. Positioning is a way of delivering information so that the audience receives the message you want them to hear. It usually involves exercising discretion in what you choose to communicate.

For example, an auto company that targets hip young buyers might tout a car's speed and style as opposed to its practical features such as gas conservation or power locks. It may have all those features, but the company selects which ones to stress, *positioning* it as a car that young buyers would want.

Similarly, you will select which features of your idea to emphasize depending upon what management will value most. Carol Coletta gave this example:

> If you were selling the concept of video conferencing to a human resources director, you might point out how it could help reduce

costs by eliminating travel. If you're presenting the concept to a CEO, however, you'll want to focus on the things that are important to a CEO, such as how the technique will help direct employees' efforts toward supporting the company's mission.

You have a limited time to get your message across, and positioning allows you to tell the story you want your management to hear.

Positioning needs to be defined, because there are many statements that sound great but are not positionings. As used in this chapter, a positioning is a benefit the company and the decision maker receive if your idea is agreed to and successfully implemented.

The key word in this definition is "benefit." A benefit positioning meets the needs of the decision maker. This may sound obvious, but you would be surprised how many times benefit positioning is ignored.

Many people become enamored with features instead of benefits. Features are descriptions; benefits meet needs.

A few examples will illustrate how tempting it can be to use features instead of benefits. We will use some familiar consumer products to illustrate the point.

- What if, for its Pentium III chip, Intel said that the processor is twice as fast as some earlier versions? It sounds intriguing, but it is a technical statement that the potential customer needs to translate into a benefit. Instead of speed, Intel's advertising focused on the new chip's ability to smoothly and quickly play video, something earlier versions of the chip were not as good at. Speed is the feature that enables consumers to enjoy the video benefit.

- Bounty paper towels could have said that a product improvement used a proprietary technology to make its paper towel. It could have gone on to mention the number of manufacturing patents it held and the millions of dollars that were invested in new equipment. These are all positive things to say and may even impress some people—for a minute or two. Instead, Bounty focused on the benefit of the new technology for the consumer. It showed the towel absorbing liquid faster than a competitive product and closed the sale by calling it the "Quicker Picker Upper." Bounty's proprietary technology allows it to make a towel that soaks up liquids faster, which is a valuable benefit among paper towel consumers. The fact that the company spent millions of dollars and has lots of patents is not a benefit to consumers.

■ When Lexus was introduced, it also could have talked about its superior technology in quieting engine noise and vibration. It uses sound- and vibration-dampening materials and technology that achieved lower levels than almost every car on the market. Instead of touting its technology, Lexus dramatically demonstrated the benefit. With champagne glasses stacked high on the hood of a Lexus, we saw the car's engine and wheels speed up to about sixty miles per hour. The glasses never moved. The consumer got the benefit message of a quiet, smooth-riding car without knowing about all the factual stuff that made it happen. A quiet and smooth ride is an important benefit for Lexus's target audience, which buys luxury cars. In advertising, you know you have a powerful communication tool when several competitors in the car industry use similar devices to demonstrate their vehicle's benefits.

Often you will hear benefit and feature statements together. When this is done effectively, it tells you what the benefit is and the feature statement gives you permission to believe it.

For example, suppose a car company tells you, "For the first time ever, your car can safely drive itself at highway speeds for hours." You might really want this benefit since it would make a 500-mile vacation trip almost effortless. Although you would really like the benefit, you doubt the company can deliver on its promise.

This is when you need the feature. Now suppose the company went on to say: "All you do is drive your car onto special computer-controlled highways with sensors that maintain the desired speeds. These systems were developed by NASA and successfully tested on one thousand miles of freeway for twelve months." If this feature was supported with demonstrations and visuals, you might be inclined to believe the promised benefit. Features help make benefits credible.

The lesson from consumer products is that if you want to persuade someone, promise him the most important benefit (determined by responses to consumer research) your product can deliver and back it up with the facts that make it credible.

We have focused on advertising because it is a very familiar form of positioning. Advertisers are trying to do the same thing you are—they want to persuade people to agree to buy a product or service. For the manufacturers, it is a very challenging form because they only have thirty seconds to position their product. They need to choose the single best positioning and make it very persuasive—and fast.

You have more time to position your idea with management—in most cases. Then there are the meetings where a senior manager walks into a meeting late and says she only has a few minutes for the meeting. You need to present your strongest positioning fast. If you have been thinking in terms of the challenge a television advertiser faces, then you are well prepared for this stressful challenge.

Meeting Audience Needs

As we've stressed in previous chapters, most people are looking for how something will benefit them professionally or personally, materially or emotionally. Any proposal you make has the potential to provide them with gain or loss in areas such as career growth, lifestyle, self-esteem, and so on. As a result, they will always evaluate what you're suggesting according to whether they stand to gain or lose, and how great a risk is involved.

To be effective, your presentation has to demonstrate, at least by inference, what the audience has to gain.

Three Audiences, Including One You Don't See

Unless you're selling directly to the board of directors, you have more than one audience. The first two audiences are the audience you're presenting to and the audience *they* will have to present to. More precisely, these audiences are the decision makers you need to appeal to. In the first audience, you want the decision maker to agree to present your idea to the ultimate decision maker. Your goal, therefore, is to provide your audiences with the ammunition they need to sell it to their audience.

The third audience is the key influencers who will be at the presentation. While they are not decision makers, they will be asked what they think of the idea and their opinions often determine the outcome. At the very least, their opinions need to be reckoned with.

For that reason, you have to anticipate not only your audience's needs, but also the needs of those at the next level of approval.

While you need to keep in mind the audience that is not present, your first priority needs to be the audience you can see. If you do not make the sale with them, the audience you cannot see will never hear your idea.

The good news is that all the work you have done so far has most of the insights you need to strongly position your proposal. To recap they are:

- Customer research told you about what is most important to customers and how well your idea delivers the benefits they want the most. In a customer-driven company, this research credibly supports powerful positioning statements.

- Allies have educated you about many points, but most valuable may be their insights about what is most important to the managers whose approval you seek. Review the input for patterns because each person's thoughts are probably part of the puzzle about what's most important.

- The key numbers needed for approval: what success looks like, what failure looks like, timelines, risks, and rewards.

Your job is to synthesize all these data and inputs into a powerful, credible positioning for your idea. It is a positioning that meets the needs of your audiences in the same way that your idea meets the needs of your customers.

The multiple audiences you face complicate your task. To simplify your task, identify your priorities. In most cases, your number one priority is finding the absolute best positioning for the strongest decision maker who is in the audience. If you do not meet his needs, you will not make the sale in most cases. This usually gives you one person to focus on.

In most cases, the next most important priority is the one or two key influencers in the audience. When you seek their opinions, you want them to support your idea. You want a positioning that meets their needs or you will find them becoming opponents who can kill your idea. In some cases where the formal decision maker is weak or uncomfortable with risk, these key influencers may be the real decision makers. If you convince them, then the decision maker always follows.

The audience that you cannot see is your third priority in most cases, even though they may be the ultimate decision maker. This audience can be a very senior executive who learns about your proposal via a one-page summary written by the decision maker you do have access to. Sometimes it can be a management committee, like the office of the chief executive that we saw at Dell Computers in Chapter 1.

In cases where this audience is isolated, you may have a difficult time ascertaining what is most important to them. In this case, you need to rely on the decision maker to become a champion with this audience. This can be a difficult leap of trust and faith, but it is one that many take in the corporate world today.

While it may be difficult knowing what is most important to this final audience, you need to give it your best shot. You do this by including in your presentation the facts and other key information that you believe appeal to this audience as a whole. If need be, these positions are secondary to the decision-maker and key-influencer positionings. In an ideal situation, one strong positioning fits all audiences.

Business Needs

Management team members have special interests related to the area for which they're responsible. Thus, some information is more important or meaningful to different team members. It's best to find out who will be in your presentation and make sure you evaluate your presentation from each one's perspective. That way you can address each person's business needs and anticipate what questions may arise. As noted, within the audience are a limited number of key influencers who deserve special focus.

The following is a brief discussion of key information important to senior management in a company. They may vary by company and the person in the job now, so be alert to the conditions in your situation.

- Chief Financial Officer—To the CFO, numbers are everything. The question a CFO will ask most frequently is: How will we fund this? Two areas that hold special interest for a numbers person are how the project will increase shareholder value and earnings per share. A CFO who aspires to general management may have additional interests. For example, if it is a marketing-driven company, he might ask questions about the process of developing the recommended advertising. These kinds of questions are not necessarily critical to deciding whether or not he gives his support, but the answers help to improve his comfort level with the project.

- President and Chief Executive Officer—The people in these positions tend to look at the overall picture in terms of risk and reward. They focus on the big picture as it relates to the bottom line, short- and long-term numbers, shareholder value, fit with long-range strategic plans, effect on existing operations, and effect on customers and employees. A CEO will ask, "How will this drive our stock?" and "Will this move our business ahead a step, or a leap?" The CEO is also likely to be motivated by the ability of a project to fulfill the spirit of the vision, since she was probably in charge of the vision creation process. This is important if the vision plays an important role in the company. CEOs can be very different. Some can be big-picture oriented while others are very hands-on and detail-oriented. This can make a big difference in the presentation you are about to make. Regardless of their personal and professional style, all CEOs will want to know the project's impact on each of the company's stakeholders.

■ Members of the Board of Directors—Board members are ideally supposed to support projects that will maintain or increase shareholder value. Naturally, they may have a bias toward information that falls within their area of expertise, and since some are from outside your organization, their interests could be quite diverse. If you find yourself presenting to this audience, your biggest help may come from peers who have presented to them before.

■ Other Management Representatives—Senior managers will first consider how the project will affect their areas. What's in it for me? Will they still be able to do the projects they want to budget; will they gain or lose power; will their personnel be required to support new processes? If these representatives are outside your hierarchy and functional area but are critical to your success, you can use the help of a joint project owner at this stage. Again, your joint owner should be someone who has credibility with this group. Similarly, if you have put together a cross-functional idea team, let them determine what needs are important to the managers in their area and what pending projects are being pushed.

If the decision maker is in general management now, consider his background—marketing, sales, development, finance, etc. This tends to be the area of greatest interest. If you're presenting to someone with a marketing background, you'd probably emphasize customer research, advertising strategy and execution, and test market results, where appropriate. With someone who has a background in manufacturing, you might discuss capital needs and timing along with installation and learning issues. A person who comes from the legal side will want everything backed up with appropriate references to regulations and case law.

There may be only two or three people in your meeting, or there may be a dozen or more. Frame what you're doing so it's in context in everyone's area; that is, help each person understand it from his or her functional perspective. How much support will it require from Human Resources? How will Marketing be involved? What will Finance have to do? What role will operations and production play? It will help to show how each area will benefit from the process, if possible, or to describe how you will mitigate the impact on some areas.

Substantive Positioning—Get to the Point

We have covered considerable ground. When you add up all that you know, you may be overwhelmed. You have so many inputs that it may be difficult to understand what is really important. It all sounds good and helpful.

But you cannot use it all. More importantly, if you try to use all of it, you will hurt yourself more than you will help yourself.

From everything you know, choose no more than three positioning statements for your idea. Your list may include twenty positions. Put seventeen of them aside for possible later use, most likely in an emergency. If you only have two, celebrate.

Take your three positioning statements and craft each of them into a single sentence. Resist the urge to load all you know into a single sentence—it defeats the purpose. You want it to be simple, clear, and powerful.

For example, "The proposed advertising scored new highs for our category in overall rating and persuasion." In less than fifteen words, you have said this is very good advertising, capable of selling product.

You could say, "The proposed advertising, developed by Hal Riney (one of the country's top creatives) and shot by Joe Pitka (award winning director of Pepsi and Nike ads), scored an overall rating of 72.3, a new high for our product category, and a persuasion score of 31.1, also a new high for the category." In fifty-two words, you get carried away with details that are not important because you are so enamored with the process. Focus on the most powerful points and do not load them up with extraneous stuff. Let simplicity be your power. Use details to support your answers when questions arise.

If you need to, be willing to make your presentation this simple: "We recommend (fill in a simple, precise statement of what you want agreement to today). We believe you should agree for three reasons. They are: (with the next one to three sentences, using less than fifty words, position the one to three reasons for urging agreement)." Draft your version of this approach and if it is more than one hundred words, sharpen and simplify.

When you take this approach, you will be pleasantly surprised how powerful your presentation becomes. The themes and positionings you establish in this process will be reprised throughout your presentation. The presentation can take three hours, but you can look for opportunities to reinforce your points on almost everything you discuss. When you can drive your points home this strongly, you will be persuasive. Your management persuasion score will set new records for the company.

Now that you have the substantive positioning determined, you can polish and strengthen your argument by digging deeper to understand your audience.

Personal Needs

Even though this is about business, it's not only about business. Every person in a corporation has a vested interest in every decision that affects him directly, and that certainly includes executives. They have an even greater personal stake in any decision they're required to make.

Always consider how your proposal will affect people personally. Yes, improving shareholder value is the goal, but if you're suggesting that the Chairman increase shareholder value by wiping out the department his son-in-law heads up, don't be surprised if your project is wiped out instead. Here are some things to consider.

- Financial Position—How will this project affect their financial position? Are bonuses based on performance, stock options, etc., or other factors that could be affected by the company investing in (and potentially losing money on) a new business?

- Ego—An executive with a good record of accomplishment doesn't necessarily have anything to prove. A newly appointed executive, however, has a mark to make. She may have her own agenda for the first year. It may be that most ideas that she did not invent will face tough questioning. Conversely, anyone with a recent (or memorable), highly visible failure may take one of two extremes: he might be risk averse, or looking for a way to redeem himself. These are difficult factors to determine with much accuracy. A consultant or other managers who have worked directly for him may be good resources, but they may be guarded with their confidential information.

■ Experience—Does this project challenge their experience? Many senior executives have risen to their current positions through time. When you challenge their establishment, you imply that their experience and achievements are becoming obsolete or irrelevant. This is a very threatening position for anyone. When you propose a project that is outside of their functional expertise it might be outside their comfort zone. When this happens you may get false objections. The manager may be trying to buy time until he can review it with sources he trusts.

■ Career Stage—Are they near retirement (they may be coasting), are they fast-trackers (who may take greater risks, or may take an adversary position to make an impression), or do they have small children and want to protect their positions (security)?

All of these can be tough to determine with accuracy. The inputs may be guesses and well-intentioned efforts based on partial information. As a result, proceed with caution. Use only information that is corroborated by several sources and is consistent with your broader positioning for the project.

Whose Decision Is It?

We keep coming back to an important point—keep in mind who the real decision maker will be. In some cases, a "gatekeeper" may appear to be calling the shots, but another person will ultimately pound the gavel. For example, you may have to sell the marketing vice president on your concept, but the division president is the person who will actually decide whether to allocate the resources or not.

Keep in mind, however, that the most senior person may sometimes defer to the judgment of a direct report when the issue requires technical expertise or when it is not a make-or-break project for the company. A decision about installing a new payroll system, for example, could be left to the discretion of the human resources senior vice president, with tacit approval from the CEO.

In some cases, an executive team comprised of the CEO and his direct reports will be the decision makers. This is usually true if the idea affects the shareholders, company strategy, or the organization as a whole.

Style Issues

Style issues can be tricky. You can work to determine what style your decision maker and key influencers have. This worthwhile exercise can provide some useful insights. Ultimately, you must determine how your style meshes with their styles.

People receive information in a variety of ways. Some of us like to hear information presented. Some of us prefer to read things for ourselves. A variation of this is that some people do not need to read the information on their own. They are very comfortable seeing the information on a screen or flip chart.

This knowledge is very important. It reflects how a person best processes information. This has its roots in how we are most effective at learning. For example, if you try to force a visual presentation with no handouts on a decision maker who learns best by quietly reading information, you are headed for a frustrating meeting for everyone involved.

If, however, you were to distribute written materials for review before the meeting and then make your visual presentation, your audience will have a proper reference point. By making this linkage, you help the decision maker feel comfortable with your presentation.

Leaders usually enjoy a presentation style that plays to their strengths. Is the leader talkative or quiet? Let a talkative leader talk. A talkative leader might make speeches in the middle of a presentation or he might prefer the give-and-take of a good discussion or even debate. Some managers like a structured approach to the conversation while others are willing to participate in a more free-wheeling flow.

It is important to know the difference. What is a fun, productive, and free-wheeling discussion for one person is an annoying distraction for another. You need to know the delivery style the top managers are more comfortable with before the presentation. If you are presenting to a manager who does not like to go off on tangents, you need to be prepared with techniques for bringing the discussion back on course. As the presentation leader, you are often expected to do this.

Give a quiet leader enough information so he can ask questions. You need to become adept at reading the body language of a quiet leader. For example, if you sense the decision maker is pondering something you said, slow down. You can ask if he has a question or let some silent time resolve the situation. This is challenging for a presenter—he can get so wrapped up in the flow of the presentation that it is difficult to be in touch with what are often subtle reactions by people in the audience. If you are skilled at this, the leader will appreciate your sensitivity to his situation.

If your leader likes to get to the bottom line quickly, then get to the bottom line quickly. Some decision makers on some projects just need a few minutes and a few numbers to make a decision. It may be because they have seen the proposal several times at earlier stages. Whatever the reason, you need to be prepared with a presentation option that quickly gets to the bottom line if needed. You know this because you learned ahead of time the decision-making styles of key audience members.

Want to have some fun? Take one of the many tests that assess your personal, social, or communications style. In Myers-Briggs, Social Styles, and several other brands of assessment, it all usually

boils down to four basic types: the introverted analyst, the concilia-
tory people-pleaser, the outgoing creative type, and the hard-nosed
decision maker.

In the book *I Wish I'd Said That!* author Linda McCallister describes six communications styles and how to adapt your style to
best deal with each.

While you probably cannot know for sure the particular personal style of your decision maker, you can get close. If you are familiar with the different styles, you can get together with a small
group who has interacted with the person. With your collective observations, you will learn some useful information.

The point of each of these exercises is to recognize that you
must honor differences and adapt your own style to suit the person
you're dealing with. It is important that you adapt your style and
not fundamentally change it.

Your audience will usually comprise a variety of the four or six
types, although we knew one organization where the leader had five
direct reports, four of whom shared his style. Focus on the one or
two key decision makers in the group and tailor your presentation to
their preferred style. As you go up the senior management ladder,
most executives want the same information regardless of their style:
an overview or executive summary specifying how much the project
will cost, what the potential rewards are, and when the initial investment will be returned. They prefer to leave the infinite details to
finance, marketing, legal, human resources, and operations.

Preferences and Eccentricities

Almost every leader has presentation preferences (or even
quirks), some of which seem utterly silly to even think about at the
senior level. But if you can control a small factor that will enhance
the decision-maker's receptiveness, why not take advantage of it?
Eliminate minor irritants and you give your idea another chance of
succeeding. Of course, there may be no rhyme or reason to a
leader's preferences, just what she prefers. For example, we know a

senior manager who only sends information in the Times New Roman font. As a result, we return any correspondence in the same font, even though our favorite font style is Arial. Now, this could truly be a preference, or he just may not know how to change the font style on his computer (we suspect the latter). The reason doesn't really matter. We simply learned to accept it without questioning and adjust to his preferences. This is what you must do with your decision maker.

We've heard of executives who:

- Don't like presenters who have someone else click their slides. Maybe this can provide a broader insight—they like for one person to be totally involved and in charge of the meeting. If so, look for other ways you can meet this need.

- Have an aversion to overheads. Dig deeper to find out what this is about. They might not like being in a darkened meeting room. Since overheads can work in a room with light, just not bright light, you might experiment with how much light you can use. If so, other darkened room presentations, like using an In Focus and computer-driven presentation, might not work.

- Like particular typefaces and colors. Sometimes an older manager has trouble seeing words on the screen unless they are a certain size. For an older manager, the colors you use may not provide enough contrast to be easily read. It is important to know this. If you don't, he is unlikely to admit his eyesight problem, but instead, simply not approve your idea because he cannot understand the presentation. The objections you receive in this situation are likely to be false and, therefore, misleading. You can waste considerable time due to a simple mistake in failing to understand your audience.

- Prefer to have things in writing. In most situations, you can also do a verbal or visual presentation if you feel it is necessary. You can distribute a written version of the presentation ahead of the meeting and refer to it as needed.

■ Have one key question they always ask that puts the presenter's personal integrity on the line, such as, "If this were your money, would you invest in it?"

When someone has a pet question (or an eccentric preference), make sure you know it. It makes preparing for the meeting easy when you know the executive will ask you a specific question or that he has an unusual, specific preference. These kinds of questions or situations can put you on the spot if they are unexpected. Your peers can be particularly good sources on this type of issue. We don't even begin to speculate on certain preferences; we just accept them as fact. You should too.

Before you start wishing you'd majored in psychology and detective work, try taking the simple way: Find someone who's gone before you. Others who have presented to these persons can shed light on how different members respond or what their hot buttons seem to be.

Whatever you do, don't forget the most important source: the administrative assistant. Few people know a person better than the assistant. He or she can enlighten you about pet peeves.

By now you see that the presentation of your idea has to meet quite a few needs: those of your company, your boss, your peers, and the key decision-makers in your audience.

Bigger Audiences

Once your idea has won approval, you may find yourself in the position of introducing it to larger groups, such as division management, or employees. The same presentation you made to the senior management team will obviously not be appropriate for these groups.

To adapt your script, take the same approach as for your management group. Begin by considering who your audience is, and what their needs are. Uppermost in your mind should be "What's in it for them?"

Once you have the time and date of your presentation and know who will be in attendance, get your team together to flush out the personal styles of who will be there, what they are likely to ask, what issues could possibly blindside you, etc. The following case examples highlight how two different teams custom designed their presentation to the audience and its needs. Don't downplay the importance of this crucial step. Assessing your audience and tailoring your presentation to their style will make or break the sale of your idea. Don't let all your hard work to date lose its impact because of inadequate planning regarding the "who" that will be receiving the information. After all, they are the next link in getting your idea implemented.

These case studies were inspired by true stories. First, Patricia's story is based on experiences in a large, publicly-traded company. Second, Dave's story is situated in a medium-size, family-run company. While there are similarities in their stories, the role and importance of different factors change because of the environment.

Case Study #1: Patricia's Story

Patricia was tired. As team leader for a major product improvement on the company's second-most profitable brand, she had worked long hours for six weeks. The team had been researching and preparing for the important management presentation coming up in another three weeks.

The team was meeting the next day to assess where they were and choose the major points they wanted to make in their presentation. It was an important meeting because it would take all of the remaining time before the presentation to finish the necessary preparation. They did not have the time to correct bad choices if they made them at tomorrow's meeting. Patricia felt the pressure.

She ran over in her mind who was going to be at the team meeting. Joe from finance would definitely be there. She was relieved because she knew the project's approval would largely depend on meeting the company's minimum hurdles. Joe was a team member she trusted, and just as importantly, someone management found credible and persuasive.

Mike's manufacturing expertise was needed to explain the new patents and equipment they hoped to use. Many issues and points

could be made. She was going to need Mike's experience and counsel to sort it out into a simple presentation. She knew this part of the
meeting had the potential to get bogged down in endless detail and
debates.

Lastly, Holland would be there from marketing. She needed to
explain the controversial advertising they wanted to use. The testing among consumers had been positive, but there were volumes of
data. They needed to determine the most persuasive points from
almost one hundred pages of data.

Patricia jotted a few notes on the agenda for tomorrow's meeting. She wanted to lead with Joe. Without the financial numbers,
they might have to put the project on hold until they could calculate
better results. The preliminary numbers had continued to look
good, but Joe was doing some final checking before tomorrow's
meeting. She then wrote down Holland and Mike, thinking she
wanted to save Mike's details until the end.

When the meeting began the next day, Patricia noted everyone
seemed to be in a good mood. After a few pleasantries, Patricia reviewed the upcoming meeting. It was on Tuesday, the 18th at 9:00.
Attending the meeting were the division president, comptroller,
and a consultant that had been working with the company for two
months.

They reviewed what they knew about each of them. The division president was the decision maker. Mike noted that in a meeting he had with her last week that she indicated she wanted meetings to be better organized. She was perturbed when someone went
into considerable detail to support a point they were making. The
comment Mike remembered was, "To tell me what time it is you do
not have to tell me how to make a watch."

The comptroller was quiet and reserved. He seemed to be there
to answer questions for the division president. Everyone agreed
that the consultant was an unknown. He worked directly with the
division president. As they pooled their learnings from their project
allies, a confused picture emerged. In some meetings, he said nothing. In others, he seemed to focus on strategy, but Mike had heard
from one person that he also probed manufacturing efficiency

data. They agreed they needed to know more. Patricia agreed to contact her boss and peers to learn more about him.

They also reviewed what they had learned from previous meetings on the project with the division vice president. He was interested and believed in the product improvement. Besides questioning whether the project was financially prudent, he was worried about two executional elements. The first was a concern about their ability to sell the product improvement. He had gone on the record as saying they needed exceptionally strong advertising. Second, the product was difficult to make. She concluded that after letting him know about the financial promise, they needed to convince him they could make and sell the product.

Next, Patricia asked Joe to update the team on the financial analysis of the project. He had a chart with six financial measures, and all of them exceeded company minimums for projects like theirs.

After Joe's presentation, Patricia asked the group what the most important measure was. Holland noted that in a meeting two weeks ago, the decision maker told everyone their projects needed to have an eighteen-month-or-better payout or they would not be considered. Mike had not heard anything and Joe said he had heard mixed messages. After a brief discussion, they agreed that the payout period seemed to be the most important measure.

Patricia asked Joe what the payout period was in their worst-case scenario. Joe reported that it was 16.5 months. The most likely was 14 months and the best-case scenario was 12 months. After more discussion, they agreed to the following positioning statement: "In the worst case, the project pays out in 16.5 months." The group liked it because it was concise and answered the first hurdle they faced—does it meet the minimum threshold. If management wanted to know more, they had the data to support their point and present a more in-depth financial analysis.

With one positioning point agreed to, Patricia suggested they tackle the marketing positioning for the project. Holland presented an updated report on the advertising analysis, which seemed to confuse things further. There was considerable good news and the bad news was minor and easily explained. From their abundance of riches, they needed to choose one key point.

Joe noted that in a meeting he had had with the division president two days ago, that he had made the point repeatedly that their advertising needed to break out of a tired mold. Joe said he spoke for about ten minutes on the need for breakthrough thinking. Holland had not heard of this conversation, but there had been requests for them to try new creative resources.

Holland noted that what made their advertising controversial to some was its unusual production style. After a discussion of what the research said on this subject, they wrote, "Personal judgment and a record-high memorability score say this distinctive advertising will break through the clutter and be remembered. The high persuasion score suggests it sells product." It was longer than they ideally wanted, but the increased length was used to address the recently revealed hot button for the division president.

Next, Mike updated the group on the manufacturing part of the plan. The patent applications were pending and legal felt they had about a 90 percent likelihood of having the patents granted. Manufacturing management was confident about their ability to bring the newly patented equipment on-line in advance of the time needed to produce their product improvement. Mike's presentation allayed many of Patricia's fears.

They agreed on their manufacturing positioning statement faster than she had thought: "The patented equipment to produce the product improvement will be operational three months before it is needed." They felt confident referring to the equipment as patented given legal's confidence. The three months early was their worst-case scenario. They were prepared for a much more detailed conversation if questions were asked.

Before concluding, they discussed other assessments they had received. They all agreed the division president liked the new electronic projector the conference room had for presentations. Holland noted she could provide animation to liven the presentation up. Everyone agreed that if the division president wanted breakthrough advertising, he would also like a breakthrough presentation. They agreed to take the risk.

They knew the comptroller did not like surprises so they agreed to share with him all their financial data a week before the meeting. Joe would meet with him three days before the meeting to address any questions.

Lastly, they agreed to share the presentation responsibilities since several people, including their peers, had indicated the decision maker liked to see teamwork in action. Since everyone on the team had good verbal presentation skills, Patricia was confident of the decision.

After weeks of hard work, Patricia felt for the first time that the project was coming together. She reflected on their agreed-to, somewhat unusual, positionings. One promised the company a financial benefit. The other two positioning statements addressed the decision maker's executional concerns. In most cases, she would want three benefit positionings. In this case, she felt their assessment of the situation had led them to the right positionings. While the presentation needed hours of work, she knew what they faced and saw a path to a successful conclusion.

Case Study #2: Dave's Story

The meeting was in two days and Dave only knew the bottom line of what he wanted to ask the chairman of the board to approve. In a few minutes, he was meeting with his marketing group to discuss their thoughts on the presentation. He was reflecting on what to say when Lindsay and Scott showed up for their meeting.

Dave asked them in and started by asking, "Lindsay, exactly what do your think we need the boss to OK?"

Lindsay said, "It is a bit complicated. We want the new flavor approved for a January introduction and the higher price plan approved for March. We could break it into two meetings, one for each topic. But he is going to be traveling and I am not sure when we could get the second meeting. What do you think?"

"Let's prepare for both in one meeting, since we need to do

both fairly soon. When we have them done, we can step back and see if it still makes sense," Dave said.

"Good. Let's start with who is going to be at the meeting," Lindsay said. They knew the chairman and their boss would be there. They thought a senior advisor and an outside consultant, who frequently attended meetings, would also be there. Scott agreed to check with one of the administrative assistants to confirm if they would be there.

Dave said that he had heard there had been a stormy meeting the day before. The chairman found the presentation confusing, at least in part because the print on the presentation was difficult for him to read. The presenter's confidence was shaken and they lost control of the meeting. Dave shared with Lindsay and Scott the font size and colors they should use. Since Lindsay had only presented twice before, Dave agreed to present a significant portion himself. They knew that they could not let the meeting get out of control.

Then they discussed the other people in the meeting. Their boss was supportive but could not be expected to lend too much support during the presentation.

That left the senior advisor, if he was going to be there. As they reviewed their prior experiences, they agreed that he was somewhat unpredictable. He might agree with your idea before the meeting and then reverse himself during it. Despite this risk, Dave agreed to discuss the ideas with him one-on-one if Scott confirmed he was going to be there. Finally, they agreed that the consultant was paid to be independent, so they would consciously avoid any attempt to influence him before the meeting.

They briefly reviewed the presentation style that worked best. They decided on a balance between a tightly controlled presentation and a slightly conversational one. If it felt too rehearsed, the chairman would get irritated or nod off. They needed to keep him involved.

They had spent almost twenty minutes discussing many nonsubstantive points. Dave knew that if they did not have these points well defined their substance would be negated.

For the next ten minutes, they discussed exactly what they

wanted the chairman to agree to. When they had a concise and simple statement, they moved to the positioning.

Dave reflected that positioning at this company was very different than at his previous company. He had worked at a large publicly held company and was now working for a private, family-run business. The family did not trust nonfamily members with profit data, so a major positioning was not available to them.

For the new product introduction, their positioning statements included projected market share and volume progress. Since executional details about how they would introduce an idea were often the most important part of the meeting, they spent almost twenty minutes reviewing their packaging, advertising, and promotion plans.

For the price increase proposal, Scott noted that he had met with his peers in finance the day before. They agreed to use the details of the price increase proposal to write a memo to the chairman detailing the profit benefits. Finance strongly supported their proposal. They agreed with marketing that the cost savings of the last two years had been totally used by sales to reduce prices while competitive products were increasing prices.

They had analyzed their competition and found substantial information suggesting their major competitors would react positively to a price increase. They had also demonstrated how the price for their product had actually decreased. Scott proposed a positioning statement: "Competitors and consumers appear ready for a price increase." With the chairman's style, he might accept this statement and they could move on to other points. The data supporting these points was a bit complex and would be challenging to present clearly.

Dave reflected that in his previous company, this simple a statement would not be enough, but it probably would work with this chairman. He usually insisted on wanting an overview and was willing in most cases to not discuss the supporting details.

Lindsay said that the sales division was against the price increase. Their opposition was strong and they were willing to fight. Dave suggested that sales be fully briefed on what they were presenting to the chairman. He did not want them blindsided. He also wanted the chairman to be told about the opposition from sales. They discussed his likely reactions. They agreed he was likely to phone the sales manager from the meeting and ask him to attend. Lindsay agreed that she would alert sales to the possibility to make sure they were reachable.

They then discussed what was likely to happen when the sales manager entered the meeting. A debate would ensue and it was likely to get emotional and volatile because of the managers in the room. They agreed to stick with their two major positioning points—finance's memo on the profit benefit (an estimated 500 percent increase in brand profits) and the positive competitor and consumer reactions.

The meeting concluded with another thirty minutes on a rough outline of the pages they would use in the meeting, including the backup data.

When it was done, Dave was struck by how different this had been from his previous company. Most of the time in their meeting was spent on style plus interpersonal and organizational dynamics. The substance seemed relatively straightforward and overwhelmed by these other issues.

Key Learning Points

1. Assessing your audience is an often-overlooked step. For those who do it well, their presentations meet the needs of the decision maker and the key people.

2. Positioning statements are powerful when they state a critical benefit, and weak when they only describe the support points or features of the benefit.

3. There are usually three audiences you need to assess. The decision maker is most important, followed by key influencers, and then the audience you will not see, which is probably the ultimate decision maker.

4. The business needs of managers vary by functional background, company culture, personal style, and preferences. Do not as-

sume that all managers look at their functional responsibilities the same way.

5. Choose a maximum of three positioning points for your idea. Keep the statements simple, clear, and powerful.

6. Personal style and preferences can be difficult to assess, but very helpful when you have accurate information.

CHAPTER 6

Designing Your Presentation

"The fool tells me his reasons; the wise man persuades me with my own."

Aristotle

Now that you've assessed your audience and you believe you understand their needs, you are ready to design your presentation. Your job is to deliver the information management feels is necessary to put their final stamp of approval on your plan. All the while you should be considering the individuals you're working with and what is their stake in the project.

Although you have an encyclopedia worth of information about your project, you'll have to pare it down to a short, compelling presentation. Like the executive overview of your business plan, it must capture management's attention in short order. Simplicity is the key.

At best, people in your audience may remember one or two key points. Think about the last presentation you attended. How much of it can you recall today? Even a fantastic presentation inspires only limited retention. If a speaker tries to convey too much information, the audience filters out everything except what they can process. Only the memorable points remain.

According to presentation expert David A. Peoples (1992), we remember:

- 10 percent of what we read
- 20 percent of what we hear
- 30 percent of what we see
- 50 percent of what we both see and hear

That's compelling evidence for using a variety of media to reach people.

Further, Peoples says an audience's attention span is about 9 seconds, and that your audience will forget 75 percent or more of what you say in 24 hours or less. That's why simplicity is the absolute essence of effective presentations. It's easier to remember something delivered in a simple way. Would you remember a slogan, "Always devote your efforts to creatively approaching every idea and finding the best solution." Doubtful. IBM got that message across in one word: "Think." That's memorable.

We used advertising in earlier chapters to understand the essence of the communication and persuasion process. This thirty-second (or less) persuasive environment teaches many important lessons. Advertisers know the value of simplicity. Nike's "Just Do It" had been the among the most powerful and simple slogans until they recently trumped it. Increasingly, Nike is now only showing its logo.

Whether you're defining what information to include or deciding how to display it, always make simplicity your goal.

What is the one thing you want the audience to do because of the presentation? Focus on delivering material that will accomplish that.

"You didn't come to your brilliant idea in an instant," says Carol Coletta. "It evolved. Developing the idea was a journey for you, and you must take your audience on a similar journey."

How you present your information says a lot about your interest level, your attention to detail, and your ability to present to perfection.

When we think of presentations we tend to think only of the presenter. In fact there are several roles that need to be filled for a successful presentation, especially the more complex ones. These roles give more people the opportunity to be a key player on the project. The roles you may need are:

- Presentation material expert—If you are using computers, overheads, or slide projectors, it is very helpful if the presenter does not have to worry about these details. You want someone at the meeting who can come to the rescue when needed, like when a light bulb burns out.

- Expert question answerer—This person has all the facts organized and accessible. So when a detail question is asked requiring a fact not in the presentation, this person quickly finds it. This helps maintain the flow of the presentation and does not overly distract the presenter.

- Materials expert—Often in a meeting you have props, like packaging and product samples. There may be displays in another room that you visit at the appropriate time in the meeting. In other cases, there may be a tasting that requires advance cooking or preparation. The presenter should not be worried about the details of this.

What Makes an Effective Presentation?

Even when a presentation is simple, it may still fall short of the mark because it's not interesting or compelling.

You'll want to consider several things before you actually sit down to design your presentation:

- Who will present?
- How long is your window of opportunity?
- When will the presentation take place?
- What and how to present?

Who Will Present?

Who can best sell your idea? That's who should present.

You may assume there are obvious choices, but before you decide, think about all the possibilities and what their pros and cons are.

Often, deciding who is best to sell the idea is a tough decision. There are several people you'll want to consider:

- The project leader is a natural candidate. If you leave him out of the presentation, there can be serious consequences. He can become unmotivated and disenchanted. Nonetheless, you may have strong concerns about his presentation skills. For example, he may be very knowledgeable about the project, but easily unsettled by pointed questions and vigorous debate. You can manage a situation like this by having him present a noncontroversial part while reserving the more difficult parts for more experienced presenters.

- Project team members may also want to be part of the presentation. The issues are similar to the team leader's issues, but the consequences are not as serious in most cases if they are not included. The positives of involving them are that management sees the team in action and the presentation benefits from the expertise of a segment expert. The downside is that they may not be skilled presenters and if you involve some team members, it may be uncomfortable excluding others. Frankly, most team members we know feel better letting others make the presentation.

- Junior managers who want experience in front of management are also candidates. If this is a need, you can usually have them first play a minor role in simple, noncontroversial presentations. Some companies believe younger managers can be seen but not heard, while others enjoy having them involved.

The profile of the best presenter is:

- Knowledgeable about all aspects of the recommendation

- Skilled presenter with a style that is compatible and effective with your audience

- Has a vested interest and passion for the idea while maintaining an objectivity that enables him to understand contrary points of view

- Has a strong, positive relationship with the decision maker and others in the meeting who will influence the decision

One extremely important consideration is, "Who can answer the questions?" You've undoubtedly spent a lot of time with experts by now, and you may feel perfectly prepared to discuss some topics, and somewhat less confident about others. For any areas you don't feel 100 percent sure of, it's always smart to have an expert at your side. Even if he doesn't participate in the formal presentation, he can at least be on hand to answer questions.

We can't envision an occasion when you should have more than three presenters. Having too many people getting up and down detracts from the continuity of your presentation.

Often it's advantageous to choose the person with the greatest influence and experience presenting to the group. If your plan affects only your department, then your boss might take the lead, along with one or two members of your team.

Certain departments tend to have more credibility than others, depending on who's leading them and the nature of their discipline. For example, in many companies the cost centers (such as communications or human resources) tend to have less clout than the profit centers (like operations and marketing). It could be smart to have the presentation anchored by the leader from the more credible area.

There could also be value to having multiple departments represented to show that the plan has support across the board. And when people present an idea, they typically become more invested in its success. Because they've played a visible role in its creation, they will be strongly associated with it when it succeeds—or fails. Vested interest can lead to greater commitment.

We once participated in a presentation in which a vice president decided to take charge at the last minute. He had little involvement before the big event, and chose not to rehearse or participate in an in-depth briefing. Fortunately, the idea was a good one and it sold in spite of his disjointed and unprofessional performance.

Whatever you do, don't design your presentation simply to showcase everyone who has contributed. A desire to share the glory is admirable; however, not at the expense of your presentation's effectiveness.

How Long Is Our Window of Opportunity?
Presentations Less than Thirty Minutes

For a very brief presentation—ten minutes or less—one presenter is preferable.

If you choose to have more than one presenter, each one should speak for at least ten to fifteen minutes in order to establish a presence with the audience. Depending on the amount of data and the complexity of the information, we recommend only one person, certainly no more than two, present. If people are bobbing up and down every five minutes, the focus will be on the activity rather than the content.

Presentations More than Thirty Minutes

For a presentation that's thirty minutes or more, it's advisable to share the duties; otherwise, the audience may become bored or lose concentration. When you share duties, the part each person takes is often critical. You want to match expertise with the content that is presented. In some cases, you may want the person with the strongest relationship with the decision maker to present the toughest and most controversial part of the presentation. Consider this even when he or she is not the number-one expert. Persuasiveness is very important and you can have your expert there to answer the questions.

There will be some instances where one person handles the entire presentation. You can do this when you have a strong presenter who is very knowledgeable. When you take this approach, it is even more important to have the support roles detailed above. Even though one person presents all of it, it is still a team effort.

Which Comes First: The Presenter or the Presentation?

In some cases, you may want to choose the presenter and then design your presentation around that person's skills. In other situations, you may develop the presentation first and choose a presenter who can adeptly deliver the information. You'll have to judge what factors are most important to your "sale."

We've seen presentations that depended heavily on a speaker's ability to express a concept in an enthusiastic—even dramatic— way. If communicating your concept is key, select a speaker whose acting ability is equal to the task. Many styles are potentially effective. You need to match the style the decision maker is most comfortable with.

For other presentations that provide more serious factual information, challenge conventional wisdom, or pose a threat to members of management, the speaker's credibility and ability to handle conflict will be more important than style. While a charismatic style is less important, you need a speaker whose style exudes confidence.

What happens if your key proponent is a poor presenter? Consider the person's importance in the management scheme. How influential is the person in gaining management's support? While you want your presentation to be flawless, getting your idea sold is more important than how it might look on video.

If the person is a poor presenter, the chances are good that he knows it and is uncomfortable presenting anyway. If this is the case, you can still convince him to be part of the presentation team. A good role for him would be the expert who answers the tough factual questions.

If someone who is not a good presenter still wants to present, it becomes a management challenge. Again, in his heart, he probably knows he is not as good as others. He probably thinks that he is expected to present and is afraid that if he doesn't, he will not get credit for the idea and the work that has gone into it. A compassionate manager can positively address all of these concerns.

Team Presentation: To Do or Not to Do, That Is the Question

It seems to be the consensus in most companies that to get an idea fully researched, developed, and implemented requires a cross-functional team to accomplish all that is required. We have discussed in detail the advantages of such a team in gathering data, building allies, assessing the audience, and putting together the business plan. But what happens when it comes time to present the actual information needed to get final approval? When you have been working closely as a team (which can be quite large with all of its subteams), how do you decide who and how many should present in the end? This will of course depend on the complexity of the idea and the length of the required presentation.

Many companies often find themselves with several smaller teams rolling up into one big team on larger ideas, observes Barbara Garner, Manager of Organizational Effectiveness for a large international corporation. When it comes time for the presentation, about one half want to be involved and the other half does not. To select the final presentation team, they often choose subject matter experts in each of the primary areas involved, as well as front line people that service customers. The team is rounded off with key managers who work closely with the decision makers and know the information needed to get the idea approved. Sometimes, these presentations can last up to three hours and have as many as 100 people in the room. While only a handful of persons may present, the rest are there as supporting team members. The process is so refined in many companies, that the decision makers have the ability to approve the idea on the spot, setting deadlines and accountabilities to ensure implementation.

While such a team approach may seem daunting and overwhelming in smaller companies, the process for selecting team presenters is the same. And, as with all presentations, there are pros and cons. The following figure highlights the advantages and disadvantages of team presentations:

Figure 6.1

Team Presentations

Pros and Cons

Pros:

Can have specialists present their information

Moral support from team members

Team can jump in when presenter is stumped by a question

Team members have to learn less information

Team members understand how idea impacts multiple areas

Represent cross-functional united front

Can be sure strong allies are available to front difficult issues

Cons:

Consensus on key issues and positioning statements to be presented
    may be difficult

Hard to develop, organize, and rehearse due to scheduling issues

Differing presentation styles

May seem disjointed to audience unless appropriate time allotted

Motivation for personal gain can reveal competition or lack of teamwork

No control over how well others present

Must have a backup in case a presenter gets sick or can't attend

When to Present

You're very fortunate if you have the option of deciding when to make your pitch; usually you'll be at the mercy of the executives' schedules. You never want to schedule a meeting or have it scheduled for you until you are ready. If someone schedules your meeting for a time that you will not be prepared, you need to push back and have it rescheduled.

The pressure can be great to "go on with the show," but you will probably only receive one quality opportunity to present your idea. Senior managers know what it takes to get ready and will respect a request to reschedule if it is reasonably supported. Always propose an alternative date when requesting a rescheduled meeting.

When you present will play a role in *how* you structure your presentation. Given a choice of times, however, keep several things in mind. There are no pat answers; you'll have to consider your company's traditions and your management's preferences to help you decide. Think through the following points before you get on the calendar.

- If you have control over when you present, try to avoid scheduling at some disadvantageous times, such as after lunch. And if the boss is just back from a trip, or is about to leave on vacation, that might not be a great time to book a meeting either.

- What is your decision maker's optimum time of day? Some people are morning people; some are not. Energy levels can lag toward day's end.

- When are other issues likely to interfere? Board meetings, annual company events, and visiting executives are times to avoid and you can often determine when they occur.

- Consider booking first thing in the morning, so management won't have time to get delayed or even completely sidetracked by fire fighting.

- In your timeline, allow time for a full rehearsal a day before and a rough rehearsal two to three days before the actual meeting.

- Is there another meeting that might be likely to go overtime and cut short your presentation?

- Are any key management people busy preparing for presentations of their own that would sap their attention or deter them from participating in yours?

- If your segment will be part of a bigger meeting, such as a weekly staff meeting, try to be first on the agenda so you have everyone's full attention and can dictate when you start and end.

- Try not to be "worked in." You want management's full attention, and if anyone is running from one appointment to the next, he is likely to be less mentally present.

In your fact finding before scheduling the meeting, the decision maker's assistant or secretary can often provide valuable counsel.

Establish a Time Limit

Ideally, you would be allowed to decide how long your presentation will last. Great! (But not likely.) You need to insist on enough time for your meeting. If someone tries to dictate the length of your meeting, you need to be willing to push back if the time is not long enough. Many times you can assemble an abridged version that may be more effective. But in situations where you cannot present your idea well in the allotted time, you will find most decision makers willing to adjust to meet your needs.

In many companies, the agreed-to meeting time and the actual meeting time have little in common. In most cases, an hour-long meeting stretches into an hour and a half or two hours. If you know this can happen in your company, your preparation needs to be deeper, especially when anticipating questions and objections. Don't let this happen because of poor time management on your part, however. Most executives tend to schedule back-to-back meetings, and may miss key information if they leave. Keep your presentation to the prescribed time, allowing for questions and answers. If the presentation runs over because the decision makers want additional discussion, fine. Be available as long as she wishes. If other managers need to leave, however, at least they have heard the critical points and positionings needed for approval.

The more effective presentations are under one hour, so keep yours to that limit. The discipline of presenting your meeting in an hour or less is a good one. Some presenters cannot resist the urge to present everything they know about a project. They do this either to impress management or to cover every conceivable point that might sell their idea. As we noted earlier, limiting yourself to three positioning points, stated simply and clearly, is all you need to sell almost every project. The challenge is choosing the right ones and communicating them well.

You may already be assigned a certain amount of time on the program. If it's enough, but is tight, then make sure you plan your presentation to conclude well within that limit and still allow time for questions.

If anyone is presenting before you, be prepared to adapt your presentation if they run overtime. You may have to compress your presentation into a shorter time frame; be ready to deliver a shortened version that still delivers punch. If you find yourself in the middle of the abridged version and you do not feel it is working, have the courage to admit that the compressed approach is not working. You may want to make a mid-course correction.

For example, you may want to stop and revise the objectives for the meeting. Consider the case where your objectives are to gain agreement to financial projections that meet company requirements and to a marketing plan, including the advertising. When you find yourself running short of time, you may consider revising the meeting objective to agreeing on the financial projections today, then reschedule a discussion of the marketing plan for the next available meeting date.

Divide your presentation into segments, or bite-size pieces that are easily digested. People's attention spans are very short, and ten to fifteen minutes is as long as you should expect to maintain someone's attention at a stretch. After each segment, use a device to break the monotony. Changing speakers, switching slide colors, changing media, or taking a break are all ways to prevent meeting fatigue.

If you write your presentation, use a rule of thumb of two minutes per double-spaced, typewritten page. Naturally, some people speak faster than others; time each presenter to make sure how long each section will last. If you do not write your presentation, then rehearse it to get your timing to fit the allotted time.

What to Present

No doubt you're proud of all the information you've collected, but you can only present a small amount of it to a senior audience. Remember, this is a sales pitch. According to the rules of effective selling in *The "I Hate Selling" Book* (Boress, 1995), if you do more than 20 percent of the talking, something is wrong.

As you begin to organize your information, remember the tried-and-true presentation rule:

- Tell them what you're going to tell them
- Tell them
- Tell them what you told them

Take your three key points, and make sure it's the information that is most critical to your audience. These are the three positioning or selling points you selected earlier. By now you have crafted them into simple, clear, and powerful statements.

Ask yourself, "What's the one idea I want them to walk away with? What's the best outcome I can hope for?" Let that organize what you will say. Know what your bottom line is and use your positioning points to get you to the finishing line.

Start by establishing what you're there for. Be very clear and ask for what you really want. Do not say, "We are here today to present the Brand A product improvement marketing plan." Rather say, "Today we seek your agreement to $20 million in marketing support for the Brand A product improvement national expansion."

Give an overview of the reasons, the benefits, and the costs of what you're proposing. Make it short and sweet. For example, "With agreement to the plan, the brand's profits will increase by $32 million in the current fiscal year." For a management group, it's usually important to get to the point in short order. "I hate the build-up," says Ken Glass. "Give me the bottom line first so I can be prepared to know how to start looking at your analysis."

Most executives say they want a balanced presentation with the risks stated up front in addition to the rewards. One said, "The biggest presentation turnoff is when people don't deal with risks head on, making the idea too pie in the sky." This is where your numbers work plays a key role. You previously determined three scenarios for your major financial measures—best, worst, and most likely. Use this framework to discuss the risks of the project. Besides the most likely option, the worst-case scenario will be most interesting to management.

Organizing Your Information—After the Introduction

By now your problem is not what to present, but what not to present. This can be very challenging for many presenters who believe the old adage about safety in numbers—in this case, number of pages and points.

If this is a challenge for you, try making your one-hour presentation last only fifteen minutes. Do not do this by saying one hour of material four times faster! Rather, make your fifteen-minute version by using only the absolutely essential information. You may want to speak more slowly in the fifteen-minute version so the major points will be strongly registered with your audience.

When you have a fifteen-minute version, ask yourself, "If I had time to make only one more point, what would it be?" Build your presentation up one point at a time, until you fill your allotted time. When you approach it this way, you avoid the process of cutting out points, which can be a wrenching experience for some presenters.

There are several organizational formats available for your presentation. You want to use the one that works best in your company. In many companies, there is either an official or unofficial format. If there is not one in your company, think about the needs of your decision maker and the points you want to make about your project. Now construct a logical, simple, and clear way of presenting them.

The following is the organization several major companies want to see their presentations follow:

- Background—Remind management of any prior agreements or key events. For example, if you are recommending expansion of a test market, remind management in this section of when and where the test market was conducted.

- Detailed recommendation—In the overview, you present a brief overview, but here you provide often-crucial detail. For example, if you said in the overview that you need $10 million in additional capital, in this section you might say more: "Of the $10 million in capital, $6 million is needed in the current fiscal year and $4 million next fiscal year." In some companies, this section also mentions the specific people who have already agreed to the plan. For example, if the consumer research director agreed to the presentation segment that discusses the results, you would discuss that here.

- Basis for your recommendations—This is where you present your three positioning points. Each one should stand out. They should be in a logical order. Think about what you need to know first, second, and third. This is where most of your number research plays out. If you have charts or tables, this is where you want to use them. This is also the section where you discuss the risks and how you plan to manage them.

- Other considerations—Often after you have made your main selling points there are additional points management needs to be aware of. This is often a short section, if it is used at all. For example, you might mention that you plan to use a new advertising agency on this project. This information is not critical to agreement but it may raise other corporate issues.

- Describe next steps—What will you do when you have agreement? Will you issue updates? Will agreement trigger other executional funding requests?

- Ask for approval—Again, be specific and do not be tentative. Some presenters tend to back off at this point by saying, "Well, what do you think?"

- Get sign-off for implementation timelines and accountabilities. Set up the next review meeting.

Presenting Bad News

Proposals that suggest a reorganization or the elimination of jobs will undoubtedly meet resistance from department heads of areas that will be negatively affected. You would never spring such a recommendation on a department head in a management meeting without prior discussion. Your best bet in these cases is to have had senior management get those people on board in advance.

Even with advance warning, however, a management team member may save a hand grenade or two for your presentation. Be prepared for the possibility. Empathize with the person and the difficulties, and then emphasize the facts that support the decision and the long-term positive outcome.

Your best safety net is to have a strong champion in your corner at the presentation, and prepare him to deal with the issue.

There is another kind of bad news. For example, suppose the purpose of the meeting is to present the results of a failed test market. For many people this can be a tough meeting. Maybe you made the original presentation that recommended the test market. Now you discover that the worst-case scenario was not bad enough.

Two lessons come from people who have presented in this kind of meeting. First, do not sugarcoat the results. Be objective, honest, and thorough. Do not get down on yourself about the results or be too apologetic.

Second, learn from the experience and share those learnings

with management. Do not make the meeting just a reporting session. Learnings often have a wonderful way of making a project even better. At Procter & Gamble, Pampers went through almost twenty failed test markets before it was successfully tested and expanded nationally. Employers learned from all of them and used those learnings to eventually create the company's largest volume brand.

Tailor Your Style to Your Audience

As you gathered information about your audience, you learned what type of "receivers" you're dealing with. Do they prefer to receive information verbally, or do they like to read it?

We knew a vice president who had a terrific sense of humor and used it very effectively... except with the CEO, who was very serious and didn't appreciate being entertained during budget meetings.

It's absolutely always necessary to tailor your style to your audience. If you have a good sense of humor, use it with caution. There are times when humor is refreshing and brilliant.

If you are serious by nature, learn to prepare and practice enough so that you can be relaxed and confident.

Maybe the most important step you can take is to personally connect with the decision maker. Establish comfortable eye contact with her. Be tuned in to her verbal and nonverbal communication. Go with her flow. Make it a conversation between the two of you.

Questions and Answers

Much as you may feel a question-and-answer session is like opening a can of worms, Q&A is very useful and necessary. In fact, you could even use it to your advantage. Plant a question that you anticipate will come up anyway, getting a friend to ask it rather than waiting for an adversary to bring it up. This way you can formulate your answer in advance.

In fact, your presentation should have almost as much backup as it has planned presentation pages. You don't want to play all of your cards in the presentation. Many presentations become successful when they accurately and fully address questions.

There are a few methods of anticipating objections you may want to use as you prepare your presentation:

- Review previously asked questions—Review the questions asked by people attending the meeting. While the decision maker's previous questions are important, do not focus your efforts only on her. People who are key influencers often ask questions that probe deeply into critical issues. Previously asked questions have a way of returning, often in slightly different form. They often signal the issues that need to be successfully addressed before you will gain the support of the questioner.

- Review the material—When you crafted your presentation, you probably included only about 10–25 percent of the total data and information you have. For example, you may present only one financial measure for the project, but it is reasonable to expect that questions could be asked about two or three more measures. Be prepared with backups that are as thorough as your presentation data. Not all of your preparation needs to be prepared as backups. As you review your presentation, look for opportunities to present the subject in greater depth, if called on to do so. It often helps if you have someone from outside the project review the material for potential questions.

- Review your logic—When you look at the overall presentation, look for logic leaps or gaps. Often you build a case a step at a time—if A and B, then C is the obvious next step. The logic may be clear and strong to you, but look for other logical steps a person might take—if A and B, then D might be right in some cases. This can produce a tough question: "If that is true, why shouldn't we be doing D instead?" You could quickly find yourself in a major detour. You can build additional safeguards into your presentation to avoid this, and you can be prepared with backups to answer this question.

Sometimes a point you make late in the presentation depends on a point you made in the first few minutes. If you do not make a tight connection, you can lose the audience. This can prompt a deluge of questions.

Anticipate other questions, especially those that may be negative, and get your team or functional experts to help you create an answer and rehearse. Consider asking your team to make a list of "The Ten Worst Questions" that you hope are not asked in the presentation. You probably know the potential pitfalls of your presentation better than your audience. When you have the list, address each one with backups. The beauty of this approach is that when you finish this exercise, your confidence can soar. You have confronted the worst possible case, and you know there is a way to respond successfully.

Select Your Audiovisual Media

What method should you use to display your information? That depends on where and what you're presenting. Certainly, try to choose media that will help you feel comfortable and confident. David A. Peoples' *Presentations Plus* (1992) points out the following benefits of using visual aids:

- Learning is improved up to 200 percent
- Can cover the same material in 25–40 percent less time
- Retention is improved up to 38 percent
- If your visual aids are in color, you will receive an 85 percent higher attention span
- Audience is 43 percent more likely to be persuaded
- Audience will be willing to pay 26 percent more money for the same product or service
- The presenter is perceived as being more professional, persuasive, credible, interesting, and better prepared

Remember that you also want the method to be comfortable for your audience. The decision maker probably sees a variety of presentations. Determine if there is a pattern to her preferences.

Whenever possible, use the highest quality presentation tools, regardless of what media you select. The highest quality method can vary by presentation. For example, if you believe you may need to respond to questions by creating a chart or table, then a flip chart needs to be considered. It can be either held in reserve or used for the primary presentation.

If your company has a meeting room with a built-in screen, LCD panel, or other tools, you may have to use them. Check them out before you create your presentation. In some cases, in-house media can be outdated or not in top-notch condition. You will certainly want to rent first-rate equipment if you find this to be the case.

Whatever you do, make sure the screen is visible from all audience positions. Often a projector obstructs the audience's view. The team member responsible for the presentation method and materials is valuable for this and other perplexing issues.

Which media are most effective? They all have benefits and drawbacks.

- 35 mm slides—With the advent of computerized multimedia presentations, 35 millimeter slides are becoming less useful. While the quality of the slide image can be very good, slides are expensive and don't offer much flexibility. It takes longer to make a slide, costs more to change, and is logistically difficult. Slide carousels are hard to transport, and if slides happen to fall out, they're very hard to reassemble quickly. You can't change the sequence of slides easily. Another drawback: Once you've passed a slide it may be difficult to go back. Lights must be lowered to show slides dramatically.

    Slides do have some benefits. They can be created in software programs like PowerPoint, saved onto a disk, and sent to an outside company for slide creation. The major benefit of slides is that the resolution is usually better than most other methods. If pictures, especially detail and accurate colors, are critical to your presentation, consider using slides as your primary or backup presentation method.

- Overheads (or transparencies)—Some experts say research

proves that overheads are the most confidence-inspiring medium. Others see them as old fashioned and cheap. Most overheads are unattractive, and they can be difficult to read. While they do allow you to write on them as you go, they're cumbersome. Moving overheads on and off the projector is distracting. That said, they do offer several advantages: They're inexpensive (color makes them more expensive); you can keep the lights up; you can write on them as you present; and you can write notes to yourself on the frames. You can use color and graphics to liven them up. One of the biggest cautions is to make sure the type size and style are readable for your audience. This is partly a function of the overhead itself, partly a result of the projector you use and the size of the image it creates on the screen. You need to keep both factors in mind. It's also easy to produce handouts from the originals. Be sure to number them. They can be produced from any source that allows you to create a printed copy. They can also be captured on a disk and printed directly from this source with the appropriate hardware—most Kinko's and Alphagraphics have the right equipment.

■ LCD panel—These slim panels sit atop an overhead projector and are hooked up to your computer for PowerPoint or other computer-based slide shows. This tends to work well for smaller audiences. Be careful about the ability to clearly view the image from the sides of the panel. Some panels have good image quality when you are directly in front of the panel, but the image quality degrades the further to the side you move.

■ Computer-based presentation—One of the most useful developments in presentations has been the option of running a presentation directly from a computer. Microsoft's PowerPoint is one example of this type of software. The advantages are obvious: Develop the presentation on your computer and make changes until the last minute without the trouble, time, and expense of redoing slides. You can quickly reorder pages and use animation to make it visually interesting. This feature is also helpful if you do not want to reveal all the information on the page at once. You can use the animation to fly each point or line of text onto the page as you want it. You can include graphics from a wide range of visual libraries—both photographs and drawings. When information is on a page, you can use a pointer in the program and underline key points for emphasis while you are presenting.

The downside is that the people putting together the visuals are not trained in the art of design. With too many words, too many bullets, and assorted clip art, slides are grossly ineffective. But you can face these same challenges with other presentation types. Computer crashes can occur but the light bulbs in the slide projector or overhead projector can also burn out.

Maybe the two biggest challenges are cost and expertise. The projector that you hook up to the computer costs about $5,000, and it is usually not as bright as many slide or overhead projectors. Their light bulbs can also burn out. You need more expertise to run the software, computer (usually a laptop), and projector than you need for any other method. While an AV team member can help, the presenter needs to be skilled enough to navigate a presentation—going forward, backward, or jumping to another section. These skills are critical when you need to quickly access backup material to answer a question.

■ Flip chart—Flip charts are great for small audiences. Pages may, however, be somewhat see-through and difficult to turn because of the flimsiness of the paper. To alleviate that, staple two pages together on each side at the bottom. Write pencil notes in the margins (where they can't be seen by the audience) to guide your discussion. You can also note audience feedback on the chart. Naturally, lights must be on.

You can create flip charts by hand, which gives them a personal touch. The quality of your handwriting is critical if you take this approach. You can also create pages on a computer, print them out, and then blow them up into flip chart pages by using special printers. Once you include them in your presentation, it can be difficult to reorder the pages. Jumping to backups can be cumbersome as well.

Some presenters find multiple flip charts to be helpful. Each is on its own stand—this can prove useful when you need to have two pages of information in front of the audience at one time. Most of the other methods would make this difficult or expensive.

You can also make surprisingly creative use of this somewhat old-fashioned method. In one presentation, the presenter wanted to convince management of the volume benefit of having one group of consumers switch one purchase a year from a competitive brand to their brand. He showed that this group of consumers purchased about four units of the competitor's product per year. He used Velcro to attach one competitive unit of purchase, pulled it off, then replaced it with a picture of their product. This made the change seem simple and the graphic use of the flip chart made it memorable.

- Video—Video is a fairly expensive way to communicate, and it's best used when you're selling a concept that is highly graphic or requires an emotional response. (Video is also a great training tool.) It's equally effective for large or small audiences, assuming you use a size format that's appropriate for the group. Showing a video on a small TV monitor to a group of fifty would be highly ineffective.

There are advances in video that make it less expensive and more powerful. Today you can input video directly into a computer. You can then edit it, including the addition of text on graphics. It can then be played through a laptop and electronic projector, the same as we used for the computer-based presentation. When you do this you can insert video into a PowerPoint presentation that also uses slides.

Separately, keep an eye out for whether your projector might be in the audience's way. The alternative is to do "rear screen projection." This requires a special projector and setup. You'll need a professional to guide you on what you need. Rear-screen projection is always preferable, but it requires about fifteen feet of space in the front of the room.

Numbering

No matter what kind of support materials you're using, find a way to keep track of what goes with what. In one nightmare presentation, we saw a division president drop his slide tray. The slides fell out. They weren't numbered, so it was impossible to reassemble the presentation quickly. This nightmare took place at a meeting with the chairman and CEO, who had little patience with such mishaps.

This risk is minimal with flip charts and most computer presentations. With the latter, you need to be careful with what version of the presentation you bring to the meeting. It is so easy to change the order of pages in a computer presentation that you may make the mistake of saving multiple versions or keeping a separate version on the desktop and laptop computers. Most presenters carefully label files and check the detailed information on a file to determine when it was last modified.

Karen Tucker of The Gary Musick Companies in Nashville, Tennessee, passed on the following true story to us. Her story, while humorous, reveals the potential disasters that can happen when a team presents using computerized, multimedia equipment in an important sales presentation:

> Our special events company opened a new division and we wanted to get the word out about our new services. The owner of the company, Gary Musick, set up an appointment with the sales and catering executives of a very large national hotel chain. Gary had worked on his PowerPoint presentation for weeks to prepare for this meeting.
>
> The meeting consisted of a team of four of us from The Gary Musick Companies and about fifteen executives from the hotel chain. We went in very prepared to impress them with our new destination management division. Gary began the presentation with his great PowerPoint presentation with me running the computer while he talked. Gary was so interesting, and I was so engrossed in what he was saying, that I fell about twelve screens behind with the PowerPoint presentation. When I realized, I quickly pushed the buttons and the graphics were flying in so fast you could barely read them. Of course, snickering came from our audience. After catching up with Gary's speech, the next few minutes ran pretty smoothly.

Then it came my turn to talk. As I got up from the computer, I tripped on the cord and shut down the whole system. Gary started crawling around my feet trying to find the plug. Needless to say, it was a bit distracting. We found out the hard way that with PowerPoint, you have to totally reboot the system, and it starts at the beginning. Gary wasn't even halfway through the presentation he had worked so hard on.

After my little speech was over, Gary decided to show them video footage of a huge convention we did for another client. He wanted to show them the video since the other interesting visuals were now dead. But, my little fiasco of tripping on the cord froze the video screen as well. We had sound, but no picture. Gary then jumped up and tried to describe what was happening with tribal dancers and actors and lights as dramatic music was blaring through the speakers. The audience burst out laughing. It was pretty comical seeing Gary out there acting out what they were supposed to be seeing. (At the very end, the hotel video technician finally got the picture on the screen, so the audience did get to see some of the footage.)

So, whether you have this kind of fiasco, or simply spill water on your script, knock over your stack of note cards, or are the victim of a computer crash, you should still be prepared to give that presentation to the audience no matter what. Number slides and overheads, mark the sequence of handouts, put the numbers on the script. Although this may not have helped in Karen Tucker's scenario, it can't hurt to do everything in your power to prevent a problem. In short, give yourself backups for dealing with almost every possible disaster.

Some backup procedures to consider for the various types of presentations:

- Slides—Be sure to have a backup projector and light bulb. To guard against dumping a slide tray with numbered slides, either have another tray ready or have a flip chart in reserve.

- Overheads—Even if they are numbered, if they get scrambled by an accident it can take too long to reassemble. As with slides, have a backup deck of overheads or a flip chart in reserve.

- Computer presentations—Backing up one of these presentations can get expensive. Computers are *usually* reliable. If it is a laptop, be sure to plug it into a power source so that you do not rely on the battery, but be sure to tape down the cord to prevent accidents. As backup for the projector, about the best you can do is have a backup light bulb (these are expensive). Again, a flip chart or even overheads can be your backup.

- Flip charts—It is tough for flip charts to pose the kinds of problems you face with the other types. About the worst we have seen is an inappropriate page numbering because of last-minute changes.

Professional Presentations Vs. Do-It-Yourself

On a limited budget, you may have to design your own slides, flip charts, etc., or ask an assistant to do it. If this is the case, we've included below a crash course in presentation design.

But if you have the budget, save yourself some headaches and hire a professional. Even a few hundred dollars worth of a graphic designer's time can vastly improve your materials. What it will add to your presentation will be well worth the investment.

The risks also need to be considered. Outside designers may make errors in entering text that can pose problems if not caught in time. If you use a designer, be sure you have enough time since they can often take longer than an in-house approach. If they are good designers, you will have to wait for them to have space on their calendar.

A designer can guide you in what layout, colors, and typefaces are most effective for presentations. This person can also make recommendations about how you should break up information to be more palatable to the audience.

Besides, your time is often better spent preparing yourself, rather than learning presentation design by trial-and-error. Make an exception, however, if you are adept with today's software. If you are skilled in word processing software, you can be effective in most of the presentation software. They often have "wizards" which help you choose themes and insert graphics.

Elements That Create Atmosphere

A well-designed presentation creates an impression that the audience should be able to describe in a word or two: serious, upbeat, exciting. That's because every element of a good presentation is deliberately selected to contribute to and convey a theme. The colors you choose, type style (or font), as well as language, and choice of media all convey a certain tone and feeling.

The nature of your project and your company's personality will dictate the look of your presentation. For example, Southwest Airlines' orientation program at one time included a comedic, upbeat video of employees doing impressions and other entertaining things. It fit the personality of the company, as well as the information that was being portrayed: We value people who can create a fun, welcoming environment for our customers.

Thus, if you were proposing a new product such as a party game, you might want to create a party atmosphere, using colorful visuals with a playful typeface to convey an attitude of fun. On the other hand, if you were introducing a manufacturing process, the topic might call for a more subdued approach. Presentations for a banking institution might typically be more conservative than for a cruise company.

Decide what impression you want your audience to leave with, and pick your media to accomplish that.

Balance

Think about a boring presentation you've attended. How long was it before you began to tune out the speaker? Now think about a presentation that you found interesting. What kept your attention? Few speakers are expert enough to keep an audience's attention much past five minutes. That's why every presentation should include a good balance of actions, words, and visuals. Remember, different people receive information in different ways: through sight, sound, touch, etc. By using a variety of tools you can reach everybody.

Audience involvement is always a plus, and you can employ questions and answers as a way to get people involved.

It also helps to include some stories to bring your points to life. For example, if you were in the test market, relate a conversation you had with a consumer or retailer that supports the overall point you are making. Make it personal; demonstrate your personal involvement in the project. Be prepared with these stories ahead of time. If you have a picture, consider including it in the presentation to help bring the story to life.

Picking the Right Medium

One thing to keep in mind as you develop visuals: What looks good in one format may not translate to another. If you're using both onscreen and printed visuals, take into account how the different media will display your information. For example, while a line graph may look stunning onscreen in color, it won't translate to an $8^1/_2 \times 11$ black-and-white page. Take the time to create materials that fit whatever medium you're using.

Using the proper charts to illustrate your numbers can make a big difference in how the information is received. Here are some tips on what charts to use and how to use them to make your presentation more persuasive.

Pie Charts

Pie charts illustrate percentages as a part of the whole. For instance, a pie chart would effectively show:

- Where marketing dollars will be spent
- How large market segments are
- What percentage of revenues is contributed by different divisions
- Budget allocations
- Expense categories
- Customer demographics
- Sales by region

Pie charts are usually most effective when they contain eight or fewer slices. If you have more than this, consider combining the smaller elements into a "miscellaneous" or "all other" segment. If you only have a small screen to work on, you may need to limit yourself to four to six slices. Again, you can accomplish this by combining segments.

When you have a "miscellaneous" or "all other" category of leftovers, you need to be careful. When pie charts show a "miscellaneous" slice that's bigger than the other slices, it leaves too much unsaid and creates questions in the decision maker's mind. Split the information out more or devise a different method of showing it. When you notice this, it often is helpful to create a backup that breaks out the various components. You can do this by showing the "miscellaneous" slice in a magnified view, or you can show what percentage each component represents of the "miscellaneous."

EXAMPLE

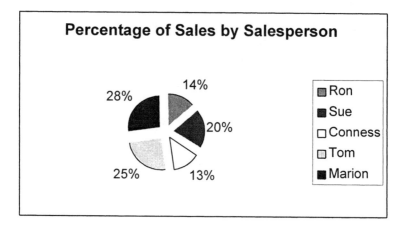

Bar Charts

Bar charts can be effective in comparing such things as:

- Year-to-year performance
- Your performance compared with the competitor's or industry's performance
- Results of one product or division versus another

These work best when you can display more than a small variance. Bar charts that are all even are unnecessary. You can just as easily make a statement that all performance is essentially equal.

You need to watch the numbers being compared and their effect on the scale. When you mix large numbers and small numbers in a bar chart, the scale flexes to accommodate the largest numbers. This can cause comparisons of small numbers to seem insignificant when there may, in reality, be substantial differences. When this happens, consider making two charts with different scales.

EXAMPLE

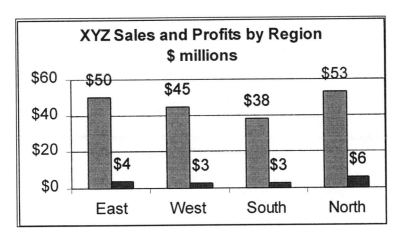

Line Graphs

Line graphs are helpful in showing trends over time in performance areas such as stock price, sales figures, and gains or losses in number of units. You can also depict different areas of performance by using multiple lines. Graphs are most effective when they feature three or fewer lines.

As with other kinds of graphs, limit the number of lines on one graph. Confusion will result when there are too many, especially when they cross over each other. The right number varies by size of the graph and the story you need to tell. In our experience, four to six lines appears to be a maximum.

Also, as we saw in the bar graph discussion, be careful about combining big and small numbers onto a graph. The scale required for the large numbers can force the smaller number trends to appear insignificant.

Because lines tend to be fairly slender, they can be difficult to distinguish. There are two ways to avoid this problem:

- Use colors that are dramatically different, and make the lines bold enough to be easily seen.
- Use a combination of dotted, broken, and solid lines, but make them bold enough so that the difference is easily seen.

EXAMPLE

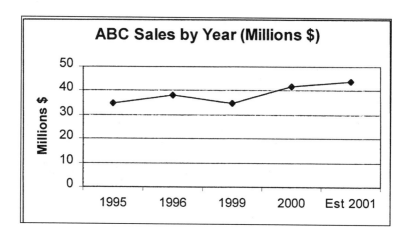

Flow Charts

Flow Charts show key process components, and are useful to show the success of a process before and after changes are implemented. For example, you might demonstrate an employee-hiring process, a manufacturing process, or a customer-complaint process.

Flow charts can be used in one of three ways:

- With fewer than eight boxes they can be effective onscreen.
- With more boxes they can be effective on paper.
- With many boxes they can be displayed on a board, as long as

the type is large enough to be read, or the color indicates areas you'll discuss.

Organization Charts

Organization charts are used to show how an area will be organized, or illustrate changes in an organization. Once again, you must limit the detail. Try to show only the key positions in the top one or two levels. If you must show additional levels, try indicating the scope of the area by adding a box showing the numbers of employees or types of positions.

Again, color-coding functions and levels can help people to read a chart. When you want to focus on one function within an organization, consider making the spotlighted function in color and the others in black.

Spreadsheets

There is only one effective way to display a complete spreadsheet: Put it on a handout that you can give participants when you're ready to discuss the numbers.

Never put a complete spreadsheet onscreen. Such detailed and complex information is almost impossible to read, and it's extremely difficult to highlight the information you're discussing. Forget the laser pointer; it won't change the spreadsheet rule.

It is possible to present portions of spreadsheet information onscreen. Pick out the critical information and show it alone.

Quality, Not Quantity

Visuals are intended to supplement a presentation; to draw people's attention to key points and to make those points more memorable. They are not intended as a means for your audience to read along as you present.

The biggest mistake most presenters make in preparing their visuals is to put *too much information on one page.* We strongly recommend:

- No more than seven words per bullet
- No more than six bullets per page

- Bullets should not be sentences; they should be key thoughts

Remember, most of the time, less is more. After you have constructed a page, ask yourself, "What is the most important few words or numbers on this page?" When you have found them, determine how effective the page would be if those were the only words on the page. Consider verbalizing the other information. Does it work? If not, add a few more words or numbers.

Remember—do not try to impress people in the audience with how much you have learned. That is NOT your goal. You want approval for your idea. You get that only when the audience is focused on what is important.

Color

Color establishes a mood, directs the audience's eye, and helps people distinguish between elements of a visual.

Colors are guides. Sections of the presentation can be in different colors. When you move onto a new section, the colors should also change.

Consider using one color to make your three positioning points. Use that color for them only, and use a different, single color for the all-supporting points.

Deeper colors such as dark blue, dark green, deep purple, or burgundy tend to create an atmosphere of seriousness or conservatism. Bright colors such as turquoise, fuchsia, bright green, or orange appear more upbeat and fun.

Choose colors that coincide with your presentation's tone. If some colors are typically associated with your business, consider using them. Can you imagine a Coke presentation that did not include red?

Red can be exciting, but it can also be difficult to read, especially on slides. Save your red for flip charts or handouts.

Slides should have a dark background and contrasting lettering. White and yellow are particularly good choices for text. The contrast is very important and often difficult to achieve. While exciting and interesting colors are important, readability is most important.

When you're using color to differentiate, be sure to use colors that are easily distinguishable. Don't put two colors that are similar next to each other. It's very difficult to tell the difference between royal blue, navy, and purple.

On flow charts, use color to highlight areas where a process would work differently in the future than it works now.

One particularly effective technique is to use "builds" (or at least highlight the bullet you're talking about). A build is when each bullet of the slide comes up as you talk about it. Thus, your first slide would have one bullet on it, the second slide would have the first bullet and the second, the third would have the first two and the third, and so on.

As the bullets build, you can also emphasize the point you're discussing by having it highlighted. On the first slide, the first bullet would come up in yellow. When the second slide is shown, the first bullet turns white, and the second bullet comes up in yellow.

You can also easily achieve this effect on the computer presentations with PowerPoint. It is an excellent method of focusing your audience on the current point.

Typeface

Select a simple, readable typeface and use it for all of your materials. On slides, use both upper and lowercase letters; all caps is difficult to read.

Never use script typeface.

Often you can use typefaces the same way you would use color to distinguish between points. For example, make your positioning statements in a particularly bold typeface and the supporting points in a lighter style. You can also make all section titles in the same typeface. Changing typefaces with purpose is an excellent method of helping the reader and keeping a presentation interesting.

You do the same with fonts and the use of bold and italics. Use the full power of your word processing or presentation software to communicate your message.

Clip Art

Pictures can make your visuals more interesting and will create a more enduring image in your audience's mind. However . . .

Clip art is a popular tool among amateur designers. If you are going to use clip art, stick with one style. In other words, don't mix cartoon images with realistic-looking drawings in the same presentation. And remember, simplicity is key. Limit your images to one per frame, and keep them in perspective. The picture should complement your message, not overshadow it.

Proceed with caution when using clip art. You can use simple art like arrows without much risk. But when considering the use of cartoons, you really need to know your audience. If there is no prior experience by your peers or others you consult with, consider using one cartoon-like figure.

If there is a history of a positive reaction to clip art, then use it prudently. It is easy to get carried away. Clip art usually livens up a page, but it seldom makes a critical point—the text and numbers are supposed to do that.

Show and Tell

If your proposal includes concepts that are best conveyed through visuals, by all means make the necessary investments to produce a high-quality tool. These might include posters, table-size models, product packaging, or prototypes. We once created a 48" × 60" color-coded flowchart to illustrate the differences between an old process and a new one.

The size of your audience dictates how large your visuals should be. Be sure you take into consideration where people will sit and how well they can see.

A variety of "props" can make your meeting more interesting and credible. In many presentations, it is necessary to review the competitor's strengths and weaknesses. For this discussion, bring in samples of their products or sales materials. If you have a food product and you are recommending a product improvement, then schedule a tasting of the old and new version versus competitive products. If packaging is part of the discussion, then bring in several design prototypes along with competitive packages.

You can do the same with advertising by bringing in video of past, present, and proposed advertising. In these discussions, management usually wants to see what competitors are doing.

Using Charts and Graphs

How your charts and graphs look is almost as important as what they say. If you design them wisely, they can create a powerful picture of your project. If you don't, they may display your information unclearly and result in your project being underestimated or completely misunderstood.

A precaution you can take with any chart and graph is to thoroughly explain the meaning of all columns, rulers, and axes.

Steps to Designing Your Presentation

1. Check out existing facilities to see the quality and type of media available.
2. Determine which media will best display your information and which media works best with your audience, especially the decision maker.
3. Decide who will present, and in what order he or she will do so.
4. Make sure every presenter feels comfortable using the tools.
5. Develop handout packets.

Again, the most common error leaders make in communicating is to focus on what they want to say versus what their audience wants to—and is able to—hear. You can lead an audience to your message, but you can't force them to swallow it.

Keep one critical factor in mind: Although you know your topic intimately, the audience may have no idea what's coming next. You must prepare the audience to receive the information by telling them what they're about to hear.

As you prepare your presentation, plan segues between sections. You want your audience to know when you are changing subjects. It gives them a chance to ask questions on the current section before moving on.

What to Include

Any proposal should include certain basic elements. A verbal presentation should follow the same structure you would use for a written proposal. This includes:

1. Your objective—Describe exactly what you want agreement with today.
2. Background information—Include information that is necessary for a knowledgeable decision to be made. For example, if there was a test market, remind your audience of the appropriate details.
3. Description of the project—This includes critical details such as timing and costs.
4. Benefits or positionings—Why should the decision maker agree? Remember to keep it to the three most important selling points for the idea. Address risks here as they relate to the positionings. This section usually includes the profit, volume, and market share benefits associated with the idea.
5. Other considerations—List here the other factors the decision maker needs to know. If there are risks that were not addressed in the benefits section, detail them here.
6. Next steps and expected completion dates—Be precise and don't be afraid to ask.

The next steps section is where you "ask for the business." This is your chance to say, "Our plan is to (describe the steps). Do we have your agreement to proceed?"

Develop Handouts

In a management presentation at the highest level, handouts merely supplement your presentation.

Prepare a separate agenda with the main points of your presentation. Avoid putting times on the agenda in case things change at the last minute. Put an agenda at each person's place before the meeting begins. If there are multiple presenters, consider listing their names with the agenda items they will present. Also, consider putting the meeting's purpose on the agenda.

If your audience needs to study any of your information in depth, create a handout packet with pertinent pieces of the presentation such as research studies or other more-detailed documents.

Some people prefer to send out packets in advance so that management may study the materials and be prepared with questions or comments. If you choose to do this, be prepared for the fact that the audience may bring the material to the presentation and flip through it as you speak. Once the materials are in the audience's hands, there is really no way to control this.

The same is true if you distribute handouts during your presentation: People will read them instead of listening to you. We prefer to excerpt what we intend to discuss and put it onscreen. That way we can maintain the audience's attention rather than having them looking down at a booklet as we talk. We then distribute handouts at the end of the session.

If you're not using any slides or other visuals, create a one-page summary of your key points in bullet format. This way you can keep the rabbit in the hat until you're ready to reveal it. An alternative is to put essential numbers on one-page handouts that you distribute as you discuss each section.

Senior level executives or board members generally will only want to see summaries of information. However, have enough complete presentation copies to give to anyone who requests the full plan.

Quality Is Everything

While the content of your presentation delivers a very obvious message about how you approach an issue, the appearance of your presentation sends a message, too. It is indicative of your standard of performance and reflects how much you care about your project, showing your attention to detail and your ability to deliver a quality product. With so much at stake, you'll want some help!

"Pretty is not important, but professional is," says Brandt Wright. "You don't need bells and whistles, but you do need everything to be absolutely accurate," says Carol Coletta.

Ask several people to proofread your slides, flip charts, handouts, or other materials to ensure that they're letter perfect. If you've changed numbers several times (as most of us do for important presentations) check that all the numbers are correct, and that your visuals and your script agree.

A professional-looking presentation binder will include a cover and tabs to indicate major sections. If different people have prepared sections, make sure all sections have the same style: margins, font, heading style, and so on. Slides and print materials should use fonts and colors that are compatible. Color copies of graphs or charts can add interest and help display information in a more dramatic way.

If your company doesn't have the facilities to produce a presentation binder, your local quick print shop can provide cardstock covers, as well as spiral or comb binding. A word of caution: Check your copies to make certain they're perfect. It's not unusual for printers to accidentally print something askew, to hole-punch incorrectly, make unreadable copies, and the like. Give yourself enough time to reprint if necessary.

Cheaters and Cheat Sheets

Have you ever sat miserably through a presentation where you couldn't hear the speaker? Or where audience members asked questions that you couldn't hear?

A team member can help you avoid losing your audience through bad acoustics or mishaps. Have someone in the back of the room in your line of sight but invisible to the audience. Give him signs or agree on hand signals for directions such as speak louder, more slowly, repeat the question, you have five minutes, or any information you may be likely to get stuck on.

Agree on the seating arrangement for other team members. The expert who looks up facts to answer questions needs to be near the presenter. She becomes a presenter when she answers a question. She may need access to a flip chart or overheads.

Your AV expert needs to be in the room but not front and center. Other support members need to be in the proximity of their tasks. For example, if someone is designated the gofer for something outside the room, position him near a door that does not disrupt the meeting (unwanted light on the screen) when he comes and goes.

You have done a lot of hard work to get you to this point—do not skimp on your presentation effort. No matter how good you think your idea is, it will not sell itself. If it is a great idea, it needs a great presentation. Even if it is a borderline idea, it deserves a quality presentation so that it can be seen in its best light, along with any risks.

If you have crafted a quality presentation, the next two steps become much easier. If you have not done a good job, you will discover this either in your final preparation or during the actual presentation.

Now that you have a presentation, let's prepare to present it.

Key Learning Points

1. If you want your audience to remember what you have said, you need both quality visuals and verbal communication. It is especially important that the words and pictures say the same thing and convey the same theme.
2. Identify your presentation team—key roles and positioning in the meeting.
3. The best presenter is knowledgeable, skilled at presenting, has a passion for the idea, and has a positive relationship with both the decision maker and key influencers.
4. Don't present until you are ready. Have a time limit when you are ready.
5. What you present is a function of what the decision maker needs to know to make a decision. You can usually satisfy this with a

clear meeting objective statement, background, project details, position statements, other considerations, and next steps. Don't forget to ask for the order at the end.

6. Select the type of media that is right for the decision maker and presenter. Choose presentation details carefully, but always make sure that readability is your first priority.

CHAPTER 7

Preparing to Present

"Memorize your lines and don't bump into the furniture."

Spencer Tracy

I f, as Woody Allen says, "80 percent of success is showing up," the other 20 percent is looking and sounding good when you do. You have only a few minutes to look like a hero . . . or not. Your appearance, demeanor, and style can all help or hurt your message. In fact, experts say that as much as 80 percent of your success is influenced by your nonverbal behavior (Claudyne Wilder, 1994).

Throughout this book you've learned techniques that will help sell your idea. You have worked hard and have gathered information, support, and experience. If you have done your work well, you are now in a great position to sell your idea.

By now, you have seen the idea through the eyes of many people. You have laid a strong foundation, incorporated others' ideas into your original idea, and received feedback on the major benefits and concerns regarding the project. If you are still convinced that you have a great idea, then this conviction will make you very persuasive in your presentation.

If you've ever dozed through a lecture by a droning professor, you understand that it takes more than intelligence and knowledge to make a riveting presentation. And, if you've ever been mesmerized by a dynamic speaker, you know what an impact a great presentation can make.

You owe it to yourself to put your best foot forward. So, although your presentation is researched and written, your work is far from over. Now you must be worthy of your material.

Few people are natural-born presenters; even fewer can critique themselves. Almost everyone can benefit from a bit of feedback and polishing.

You need to have a deep belief in the benefits of preparing and practicing. There is a tendency after you have worked on the presentation for so long to believe that you know the material so well, you do not need practice. This is an understandable attitude, but a potentially disastrous one. There is a big difference between knowing material and presenting selected portions of it in a simple, clear, and powerful presentation.

Experienced presenters run the greatest risk of falling prey to this attitude. They feel that they have presented many times and are experts. Unfortunately, they forget what made them good—preparation and practice. Consider the following real story.

You wouldn't want to suffer this indignity: Several corporate executives were booked to deliver a presentation for a group of hundreds of conference attendees. Most of the presenters spent several half-days practicing their one-hour scripts. One man, however, was reluctant to do so. He made the deadly mistake made by many inexperienced speakers: he believed he knew his subject well enough that when he got in front of the audience he would be able to speak.

Instead, his nervousness was only worsened by the crowd, and the presentation was a disaster. Less-fortunate people have found such a mistake to be a career ender.

The lessons can be painful—or you can remember that preparation and practice are crucial. We know of senior managers with over thirty years of experience who spend two or more hours practicing before giving a thirty-minute presentation or speech. The people in the audience who then hear these managers believe they are natural presenters. The fact is that they know what it takes to give a persuasive and motivating speech or presentation.

Polishing Your Style

Emerson said, "All the great speakers were bad speakers at first." Practice is what will move you from one extreme to the other.

Painful as it may be, feedback from anyone will improve your presentation 100 percent. Feedback from a professional may improve it another 100 percent.

We become so accustomed to hearing ourselves talk, we seldom hear what we say, and we almost never notice how we move. If you question whether you need help, record yourself on audio or, better yet, video. Listen to your tone, pacing, accent, pauses. Do you use dead words or phrases such as, "You know," or "um"?

If you have the advantage of seeing yourself on video, watch your movements and gestures. Note distracting habits such as swaying back and forth or scratching your nose. Do you look at the audience, or do you intently read from cards or a script?

Of all the methods you can use to improve, watching yourself on video is the best. You do not need a professional to run the camera. Set up your home VHS camera on a tripod or table, or have a friend hold it.

Mix in a combination of wide and closer shots. The wide shots let you see your whole body in action. You will see what you do with your hands. Remember, hands can be very powerful "props" in your presentation. They can also work against you if they are pushed into your pockets, or if your actions in general are awkward. Check out your posture. Do you look comfortable? If not, find a posture that is comfortable. This can be critical to your overall comfort and confidence.

On the closer shots, check the expression on your face. Is it serious? Does it reflect the tension and anxiety you feel on the inside? Facial expressions are crucial. Your audience will focus more on your face than any other part of you. You want your expression to be friendly and confident.

Saying so is easy, but achieving that look can be very difficult if your inner storm of anxiety and fear is raging. If so, you need to remedy it. It can be difficult since in the presentation you cannot see yourself. But you can sense what your face feels like when it is tense and how different that is from a friendly, confident feeling. The facial muscles feel very different. Since your facial expression is so important, have your friends and coaches focus on this aspect of your presentation until you master it. We will discuss later in this chapter thoughts on calming the inner storm, which will help to achieve that positive facial expression you want when you present.

Your spouse or friends can offer useful input. Of course, sometimes performing in front of people you know is more intimidating than doing so in front of strangers. And there's also the chance a friend won't feel comfortable giving you honest feedback.

Friends and work associates can be trained to be great coaches. Consider putting together a personal checklist of things that you want them to look for in your practice presentation. Tell them how important their honest and constructive comments are to you.

Set ground rules that you are comfortable with. Some people are more comfortable with having their friends and coaches record their comments and wait until the presentation is completed to share their observations.

Others feel more comfortable receiving the comments as they come up. This can be very beneficial. First, it gives the presenter the immediate opportunity to try it again and receive feedback on how the new way worked. It also helps the presenter identify with the comment since it is fresh in his memory. There are powerful advantages to this approach.

The second benefit is that it prepares the presenter for interruptions from the audience while he is presenting. This emulates the real world he faces during the presentation. In most cases, he will be interrupted with comments and questions. After addressing them, the presenter then needs to get back into his presentation. For someone who has trouble getting back on track after an interruption, this can be a very valuable part of his preparation and practice.

A professional can help in several ways. He or she will:

■ Give you an unbiased opinion
■ Offer simple tricks to help you improve
■ Be patient and work with you as you learn your new skills

Where can you find such a resource?

If your company has a corporate training department, seek out their help. These staff members are professionals, and they can undoubtedly offer you some tips. The same is true for the corporate communications department. When you're building your alliances, someone in those areas would be good persons to cultivate!

If these departments can't spare the time, they can probably direct you to a professional speech coach. For an hourly fee, a coach will observe you, give you assignments and feedback, and offer tips of the trade.

When a professional coach isn't in your budget, try your local college or university's speech or drama department. You may be able to hire a teacher or advanced student for a smaller hourly fee.

Another source of help is Toastmasters. Most communities have one or more chapters. The more experienced members can be a good feedback resource for you. You will usually find a mix of presentation styles in this group, which provides you with some of the broadest feedback you can receive.

Another source is a personal coach. This relatively new field (started in the 1980s) has experienced explosive growth. A personal coach works with you one-on-one to achieve your objectives faster and easier than you could accomplish them by yourself. You can find a coach to help you in a couple of ways. First, check with friends to see if they know of a coach they would recommend. Second, consult with the Internet coach-referral sites. Coach University (*www.coachu.com*) and the International Coach Federation (*www.coachfederation.org*) have excellent coach-referral systems.

Many personal coaches work for companies to provide just this kind of support to employees. You can use the referral services noted above if this is right for your situation.

Although this may sound like a lot of trouble to go to, consider what may be at stake. Spending the time and money to improve how your management perceives you could be the best career investment you make.

One caveat, however, on polishing your style: Although you want to present yourself and your team in the best light while appearing and feeling confident, be careful not to become *too polished*. Presenters that come across too "slick" and polished can have just as negative an effect on executives as someone who doesn't know his material. In the corporate world, substance counts, whether in the content of your idea or the integrity and sincerity of your presentation style.

Learn Your Material

At least several days before your presentation, run through your script out loud either by yourself or in front of someone who can critique the material. You'll undoubtedly find a few snags in the flow or the words, so give yourself plenty of time to revise your script and to adapt visuals or handouts.

This practice can happen in stages. For example, you might do your videotape practice session first and follow that a day or two later with practice before a group of people who will provide constructive feedback.

When you're comfortable with your content, you're ready to

begin learning the presentation material. Your goal is to know your plan inside out, and to speak on any point with ease.

You can take one of two approaches:

- Memorize your material and deliver it word for word.
- Become so familiar with it that you can speak comfortably from bullet points.

Either way works as long as you are a skilled presenter. Here are some benefits and disadvantages of each approach.

To Memorize or Not

If you have a great memory, you may feel most comfortable with this approach. You won't have to improvise, and you'll be sure you make all the points you want to make. On the other hand, there are five potential downfalls to memorizing:

- Memorizing means really learning every word, and for most people that means lots of rehearsing. Presentations tend to change up to the last minute, and often it's difficult to un-learn parts that you've already memorized and replace them with new information.

- Sounding too pat: Unless you're an experienced and skilled speaker, your presentation may sound memorized and ele-mentary. Only the best speakers can make a memorized pre-sentation sound professional.

- Dealing with interruptions: If a conversation breaks out in the middle of your recitation, can you find your place again?

- If interpretations and conclusions that are different from what you had planned are made early in a presentation, it can substantively change later parts of the presentation. In-corporating these changes on the fly in a memorized presen-tation can be very difficult. If you fail to make them, your au-dience will likely notice and the failure to adjust will undermine your credibility.

- Dealing with mental blank-out: Unless you are an experi-enced presenter and confident that you will not go blank and forget part of your presentation, you run the risk of such a situation and may not be able to recover gracefully. Maintain a sense of lightness and humor in these situations. Know that virtually everyone in the room has had a similar experience.

The time investment for a forty-five minute presentation can be very high. To memorize this much material can consume several days. You need a good memory or it will be even longer. During the period you are memorizing, you may not be effective at any other important tasks.

If you choose to memorize, you may find several tools helpful. First, some people benefit from writing the presentation in their own handwriting, or, at least, making handwritten notes on it. You'll remember things better this way. Second, record your presentation in pieces, listen to it in the car, and practice the sections. Practice out loud, because hearing your own voice will help you commit it to memory. Third, record key points on a card so that in case you get lost you'll have a few bread crumbs to help you find your way back. Fourth, master segments at a time. Look for opportunities to create repetitive themes to aid your memorization.

A much-used alternative to memorizing the presentation is reading from your prepared script. To be done well this also requires considerable practice. You want to be so familiar with the material that you can deliver long phrases and sentences without looking at the script. Instead your focus is on the audience.

You can even incorporate planned time for ad libs. You can also plan time to wander away from the podium, maybe to emphasize a point on the screen. If you do this, you may want to insert highlighted sentences into the script so that when you return to the podium you can quickly see where you want to resume.

While this approach requires less time to prepare than the memorization method, it shares many drawbacks with the memorization method. It is difficult to establish a strong connection with your audience when so much of your attention is focused on the script. It is almost as if you are held prisoner by it. For most of the presentation you are tied to the podium.

Having said this, many wonderful presentations are made this way. If the quality of the material, writing, and delivery are high, you can have a very memorable and persuasive presentation.

Developing Familiarity with Material

Some speakers prefer to learn their material so well that they can ultimately speak from bullet points. Although there's tremendous preparation required, speaking that way sounds extemporaneous and can be very effective.

One way to do this is to start by writing a complete script. Once again, writing it in your own handwriting can be very helpful, although as more people become comfortable with computers they become the preferred writing method.

Practice in sections. As you become more comfortable with the script, pare down the notes you speak from. Rehearse. Cut your notes even more, until you're speaking from a list of key points. If you want to eliminate cards altogether, you may do that, but it's really not necessary. You can easily use one or more cards either in your hand or on the table beside you as a cheat sheet just in case.

Without sufficient preparation, this can be a risky technique, for you may forget what you intend to say. If you're using slides, you might be tempted to look at the screen instead of at your audience. Cards can come in handy for keeping you on track and breaking your dependence on the screen to know where you are.

Another way to use this approach is to key off the presentation pages. Use the visuals on the screen to make your key points and use either note cards or your memory to remember the fill-in points you want to make around the key points on the screen. If you can memorize a script, you can easily master this approach. It takes a fraction of the time memorizing does and usually produces a better presentation.

While it may seem risky versus a completely scripted approach, it actually has fewer risks when done well. First, the points on your slides are the most important points you want to make or they would not be there. Theoretically, you could only make these points and no more in your presentation. If you did that, you would probably have a jerky presentation that did not feel complete. All you need to do if your presentation materials are strong is use some fill-in facts and transitions and links between points.

When you can do this, you have a very free-flowing presentation that feels more like a personal conversation than a staged, memorized performance. You bring the audience's attention to the points on the screen for a moment and then you speak directly to them. There is some spontaneity to this approach that keeps it fresh and alive. It also allows for the occasional, appropriate dose of humor that fits the moment.

This approach is the most personal of all the methods. You are not tied to a script; this affords you the mobility you may not achieve with other methods. Also, your mind is more into what is happening in the moment. You do not have 100 percent of your brain tied up in replaying the memorized speech. You have a greater ability to tune into the nonverbal communications from your audience.

This approach requires practice like the others. The main task is to become very familiar with the points on the screen and the flow between them. Some people who use this approach only use notes to make sure they remember the transitions between pages and sections of the presentation. These are usually crucial to maintaining a smooth flow.

If You Must Read—Use Cards or Notes

If you're speaking at a podium, you may actually have your entire script in front of you (with the warning below). As you read the script, don't flip pages over or move a page to the back of the stack. Slide a page to the right where it's out of the way. You can rearrange and stack your pages after the presentation.

While you may wish to have your entire script in front of you while you speak, it can be a dangerous crutch for several reasons:

- Unless you're extremely familiar with the material and are an expert at reading a script, you'll be tempted to read directly from it. This means you would be staring at the pages in front of you instead of looking your audience in the eye.

- Reading will give your audience the impression that you're not very familiar with your material.

- If you lose your place, you may have difficulty finding it.

Instead of using a complete speech, write your key points on index cards. Number the cards. If they get out of sequence they'll be easy to arrange. As you're speaking, hold the cards in one hand. When you finish a key point, move to the next card.

Whatever you do, don't fidget with the cards.

All Points Are Not Created Equal

It is very important to recognize the most important points in the presentation. By this time in your preparation, everything in the presentation is necessary to make the sale. You have rigorously edited to the clearest, simplest, and most powerful presentation you can craft.

Within these pages there are some points that are more important than others. You need to know which ones they are within the presentation. In your script or hard copy of the slides, circle the most important ones. When you get to these points use your voice, gestures, and props to underscore their importance.

Taking this approach one step further, identify the most important point on each page. If you had to rush, what would be the only point you would make on the page? What will you say or do to make sure your audience recognizes that this is the most important point? Have a plan. Do not let the vital point get lost among the others.

When you take this approach, you can be sure that the points that are critical to selling your idea will be in the spotlight. They will not be lost. Here is what you want—if your audience only remembers three (or whatever number is right for your presentation) points, you know what they will be. One CEO we know prefers to have one card that contains only the key bullet points. That way, when he gets sidetracked, he refers back to his card to stay on task.

A simple way of remembering this technique is with this saying: "All points in a presentation are not created equal and all points on a page are not created equal."

Your Voice

Some voice coaches teach singers to use their voices like an instrument. The same lessons apply to speaking. Your audience will remember little of what you say, but they will have a distinct impression of how you say it. Here are a few pointers that will help you put your best voice forward:

- Modulate your voice so that you don't lull your audience to sleep.
- Speak slowly. Many speakers speed through presentations, never realizing that the audience was left behind. (In one case an interpreter for the hearing impaired stopped a speaker who was going too fast to be interpreted.) Remember, you know what's coming next, but your audience doesn't. You must prepare them for what you're about to say, and then say it slowly enough for them to digest your point.
- Vary your pace, slowing to emphasize points. Use your voice like a musical instrument. For your normal voice, have a level and pace that are comfortable for you and the audience.

For portions of the meeting with useful but not critical information, you can usually speed up. If the information is on the screen, you may be able to point to it and invite the audience to review it. They will do this faster than you can speak. In fact, David A. Peoples, in his book, *Presentations Plus*, 2nd ed., says that most people speak at the rate of 120–200 words per minute, yet the human mind can comprehend 600 words per minute. If it is important information, slow down. You can then speak either softer or louder, depending on what you are most comfortable with. Plan to use a pause in places where you transition between segments, i.e., positionings, or when you have made an important point that you want your audience to reflect on for a few moments.

Watch the audience to make sure they're not straining to hear you. Even in a small group sound may not travel well.

Watch them also for other reactions. If you see an obviously perplexed member, especially the decision maker or a key influencer, then consider pausing. You can ask the total audience if there are any questions or, if you are comfortable, ask the person with the perplexed look if you can help him.

If an important member of the audience is looking through handouts, you need to decide whether to pause to let him finish or to move on. If you are covering an important point and the person shows no signs of finishing quickly, then pause. Do not make it uncomfortable for the person. You can also offer to help him find what he is looking for. This may be one of the more important decisions you need to make during the presentation. The bottom line is that you cannot afford to have an important person distracted when you are making crucial points.

Movement and Gestures

If you're not an experienced speaker, you're likely to spend the majority of your time learning your material. That's good. However, take some time to evaluate how you look when you present. Watch yourself in a mirror or on video.

Here are some frequent mistakes inexperienced speakers make:

1. Clutching the podium—The audience can sense your uneasiness. You also remove one of your better "props," your arms and hands.
2. Pacing—It is a distraction. It can tire your audience out. They are more likely to focus on your movements than on what you are saying.

3. Swaying back and forth or side to side—This is very similar to pacing. Most of the time you do not know you do this. This is an area that can be helped by a video or friends.
4. Putting hands in pockets, or jingling change—Why? Does it help you sell your idea? It is another one of those distractions.
5. Constantly gesturing—Gestures are best used like exclamation marks in writing—sparingly.

How should you use movement and gestures to enhance your presentation?

Rent a video of a sales guru or other professional speaker and see how they move. Notice when they walk and when they stand still. When you're making a key point, you should stand still. When you're delivering information that's not essential, that's the time to walk.

Move toward a visual aid to point things out (but don't turn away from the audience to read the information). Walk toward your audience; be one of them. Be willing to walk into your audience or come on their side of the table to see it from their point of view. Again, be sensitive to how your audience reacts and stop anything that makes them uncomfortable.

Hand movements help emphasize a point. Use a variety of very deliberate (but not exaggerated) movements rather than the same movement over and over.

A podium is like a protective shield: It may give you comfort, but it creates a barrier with your audience. If you can feel comfortable without it, don't use one. We have seen a wide variety of effective alternatives to a podium. Two are notable:

1. In some situations, you can sit down at a table with the audience. This approach is especially effective when you can control the change of visuals from a laptop or slide projector. It makes the presentation more friendly and conversational.
2. With larger audiences, a presenter can walk into the audience area. The impersonal nature of a podium in a large audience is overcome with this approach. This is especially effective when you have strong visuals and do not need to be

near the screen to emphasize points. You can be with your audience regularly or occasionally. In either case it tends to make it friendlier and puts the focus on the facts and statements on the screen.

Check Your Location and Equipment

Anyone who regularly makes presentations has at least one horror story to tell. Often it relates to equipment: slide trays not advancing, projector lights burning out, overhead gels melting onscreen. In any meeting there are a million details that can go wrong, so always assume Murphy's Law will prevail. There's no foolproof safeguard against disaster, but three steps will help:

1. Double-check and rehearse with all your equipment in advance.
2. Leave yourself plenty of time to fix things. At a minimum, be completely ready a day before the meeting.
3. Always have a backup. We discussed these earlier and it cannot be overemphasized. If you have not needed backups yet in your career, you will.

If this seems like paranoia, imagine yourself in this situation:

You're scheduled to deliver a day-long survival workshop at a beautiful off-site lodge. An associate makes all the arrangements and assures you that the room is cozy and ideally suited for such an event. Decorations including an old canoe, mosquito netting, and assorted camping gear complete the atmosphere.

The day before the meeting you visit the location to become comfortable with the surroundings. You discover that a vital part of the rustic ambiance of the room is four real-wood columns that divide the room in such a way that no matter where you set up your audiovisual equipment, it cannot be seen by the entire audience. It's too late to change locations. Your only course is to reset the room and work around it the best you can. Talk about survival training.

The worst part of that story is that while you should be thinking solely about your delivery, you're still trying to troubleshoot details.

Here's another true life adventure: A presentation is scheduled in a brand-new, state-of-the-art training room. A last minute discovery: When you turn on the video, the room automatically goes completely black. This would be great if you're watching *Titanic*, but not so great if you're trying to talk from slides and asking the audience to complete a written exercise. It took several hours to override the system, which dramatically cut short rehearsal time.

No matter how detailed a room diagram, or how many times you've sat in a place, you will never truly know that everything is working until you're in the location, pushing buttons, and seeing things in action.

Here are some things to consider:

- Lighting—Use colors for your visuals that can be easily seen. If a room is somewhat light, or if there is a light directly in front of the screen, your slides may be washed out.

- Gauge what lighting level is appropriate when you are and are not showing slides or other AV. If there are many light switches, mark the one you'll need to adjust. Put a strip of tape on a sliding adjustable light switch to indicate at what level the lights should be set for playing video or showing slides.

- Viewing obstacles—Can you set up your AV equipment so that everyone can see the screen? Does the overhead projector block anyone's view? Get creative if you need to. There are stands you can buy or rent that elevate the projector about as high as you need. Often you can also move the screen. Usually the combination of moving the projector and the screen results in a clear view.

- Nonfunctioning (or nonexistent) AV equipment—If at all possible, set up your equipment well before the meeting and leave it. Once you arrive at the meeting you should spend your time thinking about your presentation, not setting up a computer or overhead projector. If you leave it in the room, be sure there is reliable security. If you leave a laptop and computer projector, you have almost $7,000 in hardware in the room.

- Cords—Can they be placed so no one will trip over them and so they won't get in the presenter's way? If cords will be in places where people must walk back and forth across them, tape them down to the carpet or floor to make them less of a hazard.

Rehearse

Each time you say the words out loud you're helping yourself commit them to memory; plan several rehearsals. As we saw earlier, the first rehearsal may be by yourself. When you do it this way, have some way to evaluate yourself. We discussed how a video, tape recorder, or mirror could make a big difference. Don't be afraid to stop and replay the tape to see how you are doing. This gives you the opportunity to incorporate your learnings into the balance of your presentation.

Your second rehearsal can be in front of associates, friends, or your coach. Again, consider receiving their thoughts as they occur. You want the rehearsal to be a learning situation. You can try out the different styles and adjustments as they are made.

One speaker skimped on preparation for a communications workshop because she believed she knew the subject well enough to talk about it in her sleep. Imagine how horrified and humiliated she felt when she realized she had skipped from section 1 to section 6 of a five-hour workshop. It's not easy to recover from a gaffe like that. Knowing your material inside out is a must.

Consider conducting your second rehearsal in the actual room where you'll be presenting, even if you have to do it a week before your scheduled event. Have all your materials there, and put them exactly where they'll go. You'll need a table at hand for your props, handouts, and script. Make sure there's room to spread everything out so you won't have to shuffle papers.

Set up AV equipment so you can rehearse with your slides or other media. You can't be certain things are exactly right until you do this. Have your team with you so that everyone becomes comfortable with his or her role. If the lights need to be dimmed, find out where and how to do that. Even if there's a remote switch near you, you may want to ask someone to assist you with this. Mark your script for when this will happen, and give a copy to the person who's helping so she can follow along and time things appropriately.

Will you be using a flip chart or dry erase board? Where will that be set up? Will you have to move it to avoid obscuring the screen? Are there markers available? Do they work? Go through your flip charts and look for opportunities to improve them. Do you want to plan a blank page in a certain part of the presentation? You might do this if you anticipate a certain question that could benefit from a hand-drawn chart. Are there pages that you can skip if the presentation goes well or badly? Paperclip these sections together.

You can do your third rehearsal alone. In this one, you use everything you have learned. You can record or tape yourself as needed. If there are props, be sure they are in the room. Plan when and how you will introduce them—one at a time, in groups, or all at once? Where do you want to put them? Is it important for the audience to touch and feel them or is this a potential distraction?

After this dress rehearsal you can rehearse a few more times in the comfort of a quiet room. Use your visualization powers to see yourself making the presentation. Often it is most productive to focus on visualizing how you will make the most important points in the presentation. Other parts you may want to visualize are the transitions between segments and asking for the order at the end of the meeting.

Visualization is a very powerful method of preparing yourself. You see Olympic athletes visualizing a ski or a bobsled run. Many presenters find this to be their single most effective learning tool.

Practice Questions and Answers

There's a big difference between rehearsing from a script and answering questions as they arise. Have an objective person practice with you, asking you tough questions. In a rehearsal, bring your list of the ten toughest questions. Have a member of your team ask them at the appropriate time. Have other team members pool their effort to ask tough follow-up questions to your initial response.

This is why you want subject-matter experts in different functional areas to be members of your team. Now let them practice their roles as fact finders and answer the question for you. Some of the questions will require facts or references that you may not have in the presentation or have not memorized. How quickly can they find the answer? How do you want to answer the question—should the team member generate a chart or table; should she get up and respond using a flip chart or overhead? Have the members of the team practice doing this so they are familiar with the materials and impromptu questions requiring their expertise. They should also have several overheads prepared to address some of the anticipated or possible questions. It's always best to answer questions without benefit of notes, if you can, because it demonstrates thorough knowledge of the subject and an ability to think on your feet . . . or at least the impression of that ability. If you've thought through all the possible objections and prepared thoroughly, you won't have to think on your feet at all.

Beyond the factual and mechanical part of answering questions, you want to know the attitude you will have when you get questions. Some presenters inwardly resent and are threatened by questions, and it shows. When your audience senses this, instead of an honest exchange of views, battles can erupt. If this happens, your chances of gaining agreement to your idea just dropped by about 50 percent.

You want to keep the attitude that questions are simply a request for more information. It shows someone is thinking about what you have said—always a good sign. Thank a person for his question and if it appears to be the least bit honest, recognize it as a good question.

In addition, think of questions as opportunities to make your idea better. This is also very tough for many presenters to grasp. Any change is seen as a threat, because they have invested so much into the effort.

They also fear that any question suggesting an alternative way of doing something probably means the idea will not be agreed to in the current meeting. They would have to adjourn and return when the alternative is fully researched, assessed, and either incorporated or left out. They then need to recycle through the complete presentation process again. They have set their mind on gaining agreement in the current meeting. Anything less, they view as failure. This attitude makes it very difficult for a presenter to see the good in a suggestion.

If you have any traces of this attitude, you could be in for a tough meeting. When your attitude makes it difficult if not impossible to see the good in a suggestion made by a key influencer or the decision maker, a spirit of cooperation is not likely to emerge.

The alternative is to see suggestions as offers of help from knowledgeable and skilled managers. These suggestions may be the most valuable you receive because of the experiences of the audience members.

Yes, if the suggestion is adopted after close examination in the meeting, it may mean that you need to fully research it before having another meeting. That is OK if you now have a better idea that has a greater likelihood of succeeding when executed.

Another major benefit is that your idea now has an important new supporter and even co-owner. When a decision maker's suggestion is incorporated into a project, that person tends to be more receptive and supportive to future requests that may be necessary. For example, you may get fast track treatment for a supplementary funding request later in the life of the project.

Changing your attitude from seeing questions as enemies to seeing them as friends is tough for presenters. If you find yourself in this predicament, seek help from your boss or other people you respect. This may be one of the most important learnings for your meeting.

Dress for Success

It always amazes us when a person arrives for a job interview dressed inappropriately. It tells us one of several things may be true:

- He doesn't take the situation seriously.
- He doesn't do his homework.
- He doesn't believe in impeccable preparation.
- He doesn't understand the importance of sizing up a situation and acting appropriately.
- He may operate under a different dress code and not feel the need to dress like the executive members. In this case, however, it behooves the presenter to put personal preference aside and model his or her dress after the intended audience.

That all holds true even when you're inside a corporation. It's not as much a matter of status as it is the subtle messages your appearance sends about how you approach things. As we said in an earlier chapter, part of success in a corporation is fitting in with the cultural architecture, and dressing appropriately is part of fitting in. As with everything, it depends on your company and what its culture and standards dictate.

You're the frame for your presentation; take advantage of every opportunity to make it—and yourself—look good. Your appearance should be an addition to the material you present, not a distraction from it.

Decide what you'll wear several days in advance. They say to dress for the position you want, not the one you have. What will your superiors be wearing? If you are not sure, call the assistants of the key decision makers in the group. If still in doubt, dress conservatively in both style and color. If you don't have a suit or outfit that's appropriate, buy something. It's an investment in your future.

Check out your clothes to be sure they fit properly and are clean and pressed with all buttons attached solidly and hems in place.

Women who plan to wear a skirt or dress should have backup pantyhose in case of a run.

Some other basics:

1. Well-manicured nails
2. Neat, stylish hair
3. Neatly trimmed facial hair
4. Unobtrusive jewelry

Once again, the key is giving yourself enough time to deal with problems.

Dealing with Stage Fright

The more prepared you are, the greater your chances of success. But even accomplished presenters may feel jumpy before a major presentation. Although there's probably nothing to quiet the butterflies in your stomach, there are a few tricks you can use to alleviate the symptoms of nervousness.

Take a few deep breaths before your presentation begins. Use the visualization skills you used earlier here. Take deep breaths, ones that fill your chest and diaphragm. You will need to be conscious of this because when you are nervous, your breathing tends to be shallow.

As you breath deeply, visualize positive feelings coming into your body, maybe through the top of your head. Do this slowly—at least a count of ten or twenty if you can. As you breath out, as slowly as you breathed in, visualize tension being released. Dr. John Gray, author of *Men Are From Mars, Women Are From Venus* (1992), recommends visualizing tension being released through the tips of your fingers.

A small amount of adrenaline is good: It pumps you up and keeps you on your toes. You are alert and prepared to do your best. What you need to watch out for with adrenaline is that when it stops pumping, you can crash. Do not get too pumped up, but have a good edge that keeps you alert and focused.

View stage fright as a friend. It is your way of getting focused and ready. If you are like most people, even people with "bad" cases of stage fright, once you start you are fine. All the anxiety vanishes and you get on a roll. Reflect on how stage fright has in the past helped focus you and contributed to a quality presentation. When you can do this, stage fright ceases to be a threat.

Figure 7.1

Curing the Physical Symptoms of Stage Fright

Dry mouth

- Keep water or mints handy for dry mouth—your number one, must-do solution

- Subtly chew on your tongue to generate moisture

- "Pump" your salivary glands to bring moisture into your mouth

Red face

- Move your hands or feet to get blood flowing to them instead of your face

- Deep breathing exercises to calm down and lower your heart rate

- Take a cool walk alone, preferably outside, before the meeting

Perspiring

- Wear dark clothing that won't show moisture

- Use anti-perspirant

- Wear underarm pads

Key Learning Points

1. Preparing before a presentation is essential to success. Meeting rooms are littered with failed meetings where the number one cause was lack of proper preparation.

2. Early in your meeting preparation, find a way to see or hear yourself delivering your presentation. It can be as simple as a mirror, a tape recorder, or a VHS video camera set up on a tripod.

3. There are various methods of learning your material and becoming comfortable with it. Ultimately, you want a method that helps you confidently deliver a persuasive presentation.

4. Within your presentation, be sure you know the most important points overall and on each page. Treat them in a special way with your voice, gestures, or props.

5. In your rehearsals experiment with different voice styles and gestures. They can be great tools to emphasize points and make the presentation flow easily and interestingly.

6. Make sure a complete room and equipment check is included in your preparation process.

7. Practice answering the list of toughest questions you developed. Involve your entire team in the process since it may take more than one person to answer some questions. When you can answer the toughest questions, your confidence should zoom upward.

8. Convert stage fright into a friend that helps you deliver the great presentation that you want.

9. Above all, know what you are talking about. It is your idea and you are expected to know it inside and out. While you may not know the answer to every possible question, you should, from all your education, data gathering, and networking, have a pretty good idea of what to expect. Have your subject matter experts on hand to address tough questions in their area.

10. Be yourself. Executives are usually turned off by someone pretending to be something or someone they are not.

11. If a major mishap occurs, don't panic. Try to make light of the situation and move on. Executives are human too, and they've made their share of mistakes in presentations as well. How you recover says as much about you as anything. Appropriate humor tends to put most people at ease in embarrassing situations.

12. Be assured and confident without being arrogant.

CHAPTER 8

Presenting Your Information

"One of the best ways to persuade others is with your ears—by listening to them."

Dean Rusk

All the work is done and now you are ready to present to those key decision makers who will give their stamp of approval for implementation. In many cases, several months, even a year, pass between the time the idea originates and the time you present it to management. You will need all the perseverance, focus, and enthusiasm that got you this far on the day that you present.

You also need the same determined, objective attitude that has served you well in the developing and positioning of your idea. Up to this point, you and your team have been strong advocates for your idea and you have gained knowledge and support from others' input.

Having the right attitude, you have embraced negative feedback and found ways to make your idea stronger. This same attitude will serve you well in your presentation. If you receive negative feedback in the presentation, you will not be able to shrug it off.

As discussed in Chapter 7, you need to have a balance between being an advocate for the idea and being open to suggestions that have the potential to make your idea stronger. You achieve that balance when you have a deep commitment to doing what is right for the project and the corporation—not just a commitment to what is right for your career and personal gain.

Getting Ready

Your presentation may be the culmination of months of hard work. When the big day arrives, you certainly want to do justice to your material. Besides the right attitude, you need the right inner conditions. While there may be a few butterflies and a certain amount of anxiety, you also want there to be an inner calm. We have already talked about the breathing exercises you can do to calm yourself. In addition, you need to reflect on all the preparation you have done and take confidence from your efforts so far. You want a calm inner confidence. You know you are prepared and will do your best.

Doing your best is different from being perfect—besides, there is no objective measuring stick for perfection. You need to know that you may say something that you will regret and that is OK. While you may be prepared and confident, you are not perfect and that is OK. Recognizing this ahead of time and truly accepting it, allows you to take a small stutter-step instead of a trip and fall when you do or say something you regret. Instead of feeling devastated, you can laugh, or at least smile at what you have done.

When you can embrace this approach, you are prepared for whatever unfolds during the course of your presentation.

Look Good

Your appearance will be the first thing your audience notices about you, so check out your overall image in a full-length mirror.

Remember, your appearance is much more than your clothes and hair style. Maybe, the most important part of looking good is the expression on your face. An honest smile and calm confidence go a long way towards establishing a positive tone for the meeting. Get those butterflies and stage fright behind you before your audience enters the meeting.

Feel Good

Watch what you eat and drink. The last thing you want is an upset stomach. You may want to avoid caffeine and sugar, both of which may contribute to jitters. You *can* get too up for a meeting. Caffeine and sugar can give you a buzz that defuses your focus and scrambles your brain a bit, just when you need it the most. Follow your normal routine. Presentation day is not the time to experiment with a new diet or amount of coffee, tea, or cola.

Often a light workout gets rid of the nervous energy. In its place is often a calm and clear energy that leaves you feeling more alert and bright.

Double Check Arrangements

If you have access to the room in advance, arrive early so you can double check everything. If you do not have early access to the room, find a way to get it. It is critical that you not find yourself scrambling because the night cleaning crew moved or changed critical elements of your room arrangements. The following figure provides a last minute checklist to use to ensure everything is as it should be.

Figure 8.1

Final Room Checklist

- ■ Does the equipment work?—Check all of the equipment. Do not assume that just because it turns on and there is light that it is working.

- ■ Is the lighting set at the right level?—You may have set the lighting in an evening rehearsal for your morning meeting. This could change all of your needs. Leave time to make the necessary adjustments.

- ■ Are the chairs and visual aids in place?—How many times have props been misplaced at the last minute? Too many. They can be damaged at the last minute and necessary repairs can be difficult.

- ■ Are cords taped and safe?—Have you thought of all the ways the audience can enter the room? Are all the entryways accessible?

- ■ Do I have all my presentation materials?—Have a checklist that you have prepared before the meeting. Many times these checks are done too quickly and a vital item is missed. Do not assume that just because someone you normally trust assembled the materials that they are all there.

- ■ Are the slides, overheads, etc., numbered and in order?—Do you have your backups? Check and recheck the order, especially the overheads which can easily be shuffled by last minute changes.

- ■ Are the handouts in place?—Revisit your plan about when and how they will be passed out. Do you have not only enough for each person in the room (audience and team members), but also extras in case you need them? Do you have any second thoughts? Revise as needed.

- ■ Does the food and beverage look fresh and attractive?—If the meeting is scheduled for more than an hour, you may want to have a water pitcher and glasses as well as a small bowl of hard candies at each table for the audience.

Figure 8.1 *(Continued)*

- Are the agendas at each person's place?—Are any last minute changes that need to be made reflected in the agenda?

- Is the seating for the team and/or presenters adequate and in view of the audience?—If several people will be in attendance, you might want to consider putting name tents in front of both the audience and team members. This way, you can control the seating arrangement of the audience and it will ensure no one's name is miscalled during the presentation.

- Is there an extra flip chart close by to record any new issues, concerns, etc., that arise during the meeting and will need to be addressed?

Open the Doors and See All the People

You have completed all your checks and the meeting begins soon. Some things you can do as people arrive get you off to a fast start.

- Someone will arrive early, so be ready at least ten minutes before the scheduled start time. Having participants watch you set up detracts from your professionalism.

- When you're all set, stand near the door and greet audience members by name as they enter. Try not to become involved in a lengthy discussion with one person while others are still arriving.

Notice how people are acting. Are they having upbeat conversation, or do they appear to be serious and concerned?

When the meeting begins, you'll be challenged to get their attention away from whatever they're preoccupied with. Observation will allow you to gauge how easy or difficult that will be.

You can also take some steps to help them defuse or let go of the situation they have just left. Ask how their day is going and give them the opportunity to share, if they want to, how they are feeling right now. Even if they say the perfunctory "Fine," you have connected with them. They know you are interested and you have started their focus shift from where they were to your meeting.

If they open up to your initial greeting, consider asking them if they have any special interests or needs for your meeting. In many cases, they will not have any needs. In the cases where they do, you are alerted and can be sure to address the need. If you've done your prep work, it should already be covered in your presentation or in your backup materials. You can alert the appropriate team member to the need and then be proactive when the time comes. Managers usually respond very positively to this effort.

Let the Meeting Begin

Your big moment has arrived. Get off to a positive start by following a few simple steps:

- Start on time, finish on time, and stick to the agenda. It says a lot about your seriousness and your respect for people's time. If you have to start late, it should not be because of your actions. Even if the entire audience is not present, wait no more than a few minutes before you begin. If you start late, do all you can to still end on time, and tell your audience of your intent. They will be thankful. Consideration for staying within the stated time is critical; be sure you have enough time for both the presentation and the question and answer period. If others want to stay and discuss the idea further, they can feel free without creating a time crunch for the others in the room that need to leave.

- Stand up straight and make eye contact with the audience. Speak in a strong, confident voice. Be sure to make strong but comfortable eye contact with the decision maker. Comfortable eye contact lasts for approximately 3–5 seconds. Less than that makes people think you are unsure and lacking in confidence; more than that becomes uncomfortable.

■ Welcome everyone and thank them for being involved. Set a positive tone. You can also share your enthusiasm and gratitude for the opportunity to share the proposal with them.

■ Introduce yourself and your copresenters. Be sure to recognize all idea-team members that may be present but not participating. Having cross-functional representation visible from all the key areas is impressive to management. It truly conveys a team effort and support base. Be sure to introduce any data or subject-matter experts that will be on hand to answer any questions. While they may not be listed as primary presenters, as we saw earlier, they may become temporary presenters when you need to answer some questions.

■ Recognize any people in the audience who have contributed to the effort. This will let the decision maker know that you have a broad base of support and can defuse objections before the fact. If you have prior agreements to the accuracy of certain segments, like the consumer research director's agreement to the research findings you will report, now is a good time to share this with your audience. It shows the audience the amount of pre-work you have done and that what they are about to see is a professional effort.

■ Begin your presentation enthusiastically. The first two minutes will determine the impression your audience will have of you throughout the remainder of your presentation. In addition, your first sentence is your most important and should capture their attention. Sustain your energy level throughout. Again, you have already analyzed the style that best fits your strengths and the needs of the key people in the audience. Now is the time to use this preparation.

■ Maintain good eye contact with the audience, looking directly at individuals for several seconds. In some business cultures, the presentation is often made directly to the decision maker. For example, if the chairman of the board is the decision maker, it may be appropriate to have the presentation be a conversation between her and you. In other cultures, this may make the decision maker feel uncomfortable and the key influencers in the meeting may feel left out. We suggest that you make comfortable eye contact with each of the audience members; they are each there for a reason and should feel included and involved.

■ When appropriate, use names from the organization (people, departments, etc.) that contributed in certain phases. Always address audience members by their names when responding to a question or a comment.

Public relations expert Jerry Daly says there are two keys to a successful presentation: "Believe passionately in what you're doing and always tell the truth." This spirit will serve you well throughout your presentation.

If You Go Blank

Every presenter's nightmare is that he will suddenly go blank. That's unlikely. You know your subject inside out, and you can talk about it intelligently with anyone. On the off chance it does happen, what should you do?

Remain calm. Take a sip of water and glance at your notes. Take a deep breath and release the tension you feel.

Remember that although time seems to be standing still for you, it isn't for your audience. What may seem like an eternity to you will go unnoticed by anyone else. Take a moment to refocus. Use your visuals to remind you where you were.

If you have copresenters or teammates in the room, they should notice the silence and be prepared to jump in with a comment that will cue you. Or, if you're still blank, say aloud, "Where was I?" and someone in the audience will come to your aid.

When to Talk, When to Listen

Selling is not about talking. Selling is about identifying your audience's needs so you can give them a solution.

In the case of a management presentation, if you've done your homework, a strong foundation of support has been built and hopefully the plan is already all but sold. This forum is mainly an opportunity to present an overview and to hear concerns and respond to them. When you have this attitude, it helps your confidence for the presentation. Watch out that the attitude does not block your ability to see new and better ways of doing what you want to do.

American industrialist Henry Kaiser said, "When your work speaks for itself, don't interrupt" (Charlton, 1993). Good advice. Nervousness and silence are two things that drive a speaker to talk more. Resist the urge to add to your script by reiterating points.

This insight also supports the preparation you have already done. You are presenting only the information necessary for your audience to make a decision. By this time, you have successfully resisted the urge to share all you know with your audience.

If someone expresses a concern or objection, listen carefully to what he says. This is a gift: You're better off knowing what obstacles stand in your way. As we have mentioned a couple of times, this gift may actually make for a stronger idea which will capture the enthusiastic support of the decision maker. If one of the key managers in your audience can address the concern in a positive light, ask her to do so. You know who your supporters are and, most likely, the same concerns that arise during your presentation are the very ones that arose earlier by someone else. Even if you know the answer, sometimes it is more effective to have one of her peers respond and let her know this peer was involved in flushing out the concern in the past.

The worst thing that can happen is that someone has objections and doesn't express them; you have no opportunity to resolve the issue before implementation. Silence leaves the door open for sabotage during implementation.

When discussion ensues, don't assume you must always counter any objection. If you have supporters in the group, let them argue with a naysayer. Sometimes silence can be a powerful weapon; take a few moments to formulate your rebuttals. Since most people can't tolerate silence, someone may jump in!

When you engage in conversation, follow one of Stephen Covey's seven habits—first seek to understand and then to be understood. Also, remember another of his habits—seek win-win solutions. When these two principles guide you, objections and comments become your friends.

Management guru Peter Drucker (Crainer, 1998) says, "The most important thing in communication is to hear what isn't being said." Learn to read between the lines. Understand that objections often don't mean what you think they mean. When an adversary says, "This plan will never work," that may mean, "I'm not in the limelight," or "That's going to create too much work for my department." Try to imagine in advance what people's concerns may be, and interpret what they say in light of their circumstances.

Don't get so caught up in your presentation that you lose sight of what you are trying to accomplish and the key positioning statements you need to make. Be careful not to get defensive and start going into too much detail about the *whys* behind certain concerns. Verbosity and defensiveness will only serve to lose your audience.

Read Your Audience

Jerry Daly recalled a nightmare when he was making a presentation to a senior management group. He was new to the division, and he barely knew any of the meeting participants. Jerry, the ultimate salesman, was eloquently making a case for a new publication. Just after Jerry unveiled the proposed name, one of the two key decision makers, Ned, rolled his eyes and shook his head. Unflappable, Jerry delivered the rest of the case despite the executive's continuing to look at the ceiling and make all manner of faces. After a painful thirty-minute presentation, management said, "We'll get back to you."

Jerry left the meeting convinced of his failure. The next day he called one ally to say how terrible he felt about the clearly ill-directed proposal. "Oh, no, you've got it all wrong," said his friend. "They loved it. Ned had lost a contact, and even though he was in terrible pain he wanted to hear what you had to say. After the meeting, he went straight to the doctor."

No matter what the audience does, keep your cool. If they react very differently than you expect, just go with the flow. If you face a situation like the one Jerry faced, consider your options. You can proceed as he did or you can deal with nonverbal feedback as if it were verbal. The latter has risks, but if handled correctly, it will bring a better result.

I am sure Jerry expected that the suggested name could be controversial. He could have said with a smile, "Not surprisingly, we seem to have some feedback on the suggested title. Can you share your thoughts?"

You are being sensitive to your audience and inviting them to share. Since the suggested name is an important part of any recommendation, the decision maker would expect and even welcome the opportunity to discuss it.

Some may think it takes guts to invite apparently negative feedback. Maybe. But ignoring what may be important feedback has its own risks, the biggest of these being that you miss your opportunity to understand and address the potential concerns of the decision maker.

It's not unusual for someone who supported you in the planning stage to change direction in a management meeting. He's in front of his boss now, and he has things to gain . . . or lose. More than one vice president known for outspoken opinions has become reserved and nonconfrontational in the president's staff meeting. Why? One told us, "I don't rock the boat anymore. I have a wife and kids to support."

When you have a supporter go silent or change his mind, your reaction is more important than his change of heart. Putting him on the spot by reminding him in front of others of his prior support is a high-risk path, both short- and long-term. If you want to address his change of heart at all, do it following the meeting in a one-on-one environment.

The best path is to treat his attitude as if you had no other expectations, and address the substance of his comments. You may even use, without attribution, some of the positive points the same person mentioned when he told you he supported your idea.

At any meeting there's always more going on than meets the eye. Brenda's vacation is coming up tomorrow, Bill's child is sick, George is worried about getting his bonus, Jack and Audrey are feuding over control of a project. People are preoccupied with their personal situations and their current business crisis or challenge. It can be a struggle to keep the cart in the middle of the road. Pay close attention and, above all, don't take anything personally.

Until you learn to read people's minds, you'll never really know what's going on. In the interim, become skilled at reading nonverbal communication. Facial expressions are especially helpful. Often a puzzled look is an invitation to clarify. Take the opportunity to ask, "Are there any questions at this point?" or "How can I help clarify this?" Remember, one of the advantages of not memorizing or reading a script is the opportunity to focus on your audience and their reactions.

What do you do if an important person nods off? It is not easy in many cases. You do not want to embarrass the person. Some things you can consider:

- Pause and ask for questions—The change of pace may be enough to jar the sleeper. Also, if someone does ask a question, a different voice could have the same effect.

- Take a break—In long meetings with lights dimmed for a projector, it can be easy to fall asleep. Take a five-minute break and let everyone freshen up. If time is tight, make sure to share the importance of reconvening in the stated time period.

- Preventive medicine—Make sure you have a cool room. A warm room is conducive to sleep. If the room and outside conditions permit, open windows and let a breeze into the room. Sunlight also tends to discourage sleeping.

- Change the subject—You may want to move up the introduction of a prop. If you have something to pass around the room, it can awaken most people. If you do not have a prop, consider changing your speaking style. You can raise your voice or pick up the pace.

Who to Focus On?

Include everyone in your presentation, either literally or figuratively. That means, at minimum, making eye contact with every person throughout the session.

When one person is clearly interested in what you're saying, and is, perhaps, even nodding in agreement, it's easy to begin leaning toward that person. After all, she shares your enthusiasm, and you hope to build a swell of support. Careful. You can alienate people by ignoring them. Not only that, but you may be losing a necessary selling opportunity. You don't need to sell the ones who are already nodding in agreement; you need to sell the ones who aren't.

Those whose nonverbal communication suggests a lack of interest or outright opposition need special attention. Build a bridge to them. At appropriate times, consider directly inviting them to comment, "Jack, it seems like you might have a question. Anything I can do to help you?" Tactically, if you invite their comments before they feel totally ready, you may receive a milder version of their opposition. Your friendly, reaching-out gesture also helps create a more positive and constructive atmosphere.

Taking Notes

Although it would seem easiest to keep track of people's concerns by recording the meeting, some people are sensitive to having their every word on tape. Instead, you need someone to sit in an out-of-the-way place and take notes. This person should first, of course, be a good note-taker, someone who can write fast and neatly, and who will be able to translate the notes after the meeting.

In most cases, do not use a computer to take notes: The clicking of the keys will be distracting and irritating to the audience. However, if a person is off to the side where he will not be a distraction, the computer can be an option. It can facilitate the production of an especially quick meeting summary when comments and agreements can be directly entered in the proper format. Later editing can polish the note.

Assign someone who is familiar with your presentation and the underlying issues. Sometimes interpretation is necessary, and unless your scribe knows the score, it will be impossible to take brief notes that are comprehensive and understandable.

The note-taker should indicate who made each comment so you will have a record of concerns, as well as who was supportive and who was not.

If a point is particularly important, or if it's made by a person of special importance, you might choose to make a note yourself, just to demonstrate how seriously you've taken the comment.

In some meetings, before you adjourn, consider recapping what has been agreed to. The notes should guide this process. Do not be surprised if the preliminary agreements are revised during the review process. This is a good sign since you are gaining clarity on the most important part of the meeting—the agreements. The end-of-meeting review is an additional sign of a professional meeting.

When the notes are typed up, distribute a follow-up document as soon as possible, preferably within forty-eight hours, answering all questions and concerns.

Dealing with Interruptions

Most interruptions are questions—requests for more information or to clarify already presented information. You have two major options to deal with them.

If someone interrupts with a question you plan to answer later, you can acknowledge that it's a good question and say that you'll be covering that later in the presentation. This approach helps you to maintain the flow of the presentation. It is especially helpful if you are in the middle of making one of the more important points.

When you delay your answer, be sure to commit to a time when you will address their concerns. Keep that commitment when you make it. When you come to the place in the presentation where you address it, refer to their point, "Mary, you wanted to know more about _____. As you can see on this slide, . . ."

The other option you have is to address the point at the time it is made. We have already discussed some of the advantages of this approach. If a person feels strongly enough to make a request or ask a question, he will feel best if there is an immediate response. In most cases, people do not like being put off.

Should you answer a question when you are in the middle of making a very important point? Yes, in most cases, especially if it is from a major player in the decision-making process.

You are unlikely to make your important point successfully if an important decision maker does not agree with or is not clear about what you have already said. When this happens, recognize that others in the audience may share the same concern.

Step back and pause. First, make sure you understand the question. People do not like it when someone spends time responding to the wrong question or request. The best way of ensuring you understand a question is to restate it: "You want to know _____," or "You are concerned about _____."

Second, respond in the simplest, most direct manner. As you have done in your presentation, resist the urge to respond with all the information you have on the subject. If your expert on the team has the necessary data, let her help you. Look for opportunities to visualize the response with a hand-generated chart or table.

Third, check to see if you have met the needs of the person who asked the question. If you have not, you may have misunderstood his request, either because he was ambiguous or you misinterpreted his question. If you have addressed his concern sufficiently, it is time to move on.

Soliciting Questions

If you can, you should control when questions are asked and how they're answered. When you're asking for questions, look directly at the audience—not at your notes.

Sometimes when you ask for questions you face dead silence. If no one has a question, try sharing previous feedback you've had and ask if the audience agrees or disagrees with it. Or, if you're in a relatively large group, you can "plant" key questions with cooperative coworkers.

The Interpersonal Dynamics of Responding to Questions

Listen carefully to each question. Do not interrupt the person asking. Even though you think you can anticipate the rest of the question, you could be wrong.

If you're in a large room, one with two rows or more, or where the audience is spread out, repeat the question for the benefit of other audience members. That's because when people speak directly ahead, those sitting behind them may not hear the remarks. (This will also buy you time to formulate an answer!)

Maintain eye contact with the person asking the question. When you begin to answer, address the person by name, and then look around at the audience. Check back with that person to make sure you've given a satisfactory answer.

Never make a joke of the question or embarrass anyone in any way. Such disrespect reflects negatively on you and will certainly come back to haunt you later. You need everyone's support when you arrive at the implementation phase.

Most presenters fear the moment when someone asks a question they can't answer. It's true, we try to anticipate every possible question so we can be prepared with an answer. If the worst happens, though, don't worry. Maintain your composure and confidence. You will find that most tough questions come from your pre-thought out toughest questions list or are variations of them. Once you recognize this, your confidence should stabilize.

Trying to cover up a lack of information is fruitless, and won't gain you management's respect. Don't try to fake it; it will show. Good decision makers almost have a sixth sense for someone who does not have the answer and is trying to bluff his way out.

If you don't know the answer, but one of your team members does, refer the question to her. For example, "Beth is our expert in that area. She'll explain." In areas where you don't feel confident, agree in advance with your team members that they'll jump in if certain questions are asked.

There may be a time when no one on your team can respond. Answer truthfully (and tactfully, of course), acknowledging that it's a good question, one you don't have the specific answer to, and say you'll get the answer. Jot a note to show you're serious. And consider the executive's point of view: Ken Glass says, "I don't expect people to know everything, because it's my job to find the holes in a plan. I do expect people to be honest and just say they'll find out the answer right away."

Keep your responses short and simple, especially if you're unsure of yourself.

In general, it's best to avoid long discussions with one person. If a Q&A session deteriorates into a one-on-one discussion that's getting far afield, tell the person you'd like to explore it in depth and ask him if you can do that over lunch after the meeting. Or, tell him you'll call him to set up a meeting.

When someone asks a question that's already been answered, don't draw attention to the redundancy. Saying you've already covered it is an insult to the questioner, and a put-off to your audience. Just restate the question and answer it simply.

Be Prepared to Negotiate

Save some energy for this important phase of the selling process. This is the stage where you'll either solidify alliances or alienate people and lose the chance for their support during the critically important implementation process.

People like to give input, and they like to win. There's a good chance that no matter how good a salesperson you are you won't get everything you want. Know that on the front end, and decide in advance what points are negotiable. Develop acceptable alternatives so you can gracefully yield on some noncritical points. Your ability to "see things objectively" and your willingness to concede will earn you friends and supporters.

This is the time you may have to think on your feet. If new concerns have surfaced during your presentation, or a previous supporter has been swayed and jumped ship, you'll have to think fast to get issues resolved so that you can move ahead with approval.

There are many good books and seminars available for teaching people how to negotiate. There are several ways of describing the process, but in all of this, there is more commonality than differences.

One way of guiding your negotiations is by using some of Covey's seven habits of highly effective people. Here are some of those habits and how they relate to negotiating:

- Be proactive—You have already done this in your preparation. You have backup material organized and ready to be presented. You have thought of the toughest questions you can be asked and you are ready with your answers. When you negotiate, be forthcoming with information that you think meets the needs. Make it easy for the decision makers to agree. Your thorough idea development should speak for itself, but don't sound locked into only one view. Know what you can sacrifice or delay if necessary without hurting the integrity of the project.

- Begin with the end in mind—When you negotiate, start by being clear about where you want to end up. When you are clear in your own mind, come to agreement with the decision maker about where you want to be. This is a very important point. Often what seems like disagreement is only differences over how to get to the same place. When everyone agrees on where you want to be, your negotiations have taken a big step forward.

- Put first things first—Agree on what is most important and stay focused on that. It is so easy to spend enormous amounts of time on trivial matters in negotiations. Apparent differences over trivial matters have the ability to sour discussions on what is important.

- Think win-win—Most people like to win and think that if they win then someone else has to lose. This does not have to be the case, especially in a corporate setting, although the win-lose view of negotiations is still strongly held by many people. We discussed win-win earlier, and noted the necessary attitude for it to work. First, recognize that win-win is both possible and desirable. If you do not cross this bridge, you are stuck in win-lose. Second, understand what everyone wants and explore the points you agree on. The remaining points usually are not mutually exclusive and often can be accommodated in a final solution. Some decision makers find a win-win approach so refreshing and nonthreatening that when they clearly see their suggested solution, they back off and accept your ideas. The reverse also occurs.

  A last note, win-win is not compromise in disguise. In compromising, each party often gives something up. In win-win, both parties often get exactly what they want.

- Seek first to understand, and then to be understood—You cannot negotiate a win-win solution if you do not understand the other person's views. When we do not understand, we tend to talk *at* another person, hoping to wear him down. When we understand, new insights and solutions emerge. The path to agreement is easy, not difficult.

- Synergize—Now that you understand and desire a win-win solution, you can mix and blend thoughts and information in creative ways. Differences become friends and giant steps forward result from your negotiations.

G. Richard Shell, in his book *Bargaining for Advantage* (1999), says effective negotiation is "10 percent technique and 90 percent attitude." Incorporating the traits highlighted above and throughout this book will help you to achieve the right attitude.

Handling Difficult Persons

It is very likely—in fact, it's almost a certainty—that someone in your audience will not support your position, or will attempt to use this forum to make himself look good. Since you've done your homework, you've undoubtedly anticipated potential problems and have done your best to pre-answer the concerns within your presentation. Nevertheless, be prepared for someone to throw you a curve.

This is the time to call upon your acting ability. No matter how intense the situation becomes, never lose your cool. Don't show anger or appear frustrated. Remember, there may be other sources contributing to this person's conflict. If your idea is competing for resources, as all new projects do, someone may be threatened that he will not get the budget dollars he needs, or may in fact have to cut his budget to help support yours. As we mentioned in Chapter 5, many people equate budget dollars and personnel with power; will they be negatively affected in any way? Alternatively, perhaps someone didn't get that recent promotion or raise she was expecting, and here you are coming across as the new rising star. Fear, jealousy, insecurity. . . all human traits that bring out the worst in a person. Unfortunately, the difficult person is the one who will lose face with the other audience members, not you. Keep your cool and save face. Be gracious and understanding without trying to address his concerns unless they truly are viable.

Here are some possible methods people will use to exhibit their resistance:

- Hostility, sarcasm, attacking details, finding fault with even small points
- Showing off, asking tough questions to put you on the spot and show how smart they are
- Passivity, silence, arms folded, not paying attention, talking to another participant, not looking you in the eye

Given a moment or two, a senior person may come to your rescue, so don't be too quick to answer. Hesitate for just a moment to allow someone else to comment. Remember, although you're the messenger, there are others in the room who believe in your idea, and who are ultimately responsible for saying yea or nay. If you've sold your idea well, you should have some people on your side who are in more powerful positions than you are, and who can take on a person of equal stature.

If no one comes forth, take your time answering. Never be defensive. Confident people don't have to defend themselves. Be empathetic, accept comments, and acknowledge this person's point of view. You can understand without agreeing. Calmly respond in one of the following ways:

- "Thanks for bringing that up. This is a good time to mention what we've done to deal with that issue," then deliver your rebuttal information.

- "You're probably in a better position to judge that; what do you think?" Compliments never hurt! And turning it back around on them often puts them in a position of creating an alternative solution, not just a complaint.

- "Thanks for mentioning that. I don't have an answer right now, but I'll get back with you within 48 hours." "Why don't we discuss this more after the meeting?"

- "We seem to have a difference of opinion here, and I'd rather not take up everyone's time since we're on a limited schedule. Let me catch you after the meeting."

- "What's your experience with that?" "What's your perspective?" "What would you do?" "What factors do you believe are important?" Turn the tables and the person will have to expose her hand or, you hope, her lack of substantive information. It buys you time to formulate an answer.

If you suspect someone of having malicious intent, do not engage in a discussion with those rules. This is as close to a lose-lose situation that there is in a meeting.

Remember the negotiation suggestions we made. Keep your eye on the ball. It is not your purpose to win personal engagements.

Your job is to facilitate the group, led by the decision maker, to make the right decision on your recommendation.

Some people will try to force you into a "yes" or "no" response, or to make you choose between two bad possibilities. Try to offer other, more desirable solutions, or steer the discussion to a broader issue.

Sometimes a person will ask a "factoid" question; something that will generate discussion and allow him to gauge the temper of the audience without committing to a position. Be aware that this is a technique. Reading how others respond to the question is more important than how you respond.

This is where your factual expert can help. While she is answering the question, you are free to read the audience. Use this opportunity to make the midcourse decisions needed to gain agreement.

In the Event of a Slipup

Some years ago, a female sales rep was working for a company that made trade show displays. During a sales call on a group of executives, she began to demonstrate the ease of changing out elements on the display. As she reached up, her half-slip suddenly slid down around her ankles. Without batting an eye, she paused briefly, stepped out of the slip, gathered it up, stuck it in her briefcase, and continued with the pitch.

When you make enough presentations eventually something will go wrong. Don't get flustered; it happens to everyone. Like our sales rep, you may be able to move smoothly along without even acknowledging the problem.

When panic sets in, use the techniques suggested to overcome stage fright. Take a few deep breaths and release your fear. Fear is the biggest crippling force there is. It can paralyze you. Let it go.

Buying Signals

Carol Coletta reminded us of a simple selling rule: When someone's ready to buy, don't take them backwards.

She recounted a particularly painful sales call. "A guy insisted on taking me through 'his' presentation. His focus was on completing what was on his flip chart versus what information would meet my needs. I appreciate when someone is prepared, but they should also read when it's important to speed up, slow down, or adapt the presentation to make it fit me."

Watch for buying signals and stop selling. When the decision maker is ready to give you the seal of approval, take it and leave. Move on to the implementation phase.

Some signs that the decision maker has bought your recommendation before you reach your close are:

- "I think I have heard enough"—Of course, this can go both ways. He has heard enough and the answer is "no" or "yes." When you hear this phrase, you should have some inclination about which direction he is going in. Previous comments and nonverbal feedback are your best indicators.

- Glowing comments—If in the early and middle parts of the presentation, the decision maker's comments are very positive, even indicating that he supports it, then it is time for a trial close. For example, "It appears that there is strong support for the idea, should we move to implementation next steps now? Or do you want me to complete the last two sections which will take about another twenty minutes?"

- Implementation questions—Often when a decision maker starts asking questions about how the idea will be executed, it is an indication that he is supportive. You do not want to move to a trial close unless it is accompanied by other positive comments.

- "Where do I sign?"—The overt indication that the decision maker agrees should receive an immediate response. "Great! Thank you," is a good first response. And like we saw above, do not continue the presentation. Instead, move directly to next steps, often in summary form.

The other time you need to look for buying signs is at the close of the meeting when you ask for agreement. After you have asked for agreement, it is time to stop talking and listen. This can be very difficult when you have become so accustomed to talking.

Listen for buying signs. When it is time for you to talk again, build on and reinforce those positives. If there are objections and it is appropriate to negotiate, then use the skills outlined above.

In many cases, the end of the meeting is when a decision can go either way. You need to be calm. You have gotten this far. Now is not the time to lose your cool and, consequently, the sale.

Listen for both true and false objections. Verify what you think you are hearing—seek first to understand and then to be understood. Outstanding listening skills are necessary for success in situations that are a close call.

Not many great presenters are also great listeners. And if they are, it is a challenge to make the sharp change from presenting to listening. Despite this difficulty, if you follow the negotiation suggestions you will be come to the right decision most of the time.

Time's Up: Now What?

Keep an eye on your time, and control the discussion so that you can complete your business and end on time. You'll need a few minutes at the end of the session to wrap up details and be prepared to move to implementation.

If you find yourself running late, make immediate adjustments to get back on track. Know from your practices where you can speed up and where you cannot. Often if there are three points on a page, you can say to your audience, "As you can see there are three reasons this is right. The most important is number one." You then cover number one and let your audience read numbers two and three. This often can cut in half the time necessary to cover a page.

Before you leave the meeting you should state the final results in a positive, confident, upbeat voice:

1. Recap any unfinished business that you'll address after the meeting.
2. Outline the next steps you've identified as a result of the discussion.

3. Get agreement on timelines, budget, responsibilities, and accountabilities.
4. Assign an implementation leader and possible team members.
5. Develop implementation timelines for three, six, twelve months, and beyond.
6. Suggest when you will present additional information or a progress report to the senior team member.
7. Let your audience know when they will receive the meeting summary.
8. Make eye contact with each audience member and thank him or her for contributing the necessary time, energy, effort, and support this project required.

Exit your presentation with your head held high and a confident look on your face. Position yourself close to the exit door so that you can shake people's hand and thank them for their valuable input and time. When everyone has left the room, give your team an extra special thanks for all their hard work. This would be an excellent time to celebrate over lunch or dinner. Know that you have just succeeded in making a difference in the world in which you work. The ripple effect from your idea will not only benefit the bottom line, but will permeate the lives of each of your company's stakeholders: employees, customers, shareholders, and suppliers.

Isn't it amazing what one little idea can do?

Key Learning Points

1. Know what mental and physical conditions enable you to do your best work. Do all of this before your presentation. Your goal is to be in peak physical and mental condition for the meeting.
2. Get to the meeting room early and double check everything. Greet people as they arrive and establish a positive, upbeat tone from the very beginning of the meeting.
3. Be ready to start on time, connect with your audience, and be enthusiastic.
4. Become adept at reading your audience, especially nonverbal

feedback, and use it to make midcourse adjustments to your presentation.

5. Focus on both the substance of the questions and the interpersonal dynamics when responding to them. Doing only one of these will usually produce more questions and problems.

6. When negotiating in a meeting keep Covey's principles of highly effective people in mind. They lead you to the path of least resistance and win-win solutions.

7. Be prepared for the decision maker to agree at any time. When she is ready to agree, move on to implementation. Become adept at reading early agreement signs.

8. Once you have agreement, assign next steps including timelines and accountabilities.

9. Pat yourself and your team on the back for a job well done!

Bibliography

Bank, David, and Don Clark. "Microsoft Broadens Vision Statement Beyond PCs." *Wall Street Journal*, 23 July 1999, sec. A, pp. 3, 5.

Bartlett, John. *Bartlett's Familiar Quotations.* Edited by Justin Kaplan. New York: Little Brown & Company, 1992.

Bennis, Warren, and Burt Nanus. *Leaders: Strategies for Taking Charge.* 2nd. ed. New York: Harper Business, 1997.

Bolander, Donald O., et al. *Instant Quotation Dictionary.* New York: Dell Publishing, 1990.

Boone, Louis E. *Quotable Business.* New York: Random House, 1992.

Boress, Allan S. *The "I Hate Selling" Book.* New York: AMACOM, 1995.

Bygrave, William D., ed. *The Portable MBA in Entrepreneurship.* 2nd. ed. New York: John Wiley & Sons, 1997.

Charan, Ram, and Noel M. Tichy. *Every Business Is a Growth Business: How Your Company Can Prosper Year After Year.* New York: Times Business Books, 1998.

Charlton, James, ed. *The Executive's Quotation Book.* New York: St. Martin's Press, 1993.

Covey, Stephen R. *The 7 Habits of Highly Successful People.* New York: Simon & Schuster, 1990.

Crainer, Stuart. *The Ultimate Book of Business Quotations.* New York: AMACOM, 1998.

Drucker, Peter. "The Discipline of Innovation." *Harvard Business Review* (May–June 1985): 67.

"Forbes 500." *Forbes Magazine* (April 1999): 256.

"Fortune 500." *Fortune Magazine* (April 1999).

Gabarro, John J., and John P. Kotter. "Managing Your Boss." *Harvard Business Review* (May–June, 1993): 150–157.

Gouldner, Alvin W. "The Norm of Reciprocity: A Preliminary Statement." *American Sociological Review* 25, no. 2 (April 1960): 161–178. Excerpt from G. Richard Shell, *Bargaining for Advantage: Negotiation Strategies for Reasonable People,* New York: Viking Press, 1999, 58–59.

Gray, John. *Men Are From Mars, Women Are From Venus.* New York: HarperCollins, 1992.

Hay, Peter. *The Book of Business Anecdotes.* New York: Facts on File, 1988.

"How Big Companies Grow." *Harvard Management Update* 4, no. 5 (May 1999): 1–3.

Kanter, Rosabeth Moss, John Kao, and Fred Wiersema. *Innovation.* New York: Harper Business, 1997.

Leslie, Joan Brittain, and Ellen Van Velsor. "A Look at Derailment Today: North America and Europe." Greensboro, NC: Center for Creative Leadership, 1996.

Peoples, David A. *Presentations Plus.* 2nd ed. New York: John Wiley & Sons, 1992.

Peter, Laurence J., and Raymond Hull. *The Peter Principle.* Cutchogue, NY: Buccaneer Books, 1996.

Peters, Tom. Foreword to *Innovation* by Rosabeth Moss Kanter, John Kao, and Fred Wiersema. New York: Harper Business, 1997.

Peters, Tom. "The Wow Project." *Fast Company* (May 1999): 118–128.

Reader's Digest. New York: Reader's Digest (July 1961).

Roth, K. Madsen, ed. *Hollywood Wits.* New York: Avon Books, 1995.

Shell, G. Richard. *Bargaining for Advantage: Negotiation Strategies for Reasonable People.* New York: Viking Press, 1999.

Treacy, Michael, and Fred Wiersema. *The Discipline of Market Leaders.* 2nd. ed. New York: Perseus Books, 1997.

"20 Years: The Entrepreneurial Decades." *Inc. Magazine* 21, no.7 (20th Anniversary Issue, 1999): 159–174.

"U.S. Housing Boom Taking Its Toll of Building Supplies." *The Palm Beach Post,* 23 March 1999.

Wilder, Claudyne. *The Presentations Kit: 10 Steps for Selling Your Ideas.* New York: John Wiley & Sons, 1994.

Glossary

accounts payable. Amounts owed to suppliers for purchases on credit.

accounts payable turnover. The rate at which accounts payable during a certain period were paid. Calculated as purchases during that period divided by accounts payable at the end of that period.

accounts receivables. Money yet to be received for goods sold on credit.

accounts receivable turnover. The rate at which accounts receivables are collected during a certain period. Calculated as credit sales divided by average accounts receivables for the period.

accrual. Recognition of revenue or expenses when incurred regardless of when cash is actually received or disbursed.

activity ratios. Internal ratios that measure various income and expense items relative to total revenue.

advocate. A well-positioned, influential senior manager who supports and promotes your idea amongst key decision makers in the company.

alliances. Strategic arrangements or agreement between firms for the sharing of some part of each business.

allies. Enthusiastic supporters from across the organization, who are highly respected by senior management, that contribute their expertise and insights in the development and selling of your idea.

annual report. A report to stockholders from management, including various financial statements describing the health of the company as well as the auditor's report.

appreciation. The increase in market value of an asset over time.

asset. Something of value that a company owns. May be tangible (machinery, equipment) or intangible (goodwill, customers). Reflected on the Balance Sheet.

audit trail. A history and financial record of a particular transaction.

balance sheet. A snapshot of a company's financial position at the end of an accounting period. Lists assets (what is owned), liabilities (what is owed) and net worth (assets - liabilities).

bar charts. A type of chart using horizontal and vertical bars to plot some measure against two sets of values. For example, sales by month.

basis for interest document. A one to three page preliminary document that outlines the parameters of your idea that essentially asks management, " If we could do this would you be interested?"

board of directors. Officials elected by stockholders as ruling body of a corporation. Responsible for appointing the chief officers (CEO, President) of the company and setting policy.

brand identity. The major characteristics consumers associate with a brand. They can be feelings or tangible performance benefits.

brand loyalty. A measure of what percentage of consumers buy a particular brand. The alternative is people who buy two or more brands to meet their needs for a type of product.

breadth. The number of concepts or ideas shared with consumers during market research.

break-even point. The volume level where the total costs per unit equal the selling price per unit.

budget. A formal statement of expectations regarding sales, expenses and other financial transactions to help in financial planning.

business life cycle. The stages of development during the life of a business enterprise, from start-up, growth, stabilization to renewed innovation or decline.

business plan. A written document detailing a proposed new venture or innovation.

capital. The total funds available to a firm from all sources, debt and equity.

cash flow statement. A financial statement that reflects the amount of cash coming in and going out of a company.

cash ratio. Used to measure liquidity and is the cash available to cover short term debt. Calculated as cash & liquid assets/current liabilities.

champion. A highly credible, respected member of the senior management team who supports your idea by assisting in the selling of the idea to other executives and key decision makers.

clip art. Cartoon and realistic images available on your computer software which can be added into any presentation to add interest. Keep images to one per visual frame.

compounding. The process of adding the interest on a sum back to the principal during a period. Thus, interest in the next period is based on the principal plus interest accumulated.

computer-based presentation. Microsoft PowerPoint or similar computerized presentation software that is flexible to change, easy to prepare, and highly professional in appearance. The only downside is if electric power is lost, it is difficult to find your place again once resumed.

consumer research. Either quantitative or qualitative research done to determine consumer feelings, habits, and evaluation of elements related to usage of a consumer product.

cost-benefit analysis. A numeric comparison of the benefit and related cost of a project.

cost of goods sold. The direct cost specifically associated with producing the items sold during a specified time period.

cross-functional teams. A team consisting of members from across the organization, such as marketing, finance, legal, operations, human resources, manufacturing, etc. Such representation offers varying skills, talents, and perceptions that provide a much bigger picture and input into a project.

current ratio.   Used to measure liquidity or how well a company can pay its bills. Calculated as Total current assets divided by total current liabilities found on the balance sheet.

debt ratios.   Calculations that compare debt relative to size (a measure of leverage) and relative to ability to repay.

debt-to-equity ratios.   The amount of debt relative to stockholder equity. Calculated as total liabilities divided by total equity.

depreciation.   Spreading the cost of a fixed asset (e.g., building or equipment) over its estimated useful life.

discounted cash flow (DCF).   A method of expressing a projected stream of cash flows as a present value.

distribution channels.   The different routes that products and services pass through from production to consumer.

dividend.   Payment distributed to shareholders as his or her share of the profits, usually paid out on a quarterly basis.

dividend yield.   The percent return each year from dividend payouts relative to investment in the stock. Calculated as dividend per share divided by stock price.

due diligence.   The process of gathering and verifying information.

Dun & Bradstreet.   An agency that publishes information on individual companies regarding their credit history, management, product lines, number of employees and any legal proceedings.

earnings.   A company's profit or net income during an accounting period.

earnings per share (EPS).   Earnings per outstanding shares of stock (not the same as how much money you made on the stock you own). Calculated as net income minus preferred stock dividends divided by the number of common stock shares outstanding.

EBIT.   Earnings of the corporation Before deducting Interest and Taxes.

EBITDA. Earnings of the corporation Before Interest, Taxes, Depreciation and Amortization.

economic forecasting. Projections of the future values of various economic variables.

economies of scale. The lowering of costs resulting from the spreading of fixed costs over increased volumes.

employee suggestion systems. A formal process for submitting ideas within a company.

entrepreneur. One who organizes, manages, and assumes the risks of a business or venture.

equity. The value of a company's assets minus its liabilities. Same as net worth.

expenses. Costs reflected on a firm's income statement during an accounting period.

expansion. Growth by increased market share or by entry into new markets.

extension. New use or application of an existing product or service.

federal reserve system/board (The Fed). The central bank of the United States whose customers are the government and commercial banks. Its functions are to help manage the currency through the monetary system (interest rates and money supply), supervise banks, and check clearing.

financial statements. A series of accounting reports designed to paint a picture of the overall financial health and stability of a company.

fixed costs. Costs that do not vary with the volume of business in the short-term such as rent, insurance, mortgage, or executive salaries.

flip charts. A presentation medium that is easy to develop and use, but difficult to transport. Good for informal presentations and small groups.

flow charts. A chart or diagram indicating the movement of an item through a process of different activities.

focus groups. A form of qualitative consumer research intended to determine consumer language and major potential benefits and issues with a marketing idea.

gross profit margin. Used to measure top line profit, i.e., what you charge over what you paid for the cost of producing your product or service (before overhead, selling, and administrative expenses). Calculated as sales minus cost of sales divided by sales as found on the income statement.

growth rate. The average change in percentage terms over some defined period, taking into account the effect of compounding. Stated as an annual rate.

horizontal integration. A growth strategy in which one company buys another company that is similar.

hurdle rate. The minimum rate of return required by a company for a new product or venture.

idea life cycle. Every idea has a life cycle and a point which a decision has to be made whether to continue the idea and evolve in a new direction to stay current or let it die.

idea team. Individuals with key areas of expertise from across the organization who contribute to the research, development, and selling of an idea.

implied internal interest rate. The internal rate of return (IRR). The rate that is calculated to equalize the investment in a project and its future cash flows.

income statement. A financial statement that measures a company's profitability by recording the company's revenues (income from sales) minus its expenses (operating costs, interest, taxes) over a specified period of time. Also known as the Profit and Loss Statement or P&L.

income statement ratios. Each item on the income statement is compared to sales. These are useful in preparing budgets, developing pro formas, and comparing with other firms in the same industry.

innovation. The creation or modification of resources to produce new products or services.

interest coverage. How many times a company can cover its interest obligations out of earnings. Calculated as earnings before interest and taxes divided by interest expense.

interest expense. The amount of interest due and payable on a firm's debt obligation during an accounting period.

interest rate (compound). Interest rates that that are calculated on the original principal amount plus the accumulated interest from prior periods.

interest rate (simple). Interest rates that are calculated on the original principal amount only.

internal rate of return (IRR). See implied internal interest rate.

intrapreneur. Internal innovators who can turn ideas into profitable activities for a company.

invention. The development of a new product, service, or process.

inventory turnover ratio. Used to measure how fast inventory turns. Calculated as cost of goods sold divided by average inventory.

inventory turn-days. The average number of days that inventory is on hand. Calculated as the number of days in period multiplied by (inventory divided by cost of sales).

joint owner. An individual in your company who can share in the development of your idea by bringing complimentary skills and expertise, and who is also highly respected by senior management.

key benefit scores. In market research, the key reasons people buy certain products or services and how your idea scores on these benefits.

LCD panel. A slim panel that sits atop an overhead projector and is hooked up to your computer for computer-based slide shows.

leverage. The amount of debt compared to other measures, such as total assets or equity.

liabilities. What a firm owes.

line graphs. A chart using a line or lines to connect two sets of values measured on the horizontal and vertical axes.

liquidity ratios. The ability of current assets to meet current liabilities when due.

management's discussion and analysis (MD&A). The portion of an annual report that gives management's analysis of results of operation.

market leader. The top firm in an industry determined by sales or innovation.

market ratios. Used to show comparisons against market values.

market share. A firm's revenues or volume in a market compared to the size of that market.

mergers and acquisitions. The combination of two or more companies in which the resulting firms maintain the identity of the acquiring company.

mission statement. A formal statement crafted by a company emphasizing key values in how it wants to do business.

modification. Alteration of some product or service to create something different.

net income. The bottom line of the income statement. The amount of profit resulting from income minus all expenses.

net present value (NPV). Calculation which takes the future value of an investment and recasts it to present value.

net profit margin. The net profit after all costs as percent of sales. Calculated as net income divided by sales.

net worth. The bottom line of the balance sheet (assets minus liabilities). Also known as shareholder equity or book value.

operating expense ratios. Individual expense items as a ratio to total expense.

operating profit margin. Measures profitability after all costs and expenses (except taxes and interest) are subtracted. Calculated as operating income divided by sales as found on the income statement.

opportunity costs. The return given up to invest in one thing instead of investing in another.

organizational charts. A diagram indicating the hierarchical arrangement of reporting relationships and responsibilities for an organization.

overall rating. In research, consumers rate an idea on a five, seven or nine point scale. In a five point scale, the highest rating is the most important. In the other two scales, the two highest ratings are the most important.

overheads. Transparencies used in presentations with an overhead projector. Convenient, inexpensive and easy to use, and are good for more informal presentations.

patent. An intellectual property right that protects the discoverer of a new and unique product or process against duplication or infringement.

payback period. The length of time required to recover the initial investment in the project.

payout ratio. The percent of profit paid out in dividends. Calculated as total common stock dividends divided by net profit.

personal coach. Usually a professionally trained person who helps people get what they want most in life faster and easier than they could achieve it by themselves.

pie charts. A chart in the shape of a circle (pie) used to illustrate percentages as part of a whole, and should contain eight or less "slices."

positioning. A way of delivering information so that the audience receives the message you want them to hear. A benefit the key decision makers and company receive once your idea is implemented.

position statements. These statements outline the known benefits of a product and the basis for expecting consumers to purchase the product.

positive and negative ratios. In market research, the ratio of the things people like to the things they dislike. An important measure of an idea's strength.

pre-testing research. This quantitative or qualitative research determines the risks and benefits a company or product will face before it introduces a product, usually into test market.

price-earnings ratio (p/e multiple). The relationship between the stock price and earnings per share of a company. Calculated as the market price of stock divided by annual earnings per share.

Ex.: If the earnings per share of a company is $1 and the stock price of the company is $10, then the p/e multiple or ratio is 10 (10/1=10).

pricing. The cost of a product to a customer, either end user or distributor/middle person.

profit. The bottom line of the Income Statement, i.e., the same as Net Income. What's left after all expenses are subtracted from income.

profit ratios. Comparisons of different levels of profits to revenues or equity.

pro forma financial statements. A projection of future financial conditions relating to the balance sheet, income statement, and/or cash flow statement. Also used to show the effects on current financial statements when specific items are changed.

pro-rata expense. An expense item that is allocated among different groups or categories.

public companies. A corporation with shares outstanding that are owned by the general public.

public data. Data on a company that is available to the public. Includes published information such as annual reports, Web sites, press releases, etc.

purchase intent. In research, when consumers are asked on a five or seven point scale to indicate their intent to purchase. The highest rating is the most important.

quality enhancement idea. An idea that improves the quality of work life for employees or enhances customer loyalty although it does not generate revenues or cost savings.

qualitative research. Research that gives suggestions of issues and benefits of an idea. The results cannot be used to reliably predict consumer response. This is often done among less than fifty consumers.

quantitative research. Reliable evaluation of what a larger group, e.g., total United States, would feel if all of them were asked. Typically more than 100 consumers are involved, the testing is done by professional organizations, and the results undergo statistical testing.

quick ratio. Used to measure liquidity and is the cash and liquid assets available to cover short-term debt. Calculated as cash, liquid assets, and accounts receivables divided by current liabilities as found on the balance sheet.

ratios. Numerous measures used to gauge the financial health of a firm, as well as how it compares to other companies. Enables analysts to compare companies within and outside their industries.

regulated businesses. Businesses such as banks, insurance companies, and others that fall under the jurisdiction of a governmental agency.

return on assets. Used to measure how well a company is using its assets to make a profit. Calculated as net income divided by total assets.

return on equity. Used to measure how much stockholders earn on their investment. Calculated as net income divided by stockholders' equity.

return on investment. Used to measure how much the subject investment generates in net profit as a percent of investment. Calculated in three ways: a) Net income divided by stockholder equity; b) Net income divided by assets; and c) Net income divided by project assets.

return on sales. Used to measure the profit on each dollar of sales. Calculated as net income divided by sales.

return on revenues. Same as return on sales.

revenue producing ideas. Growth-oriented ideas that contribute to the bottom line of a company by generating revenues.

risk. Exposure to loss.

rough volume estimates. Estimates based on either qualitative or quantitative research and often can have a wide variation between high and low.

sales patterns. Characteristics of daily, weekly, or monthly sales. These are often best viewed on a chart.

sales-to-assets. How well total assets are utilized in generating sales. Calculated as sales divided by total assets.

sample size. Usually associated with quantitative research. It is the number of people needed to make the research statistically representative of a large group.

scope. The extensiveness of marketing research.

securities and exchange commission (SEC). The primary regulatory body for security offerings in the United States.

SEC Reports. Reports that public companies are required to make to the Securities and Exchange Commission.

service data. This data represents both company data, e.g., order fill rates, and customer satisfaction with a company's service.

service improvements. These are usually improvements taken in response to consumer problems.

shareholders. Owners of a company.

silo or bunker culture. A characteristic of a company that keeps its functional units, like marketing and accounting, separate and often competitive. In this culture there is little sharing and trust between functions.

slides. 35mm slides are effective presentation tools, but are becoming less used with computer-based presentation abilities. While the quality is very good, they tend to be more costly, less flexible if change is required, and logistically difficult.

sources of funding. Avenues for raising capital such as initial public offerings (IPOs), debt, bonds, and venture capital.

spreadsheets. A table of figures used for making financial and accounting calculations.

stakeholders. All constituencies who have a vested interest (or staked claim) in a business. Includes shareholders, employees, customers, communities.

start-up venture. A newly created business.

status quo. To remain in a constant state; change resistant.

stockholder's equity. Same as net worth (assets - liabilities) and is reflected on the balance sheet.

stockholders. Same as shareholders.

stocks. Shares issued by a company to raise money for expansion, etc.

subgroup evaluation. In consumer research, this is an analysis of groups within the total research, like heavy versus light users of a product.

subject matter expert. A specialist or technical expert in their professional field.

synergy. The benefit of combining resources so that the output is greater than the individual resources could do individually.

threshold rate. See hurdle rate.

time value of money. The changing value of money from one time period to another which results from the interest rate applied against the principle.

total debt ratios. A leverage ratio that measures the amount of debt used in relation to assets or stockholder's equity. Calculated as total debt divided by total assets, or total debt divided by stockholder's equity.

trend analysis. An analysis of performance that is made over a number of years in order to ascertain significant patterns and trends.

variable costs. Costs directly related to the volume of business, such as raw materials, production labor, or delivery expense.

vertical integration. Expansion within an industry by acquisition of support services such as suppliers, wholesalers, or retailers.

video. A fairly expensive presentation medium, but one that is highly effective and easily transported. Very good for multiple, small audiences.

vision statement. See mission statement.

Index